Reinventing the Workplace

Reinventing the Workplace

How Business and Employees Can Both Win

David I. Levine

THE BROOKINGS INSTITUTION
Washington, D.C.

About Brookings

The Brookings Institution is a private nonprofit organization devoted to research, education, and publication on important issues of domestic and foreign policy. Its principal purpose is to bring knowledge to bear on current and emerging policy problems. The Institution was founded on December 8, 1927, to merge the activities of the Institute for Government Research, founded in 1916, the Institute of Economics, founded in 1922, and the Robert Brookings Graduate School of Economics, founded in 1924.

The Institution maintains a position of neutrality on issues of public policy. Interpretations or conclusions in Brookings publications should be understood to be solely those of the authors.

Copyright © 1995

THE BROOKINGS INSTITUTION

1775 Massachusetts Avenue, N.W., Washington, D.C. 20036

Library of Congress Cataloging-in-Publication data:

Levine, David I., 1960–
    Reinventing the workplace : how business and employees can both win / David I. Levine.
        p. cm.
    Includes bibliographical references and index.
    ISBN 0-8157-5232-6 (alk. paper). — ISBN 0-8157-5231-8 (alk. paper : pbk.)
    1. Industrial management—Employee participation. 2. Labor productivity—Psychological aspects. 3. Job satisfaction. 4. Work groups. 5. Total quality management. 6. Industrial management—Employee participation—Japan. I. Title.
HD5650.L437 1995
658.3'14—dc20   94-24066
                                                                        CIP

9 8 7 6 5 4 3 2 1

The paper used in this publication meets the minimum requirements of the American National Standard for Information Sciences—Permanence of paper for Printed Library Materials, ANSI Z39.48-1984

Set in Garamond Book

Composition by AlphaTechnologies/mps, Inc.
Mechanicsville, Maryland

Printed by R. R. Donnelley and Sons Co.
Harrisonburg, Virginia

To my father
and
the memory of my mother

Preface

When I entered my economics Ph.D. program in 1982, few economists studied organizations. Although several conservative Chicago economists and several radical economists had written seminal articles, the mainstream largely neglected the field of organizational economics. Fortunately, since the early 1980s there has been a remarkably interdisciplinary blossom of interest, leading to what Oliver Williamson described as "the new science of organization."

This volume pulls together many of the insights of this new interdisciplinary science. My job title at the Haas School of Business at the University of California, Berkeley, gives a feel for the breadth of fields I draw from, since I am an associate professor in both the Organizational Behavior/Industrial Relations group and the Economic Analysis and Policy group. This volume draws on the insights of a broad array of social sciences and business experience, coupled with the tools for analyzing public policy that are the hallmarks of economic analysis. This book is intended for anyone interested in workplaces, including managers, workers, and union leaders. Those with an interest in public policy toward workplaces should find that this book brings together the relevant theory, evidence, and prescriptions.

Much of this volume derives from research that was undertaken with coauthors: Paul S. Adler (chapter 2), Douglas Cowherd (chapter 3), Barbara Goldoftas (chapter 2), Susan Helper (chapters 5, 6, and 7), Douglas L. Kruse (chapter 4), Edward E. Lawler III (chapter 4), Gerald Ledford (chapter 4), Susan A. Mohrman (chapter 4), Richard J. Parkin (chapter 6), George Strauss (chapters 1, 2, 3, and 8), and Laura D'Andrea Tyson (chapters 3, 5, 6, and 7). The structure of the argument draws on the articles coauthored with Strauss and Tyson, amplifying my debt to them. In addition, I revised the volume while I was visiting the Department of Labor's new Office of the American Workplace, where I learned a tremendous amount from my colleagues. Many spillovers occurred in both directions between this book and publications of the Office of the American Workplace. Nevertheless, the opinions expressed in this book are solely my own and do not represent the official policy of the Department of Labor or the Council of Economic Advisers.

Large portions of the text derive directly from these coauthored articles. Furthermore, these colleagues provided many of the ideas even in the sections they did not coauthor. In short, I could not have written this volume without their help, and I am grateful for the opportunity of working with such outstanding colleagues. In addition, Helper, Lawler, Ledford, and Mohrman also provided some of the data, as did my Berkeley colleague James R. Lincoln. As an added contribution, most of these colleagues have read drafts of this volume and greatly improved its entirety. The research would not have been nearly so enjoyable without their participation.

I also received valuable comments from George A. Akerlof, Eileen R. Appelbaum, Rosemary Batt, Elizabeth Bishop, Clair Brown, Rebecca Brown, Peter Cappelli, Beth Clark, Robert E. Cole, Mark Gilkey, Jody Hoffer-Gittell, Lawrence F. Katz, Morris M. Kleiner, Jeff Kling, Douglas L. Kruse, Jonathan S. Leonard, Daniel Levine, Nancy Levine, Sue Levine, James R. Lincoln, Jonathan Low, Michael McGregor, Martin Manley, Steve Marler, James Rebitzer, Annalee Saxenian, Nancy E. Wallace, and Janet L. Yellen, as well as three reviewers for Brookings.

Elizabeth Bishop and Steven Raphael provided expert research assistance and a number of important insights. Colleen McGuiness edited the manuscript, Laura Kelly verified it, Trish Weisman proofread the pages, and Rhonda Holland prepared the index. Nancy Davidson shepherded the book through many stages. I appreciate the hard work of all these people.

I am saddened that the book has not incorporated all the good ideas of these friends and colleagues. I can only take solace that it is much improved thanks to their hard work.

Over the years this research has been supported by funding from the Institute of Industrial Relations at the University of California, Berkeley, the Sloan Foundation, and the Consortium on Cooperation and Competition. I appreciate their support.

Finally, Vicki Elliot lived through the process of my writing this book and tolerated the many hours that it kept us apart during our newlywed year. I missed her those hours, and the prospect of spending more time with her is one of the great rewards of finishing this project.

Contents

Reinventing the Workplace

1

Introduction

*An American, a Japanese, and a Frenchman were captured by
hostile forces that intended to execute them immediately. Each
was granted a last request. The Frenchman asked to sing "La
Marseillaise." The Japanese asked to give his lecture on employee
involvement. The American asked to be shot right away so that
he would not have to listen to one more Japanese lecture on
employee involvement.*

Extraordinary claims have been made about employee involvement for
generations. The reason is simple: Employee involvement works—at
least, some of the time. Providing frontline employees with the skills,
motivation, and freedom to improve how they do their jobs can greatly
increase both productivity and worker satisfaction. However, substantive employee involvement remains the exception in the U.S. work
force.

The New United Motor Manufacturing Inc. (NUMMI) auto plant, a
joint General Motors (GM)–Toyota venture located at a former GM plant
in Fremont, California, is a suitable case study of the potentials and the
pitfalls of employee involvement. The old GM plant had been plagued
with serious problems of low quality, high absenteeism, and very poor
labor relations. Although most of the technology and most of the workers were the same as in the old plant, and the same union was in place,
NUMMI in its first few years reduced worker-hours per car by approximately 40 percent, zoomed to the top of U.S. auto plants in quality, and
enjoyed the lowest absenteeism of any U.S. plant. Work teams were
responsible for planning job rotation, balancing assignments to equalize

1

workloads, and engaging in continuous improvement of the safety, quality, and efficiency of the jobs. A joint union-management committee selected team leaders.

Establishing and maintaining employee involvement at NUMMI was not easy. A host of additional management practices were required. For example, NUMMI changed how pay was set, the role of the union, the number of middle managers, and the process by which the assembly line was designed. Despite the improvements, some problems did persist.

The substantial increase in productivity experienced at NUMMI, as well as other companies, was linked to employee involvement. The question thus arises, Why has substantive employee involvement remained relatively rare? One possible answer is that employees do not want more involvement at work. However, more than 80 percent of Americans participating in a 1994 poll agreed that most companies do not give workers enough say in decisions that affect them.[1] Another possible answer is that American companies have access to monopolies, patents, low-cost labor, or low-cost raw materials and find hiring workers hands' alone cheaper than their heads as well. Although this situation does exist, global competition, deregulation, new technologies, and new market pressures are requiring more companies to change their way of doing business.

A third answer, which is the focus of this book, is that a number of obstacles in the American economic and political system increase the costs of implementing a high-involvement workplace. They include laws forbidding many forms of employee involvement, a financial system that fails to reward companies making hard-to-measure investments in their work force, and macroeconomic policies that penalize companies that try to provide long-term commitments to their employees.

New public policies can be derived from the obstacles that need to be overcome. Although employee involvement is not a panacea for all of America's ills, the policies can provide a coherent structure to support changes in work organization, to improve the productivity and profitability of business enterprises, and to create better and more rewarding jobs for the work force.

Brief History of Employee Involvement

In the 1990s employee involvement is often introduced in the guise of high-performance workplaces, business process reengineering, continuous improvement, or total quality management.[2] Although the particulars of employee involvement have changed, certain underlying themes have remained the same since the 1940s. The strongest is that frontline employees who are actually performing the work will have insights into how to improve their tasks. Employee involvement encompasses a range of policies that, at the minimal end, permit workers to suggest improvement and, at the substantive end, give all employees the ability, motivation, and authority to continuously improve how the organization operates.[3]

In the 1920s the British Industrial Health Research Council's pioneering research showed that work could become more meaningful in ways that would increase satisfaction, productivity, and quality.[4] Large-scale academic interest in participation dates from the famous Hawthorne–Western Electric experiments of the late 1920s through the 1930s.[5] In these experiments, a small group of workers who were given increased control over the work process, felt that high productivity was a group goal, and were highly cohesive increased productivity substantially; groups that feared that high productivity would lead to layoffs restricted their output.

During the post–World War II period, employee involvement spread in different fashions. West Germany was the first nation to require many companies to create and consult with works councils of elected worker representatives. This form of mandated involvement subsequently spread to all of continental Western Europe. In most nations, management is required to consult with works councils on many employment-related issues; in some cases, management cannot move ahead without the council's approval.

Worker or union representatives serve on company boards of directors in many European countries. Worker representatives are almost everywhere in the minority. They sometimes have considerable influence on broad policies. In West German coal and steel industries, for example, labor and management are equally represented on the board, with a neutral third party breaking deadlocks. In most European nations, these forms of employee involvement have been viewed primarily as means of bettering the condition of workers, although proponents also have hoped for increases in productivity as workers are empowered.

In Japan, employee involvement grew from the bottom up, as companies fought against radical unions partially by creating an industrial relations system that incorporated many of the unions' demands: increased employment security, seniority-based pay, and relatively high levels of training. Union-management joint consultative committees are common in Japan. In some companies, the committees engage in traditional collective bargaining; in others, the bargaining and consultative functions are kept separate. Management often shares confidential information with the committees, including details of major new investments and changes in policy. Furthermore, management normally revises its plans when faced with strong union objections.[6]

Worker-owned and -controlled producers' cooperatives are common in Europe and Israel, with the most famous being the Israeli kibbutzim. Among the most successful worker-owned and -controlled organizations is the Mondragon complex in Spain, a large federation of more than one hundred employee-owned companies, with associated educational and financial institutions.[7]

In the early 1950s a series of experiments by Kurt Lewin and his students contributed to the belief that participatory groups were more productive than nonparticipatory ones and that decisions made collectively were more likely to be implemented than those made autocratically. The results of subsequent studies by a group in Michigan, headed by Renis Likert, were consistent with Lewin's findings.[8] Since the early 1960s the advantages of worker participation have been widely taught in business schools.

The 1970s brought widespread national concern with the "blue-collar blues," triggered in part by a strike at a Lordstown, Ohio, GM plant over the alienating conditions of assembly line work. Some observers noted a "revolt against work," particularly among younger, better-educated workers.[9]

Meanwhile, highly influential studies by J. Richard Hackman and Edward E. Lawler III found that some job characteristics such as autonomy were closely connected with both productivity and satisfaction.[10] Thus, they concluded, job redesign might increase job satisfaction and raise productivity. At the same time, interest arose in "socio-technical systems" integrating employee involvement with new technology, which contributed to the introduction of autonomous work groups into the assembly lines at Volvo and Saab.[11]

A few progressive U.S. companies in the 1940s, 1950s, and 1960s had begun to experiment with various forms of participation. Typical results included a positive impact on productivity, satisfaction, and adaptability to change.[12] By the 1970s the terms *job enrichment* and *quality of worklife* (QWL) became popular, and experiments in workers' participation began to spread to mainline companies such as American Telephone and Telegraph (AT&T), Texas Instruments, and General Foods.[13]

Aside from AT&T, much of the early experimentation was in new nonunion plants, especially in the Southwest. Unions remained generally skeptical. By 1973, however, the national agreements negotiated by the United Auto Workers (UAW) and the major auto manufacturers contained provisions endorsing QWL programs. While some QWL experimentation went on, widespread adoption of QWL programs in unionized plants had to wait until the recession of the early 1980s.

Since 1980 consultative participatory schemes such as quality circles have emerged from the experimental stage and have been increasingly adopted by industry. (In consultative participation, workers are consulted and can make suggestions; in substantive participation, workers make decisions and implement them.) Quality circles typically involve volunteers from a work group meeting an hour every week or two to come up with recommendations to improve the work process. Quality circles spread in large part because they were associated with the dramatic inroads Japanese companies had made in industries such as consumer electronics and automobiles.

By the late 1980s the term *quality circle* became unfashionable, as managers realized that quality circles were but one aspect of Japanese success. Total quality management (TQM), along with variants such as total quality control and continuous improvement, arose as a replacement. Employee involvement is a key aspect of total quality management, which recreates quality circles under new names such as quality improvement teams.

TQM programs in U.S. organizations vary enormously. Under pressure from Japanese competitors (whose defect rates may be a tenth of their American competitors'), most large U.S. employers adopted quality programs. Moreover, the quality programs at companies as different as Ford, Xerox, and Florida Power and Light led to dramatic increases in quality and productivity, while also increasing worker participation and satisfaction.

All quality programs involve a set of tools that are intended to achieve continuous improvement in quality and efficiency. Unfortunately, only the best programs integrate these tools with a managerial philosophy and with fundamental changes in management practices. In successful TQM programs, efforts at continuous improvement are based on customer focus, empowered employees, close customer and supplier relations, and management based on facts and data. TQM is also associated with reduced inventory so problems are not hidden by buffers (often known as just-in-time production, or JIT), statistical process control

(SPC) to track the number and timing of problems, Pareto diagrams to identify priorities, brainstorming and cause-effect diagrams to analyze sources of errors, and a systematic problem-solving method that ensures that the proposed solution works and that the new solution is systematized and disseminated to those who need to know about it.

Throughout the 1980s a modest but steady increase was seen in more substantive participation, such as self-directing work teams. Workers were implementing many of their decisions, not merely making recommendations. Most of these programs have also drawn on the quality movement's tool kit.

More recently, process reengineering—in which frontline workers (either individually or in groups) perform complete tasks without departmental boundaries or supervisory checks dividing and slowing down the operations—has become more popular. Although often touted as a new idea, process reengineering grows directly out of the concept of just-in-time production pioneered at Toyota in the 1950s.[14]

Several related factors have spurred interest in participation among American managers, unions, and workers. New technologies open up new possibilities for higher productivity, but they often fail to increase performance. The disappointing productivity performance, in turn, has led managers to realize the old ways are not working well. At the same time, the success of Japanese and other foreign companies with more participatory industrial relations systems has shown that alternatives exist. Perhaps most important, the loss of markets by U.S. companies has increased both the need for and receptivity to change.

Extent of Employee Involvement

Obtaining reliable data on the extent of employee involvement in the United States is difficult. No standard definitions of what is to be counted have been devised, determining the proportion of employees involved is problematic, and many defunct programs are still reported as active.

In spite of these limitations, the evidence is that most large American employers have employee involvement somewhere in their organizations and that the incidence has spread rapidly since the mid-1980s. A 1992 representative survey of U.S. establishments with more than fifty employees found that more than a third involved most of their core employees in two or more of the following high-involvement practices: work teams, quality circles, job rotation, or total quality management.[15]

In a 1990 study of the Fortune 1000, 88 percent of the responding companies had at least 1 percent of their workers in employee involvement programs. The programs included quality circles (groups of workers meet regularly to solve quality, productivity, and safety problems); autonomous teams; job enrichment (jobs are enlarged to include a broader array of tasks, such as checking one's own work); employee surveys that also relay the results to employees; and other participative groups such as cross-functional teams, minienterprise units (small groups of workers form a small profit center within the company), and union-management quality of worklife committees.[16]

The proportion of employees in an employee involvement program at responding companies rose from 22 percent in 1987 to 31 percent in 1990. The increase was attributed to a combination of more companies with employee involvement and a higher proportion of workers in employee involvement programs.

Although the numbers were rising, only a minority of workers at most companies were active in employee involvement programs. Of the 6.5 million employees in the responding companies, 1.2 million were covered by quality circles, 800,000 by cooperative union-management programs, 400,000 by mini-enterprise units, and 300,000 by autonomous work teams. Of the companies with involvement policies, the average percentage of employees covered was 24 percent for quality circles and 16 to 18 percent for cooperative union-management programs, minienterprise units, and autonomous work teams.[17]

Most of the plans are fairly new. According to the 1990 study, the median number of years the programs have been in operation ranges from a high of six for quality circles down to only three for autonomous teams. This result is consistent with a rapid diffusion of employee involvement programs, as well as with high death rates for programs. Most of the companies reported that they planned to expand their employee involvement programs. Employee involvement grew to cover about an additional 10 percent of the work force between 1987 and 1990—a fast pace.

At least half of all unionized companies have union-management committees intended to promote employee involvement and quality of worklife.[18] If quality of worklife committees have been formed at a company, usually about half of all union members are covered by the program.

In short, participation plans spread rapidly during the 1980s. By the early 1990s a majority of large companies had introduced employee involvement somewhere in their organizations. Nevertheless, functioning plans currently exist in only a minority of individual plants and offices. Moreover, even in worksites with employee involvement plans, often a minority of employees participate.

Ethical Arguments for Employee Involvement

But profitability is not the only indicator of a firm's conditions. It is possible for the financial accounts to be in order, and yet for the people—who make up the firm's most valuable asset—to be humiliated and their dignity offended.

—POPE JOHN PAUL II

Virtue has never been as respectable as money.

—MARK TWAIN

The ethical arguments for employee involvement and a democratic workplace parallel those for democracy in the political realm. The most common argument for political democracy is not that it leads to the most efficient economy (although that argument is often made) but that citizens have an unalienable right to influence the laws that govern them—people bound by rules have a right to influence those rules. Tyranny results when citizens do not have substantial control over their government. Following this political argument, the ethical argument for employee involvement assumes that when a company can punish or control an employee, that employee has a fundamental right to democratically influence the company.

Corporate tyranny reigns, however. In the United States, workers have no rights to influence their conditions of employment. For example, any employer can dismiss an employee for complaining about unpleasant working conditions, for speaking too loudly or too softly, or for almost any other reason (except on the basis of race, color, or creed). Some observers concluded: "If one is a democrat, facilitating collective representation [within organizations] is 'the right thing to do.' "[19]

Marshall Sashkin made a related ethical argument in favor of employee involvement. He maintained that a positive moral injunction exists that managers must "Do no harm." He provided evidence that work with little opportunity for employee involvement increases stress and alienation, thus harming employees both psychologically and physiologically.[20]

One defense of the tyrannical form of companies is that employees can freely and easily leave organizations that make decisions they dislike.[21] An early analysis of the economics of the employment relationship argued that an employer has no more power over employees than does a customer over a grocer.[22] According to this line of reasoning, the employer has no tyrannical powers.

Unfortunately, most workers do not have the luxury of being able to freely leave. For example, in the United States workers can expect a substantial period of unemployment if they are dismissed for protesting working conditions. In recent decades, the average cost of job loss following dismissal has varied from five to fourteen weeks' pay. Furthermore, dismissal is not an idle threat—each year in the United States, approximately 1 million firings take place in which the employer was unable to show a legitimate cause.[23]

In addition, the possibility of costly exit does not preclude the relevance of ethical arguments. Citizens can move from town to town if their local government is unsatisfactory. However, the possibility of leaving is never seriously offered as a reason to deny citizens the vote.[24] In some sense, citizens have an advantage when moving, because the new town must (in short order) give them the privileges of citizenship. In labor markets, by contrast, workers who quit one unsatisfactory workplace have no guarantee that a future employer will grant them membership (that is, employment).

A more serious critique of the ethical argument is that employees have freely chosen to join their employer. Workers should have the right to choose workplaces that have little employee involvement; signing on with such an employer implies that any reduction in satisfaction resulting from a loss of participation is more than outweighed by the higher wages made possible by the efficiency gains of central direction and control by managers. Markets efficiently determine the level of employee involvement that optimally balances employees' desire for involvement with their desire for efficiency and high wages. To evaluate this critique, an examination must be made of whether markets select the most efficient work organization. The task thus becomes understanding what is required for employee involvement to succeed, the barriers to successful involvement that may lead the market to select inefficient organizations, and the public policies designed to reduce those barriers.

2

NUMMI: A Case Study

*The average man won't really do a day's work unless he is
caught and cannot get out of it.*

—HENRY FORD

The experience at NUMMI provides an illustrative case study of employee involvement. At the NUMMI plant, a joint venture, Toyota had taken over management of a GM factory and greatly improved productivity, product quality, and worker quality of life—even though the same union and largely the same work force, plant, and equipment were in place. NUMMI changed virtually every human resource and management practice, including training, compensation, union relations, supplier relations, and product development. Implementation of employee involvement is not foolproof, however. For example, repetitive motion injuries and problems with unsafe work practices arose at NUMMI.

GM-Fremont, 1963–82

GM management of the plant in Fremont, California, was based on the premises of scientific management, developed by F. W. Taylor at the turn of the twentieth century. Scientific management emphasizes the division between planning and doing—managers and engineers make all

This chapter was coauthored with Paul S. Adler and Barbara Goldoftas. The appendix has a description of the methodology and sources used. See Paul S. Adler, Barbara Goldoftas, and David I. Levine, "Ergonomics, Employee Involvement, and the Toyota Production System: A Case Study of NUMMI's 1993 Model Introduction," University of Southern California, Graduate School of Business, 1995, for a more complete discussion of the NUMMI case.

10

the plans, while frontline workers perform all the work. Successful work by those at the bottom leads to bonuses, promotions, and continued employment.

Although associated with assembly lines, scientific management underlies the design of many jobs throughout the economy. Examples include McDonald's hamburger flippers, data entry clerks in banks where computers monitor output, and textile workers paid piece rates for sewing high-fashion blue jeans. In all of these cases, managers and engineers design the work, while employees with little opportunity for being creative or improving their jobs perform the tasks.

Scientific management has important advantages, particularly when technology changes slowly and the product or service provided does not need to meet exacting quality standards. In these settings, managers and engineers can design the work rationally and train workers quickly. Because tasks are simple, workers are easy to monitor and are rewarded for the quantity they produce. Unfortunately, product quality may be unreliable.

Scientific management grants workers little discretion because of a belief that they will slack off. As a former GM executive wrote, "Among all layers of management at GM, there are those with outright contempt for the working person. To them the worker is devoid of integrity and purpose."[1] One NUMMI worker related the message he received on his first day of work at GM-Fremont: "You new employees have been hired in the same way we requisition sandpaper. We'll put you back on the street whenever you aren't needed any more."

In addition to the belief that workers will not work hard, workers are assumed to have no ideas about how to increase productivity or quality. Employees fear that if they do come up with improvements, management will raise the speed of the line and fail to offer rewards. Furthermore, because workers usually receive minimal training and do not see how their work fits into the larger project of the factory, coming up with improvements is difficult.

Even when workers want to share ideas, scientific management at GM, for example, provided no mechanisms for doing so. One worker from a GM plant in Michigan described a plant manager's orientation talk for new employees:

Sometime during his spiel, he's gonna tell us that he will be regularly touring the plant, pausing to listen to any of our gripes and suggestions. He will pledge to be visible and accessible. . . . In all of my years

here, I've yet to see his face in the factory. He's probably afraid he'll
scuff one of his cuff links or something.[2]

Finally, under scientific management, group pressure is to reduce
performance. Workers fear that a highly productive single worker would
raise management's standards of performance for all employees. Thus
high performers at work, like teacher's pets in school, are socially
isolated and punished by their fellow workers.

Even when workers want to do quality work, the line does not permit
it. As one GM worker explained in the 1950s, "The bad thing about
assembly lines is that the line keeps moving. If you have a little trouble
with a job, you can't take the time to do it right." Another echoed, "I try
to do quality work, but I'm too rushed. This keeps me from getting
pleasure from the work. They say 'haste makes waste,' and they're
getting plenty of both."[3] A generation later, the ability of GM-Fremont
workers to produce quality products was essentially identical.

The distrust between manager and worker is magnified at the union-
management level. For example, relations between union and management at GM-Fremont were close to disastrous. Managers often acted
arbitrarily, played favorites, ignored safety issues, and pushed workers to
increase productivity. When a worker complained about any of these
actions, a manager's typical reaction was to say, "If you don't like it,
grieve." Grieving—writing up formal grievances that a manager had
broken the union contract—became a full-time job for the elected union
representatives. Having carefully specified job duties in the contract
became the only protection workers had from arbitrary foremen.

The union, meanwhile, was purely confrontational, defending all
workers against managerial discipline. Even workers who were known
to have stolen goods or to have shown up repeatedly too drunk to work
were defended by the union. At contract time, management and the
union typically agreed to dismiss all of the thousands of outstanding
grievances. This solution left numerous irresponsible and illegal management actions unchanged and irresponsible and criminal workers retained.

NUMMI's Arrival

The GM-Fremont plant closed its doors in 1982, idling fifty-seven
hundred workers. As one NUMMI manager reported, "We were told . . .
that's the worst plant in the world."[4] In a troubled company, Fremont
was the most troubled plant. Unexcused absenteeism often ran more

than 20 percent, with levels so high on some Mondays and Fridays that the assembly line could not start. During the three years between contract talks, the accumulation of more than four thousand unresolved grievances was not unusual. Quality levels and productivity were far below the GM standard, which itself was falling ever further behind the world-class standard being set in Japan.

In 1983 GM and Toyota signed a letter of intent to open a joint venture to produce small cars at the Fremont site. Each partner provided half the $200 million in investment and was a half owner of the new company, New United Motor Manufacturing Inc. Toyota agreed to supply the car design and to manage the factory, while GM would provide the building and sell half the cars.

Although Toyota was initially reluctant to work with the United Auto Workers, in September 1983 the company agreed to recognize the union and give priority to rehiring laid-off GM workers. Of the twelve hundred workers employed when production began in December 1984, 99 percent of the assembly workers and 75 percent of the skilled trades workers, such as electricians, were former GM employees and UAW members. The selection process was done jointly by the union and management. Very few workers who applied were rejected; the union even arranged a second chance for some applicants who failed the drug test.

Like the work force, the factory underwent minimal modifications. When NUMMI began producing the Chevrolet Nova and Toyota Corolla in 1984, it was at best a mid-technology factory, with a few robots but little of the high-tech equipment in the newer GM factories.

Nonetheless, with largely the same work force and plant, NUMMI soon achieved productivity levels almost twice those of GM-Fremont in its best years and 40 percent better than the typical GM assembly plant. It was producing not only the highest quality levels GM had ever known but also the highest of any domestic auto plant.[5] Through the early 1990s the plant continued to excel in quality and productivity.

Worker satisfaction at the plant was also high. In the late 1980s, when researchers asked NUMMI workers whether they would switch jobs if a GM plant were across the street, the response was uniformly negative.[6] According to surveys conducted in the plant, the number of workers who said they were "satisfied with my job and environment" increased from 65 percent in 1985 to 90 percent in 1991.[7] In 1992 NUMMI had an absence rate (excluding only scheduled vacations) of 3 to 4 percent, compared with an average of nearly 9 percent at GM and close to 20 percent at GM-Fremont.[8]

In 1988 the company switched from the Chevrolet Nova to the new Geo. By 1993 NUMMI was producing about 200,000 cars a year, with a capacity of 220,000. Toyota had announced in 1989 that it would invest $350 million to expand the plant and begin production of Toyota pickup trucks. With a capacity to build 125,000 trucks, the new line opened in September 1991, adding seven hundred workers to the factory. By 1993 NUMMI was producing 120,000 trucks, which were rated number one in initial quality by the respected J. D. Power survey.

Toyota Production System

The extraordinary turnaround was brought about by NUMMI's management practices, which were based on the Toyota Production System.[9] While the closing of GM-Fremont unstuck the attitudes of workers and union leaders, most observers agreed that had the workers returned to a plant managed in the old GM style, productivity, quality, and morale would have rapidly returned to their previous levels.

The Toyota Production System has three pillars: just-in-time (JIT) production, the jidoka quality principle, and standardized work and kaizen (continuous improvement). Employee involvement is an integral part of each.

JIT production attempts to eliminate all work-in-progress inventory. Ideally, each part is delivered to the work station just as it is needed. In practice, the plant holds an average of about two days' worth of inventory. Nearby suppliers deliver several times a day, while more distant suppliers, mostly in Japan and the Midwest, deliver every few days.

JIT lowers inventory holding costs and increases the rate of organizational learning. Ordinarily, inventory buffers can hide a problem at one work station because it does not affect other parts of the production process. Without buffers, workers and engineers can quickly identify production glitches and reveal their root causes. In the short run, those further along in the process might not receive the components they need, but in the long run, costs fall as problems are discovered and resolved.

The JIT system creates considerable pressure on workers. Any production problems will bring the entire line to a halt. A high level of worker involvement is necessary to ensure a timely response. Delivery of the end product is at stake.

The jidoka quality principle dictates that, as much as possible, the production process should be error-proof. Under the GM system, defective parts proceeded from one manufacturing process to the next; management did not trust workers to examine the parts and instead relied on teams of inspectors to catch and repair defects at the end of the assembly line. By contrast, NUMMI aims to find defective parts immediately so that more can be detected and the root cause of the problem can be fixed sooner. Certain automatic wrenches, for example, are programmed to tighten four bolts per car. If the car moves on and only three bolts have been tightened, the system sets off an alarm.

Such mechanical systems are coupled with a direct form of worker control over quality and the work pace—the andon cord. Located above each work station, the andon cord permits each worker to stop the assembly line when problems arise. When the cord is pulled, a musical tune plays and a flashing light on an overhead board signals where the line pull occurred, alerting the group leader and the team leader. If the cord is not pulled again within a minute, the line shuts down until the problem is fixed. On average, NUMMI workers pull the cord about 150 times per eight-hour shift, and the line is stopped approximately 20 minutes each shift. (Approximately $8,000–$10,000 is lost per minute when the line is stopped.) The NUMMI-UAW contract stipulates that when workers fall behind or see a defect they cannot repair, they are "expected, without being subject to discipline, to pull the cord."[10]

NUMMI executives have said that the ability of ordinary workers to stop the line symbolizes the relationship of trust between management and labor. "We had heavy arguments about installing the andon cord here," said NUMMI president Kan Higashi. "We wondered if workers would pull it just to get a rest. That has not happened." (In contrast, at traditional GM factories, workers are not permitted to or able to stop the assembly line under virtually any circumstances.)

Standardized work and kaizen form the third pillar of the Toyota Production System. Following the precepts of scientific management, each task is designed to be performed in a standardized fashion, with motion-by-motion instructions that describe exactly how a job should be done. NUMMI's approach to scientific management differs from GM's in two crucial ways. First, workers, not industrial engineers, define the procedures. At GM-Fremont, eighty industrial engineers designed the work process, monitoring and timing workers at specific jobs. At NUMMI, team members carefully design the optimal procedure to do each task. Second, at NUMMI the best procedure remains an ever-shifting target. That is, workers are encouraged to improve, or kaizen, their jobs. Suggestions that pass muster with their team and group leaders are then standardized and become the new best procedure—until the next suggestion renews the kaizen cycle.

NUMMI has a number of mechanisms for stimulating and capturing these kaizens. The line speed is altered every few months with changes in the production schedule; workers thus must redefine their work procedures.

NUMMI also has an active suggestion program. In 1992 more than 94 percent of workers contributed at least one suggestion, earning an average award of $25 per suggestion, and about fourteen thousand suggestions were implemented. (The proportion of employee participation is somewhat inflated because team leaders or an entire team sometimes put multiple names on a suggestion, even if only one person contributed.)

Building on the culture of improvement, in 1991 NUMMI introduced problem-solving circles (PSCs). Volunteers work with others from the same group, studying a problem for several weeks or months, typically working over a company-provided lunch. A circle picks the problem it wishes to work on, subject to the constraint that it be within the group's span of control. Most circles succeed in solving at least one problem, and some continue working on additional problems.

Although PSCs usually work on problems relating to quality and productivity, safety is also a legitimate topic. For example, one PSC met in the Wet Sanding Group. (Wet sanding smooths down the car surface before painting.) The group had two main problems: bends in the sanding screens that scratched the undercoat, and back problems caused by reaching over the top of a car to sand. The circle chose the second problem to tackle and began a systematic analysis of its root causes. The PSC's preferred solution was to provide a stand for employees that automatically lowered and raised as the car went by, to minimize stretching. Management deemed the solution outside the circle's span of control because it involved a major new piece of equipment. In addition, a group of engineers was studying the idea. The PSC's second-best solution involved implementing job rotation, so nobody needed to stretch in one direction for the entire eight hours. A subset of the affected team (three out of five members—one was injured and could not perform some jobs, and one liked his job) participated in the rotation.

In addition to the formal mechanisms for employee involvement, NUMMI workers have influence through a variety of informal means, including talking to the company or union president in the cafeteria, informally calling over a skilled trades worker to modify a machine, and writing to the union newspaper.

NUMMI's Management System

The Toyota Production System and its employee involvement practices are buttressed by other management practices and policies. They create different incentives and broader opportunities than those at GM-Fremont, including greater worker involvement, more job security, and a relatively larger amount of career mobility. NUMMI has also redefined the roles of managers and unions.

The initial contract embodied a very different role for the union than in the former GM plant. The introduction stated, "We are committed to building and maintaining the most innovative and harmonious labor-management relationship in America."[11] The union was given a formal role in consultation on matters ranging from the pace of work to major investments—areas of decisionmaking usually reserved solely for management. Union and management dedicated themselves to ongoing worker training and kaizen efforts.

NUMMI workers receive more than 250 hours of training during their first six months on the job, while a typical auto worker is lucky to receive 40 hours in the first year. About 75 hours of training at NUMMI take place in the classroom, where workers learn the company's management philosophy and study techniques for control, safety, problem solving, and work standardization. In each subsequent year on the job, they receive 50 hours of training in areas such as standardization techniques, the principles of kaizen, and leadership development, far more than the 20 hours that is standard at the Big Three automakers (GM, Ford, and Chrysler).

The NUMMI contract also promises a measure of job security, stating that before laying off workers, the company would cut managers' paychecks and bring in work contracted out to suppliers. Many workers initially doubted the credibility of this commitment, but slow sales in the late 1980s afforded a test. During much of 1987 and 1988, demand for the Nova was weak, and production at NUMMI was running at a mere 65 percent of capacity. Instead of laying off shop-floor workers, the company sent the entire work force to training classes, increased maintenance chores such as painting, and placed surplus workers into teams that designed the production process for the next model car.[12]

NUMMI has much different guarantees of fair treatment than did GM-Fremont. The dispute resolution procedure at NUMMI emphasizes solving problems quickly and at the lowest level possible, without filing a formal grievance. For example, if a worker has a dispute with her team leader, she can call on her work group's union coordinator (a regular worker who works a few hours a week resolving disputes); if they fail to resolve the dispute, they call over a representative from the Labor Relations department and an elected full-time union representative. Only after these informal means are exhausted is a formal grievance written up. As in most union contracts, the grievance procedure includes a series of appeals to higher levels of the company and union, culminating in a few cases a year that go to binding outside arbitration. The UAW files about fifty formal grievances against NUMMI a year, about as many as were filed every few weeks at GM-Fremont.

An important aspect of the success of NUMMI is that workers feel they benefit from it. Although the plant had been opened for almost a decade and no layoffs had occurred, job security is an important reward. The threat of a plant closure is salient in all workers' minds.

At the plantwide level, a formal bonus system is in place. The bonus is based on the improvement in the proportion of the time that the assembly line is running and on three surveys of customer satisfaction (the New Vehicle Sales and Delivery Survey, the Continuous Automotive Market Information Program, and the J. D. Powers Quality Survey). In addition, collective bargaining creates implicit gainsharing, because high quality and productivity provide more profits for the union to bargain over in the next round of negotiations.

Compared with GM, rewards are different for NUMMI managers as well as for NUMMI workers. Senior executives and workers park in the same lots and eat in the same cafeterias as line employees, and they work in accessible open offices. Managers (and those workers who choose to) wear the company uniform. Wage differentials between workers and managers are also smaller at NUMMI than at GM.

NUMMI stresses cross-training. Ideally, all workers learn the four or five jobs performed by their team and rotate among them several times a day. This rotation, which until recently has not been part of the Toyota Production System as practiced in Japan, does not always operate as planned. Sometimes only part of a team rotates, for example; other times, absenteeism or incomplete cross-training makes switching jobs on a regular basis impossible for team members. At its best, however, rotation builds up group cohesiveness; mollifies team members' concerns over which jobs are overloaded (more work than the pace of the line allowed for completion) or underloaded (more time available than was necessary to perform a task); and gives workers a broader understanding of their jobs, which can serve to facilitate kaizen.

Promotions provide another form of mobility. Team leaders are union members. Their responsibilities include many tasks formerly performed by GM-Fremont's first-line supervisors. The team leader job provides an intermediate step to the position of group leader, the counterpart of GM foremen, who supervises three to five teams. Team leaders, who receive a slight increase in pay, are selected by a joint management-union committee based on a negotiated set of explicit and largely objective criteria. Almost all team and group leaders are promoted from within.

Finally, team members and team leaders also work on special project teams, which handle tasks ranging from safety problems to the design for the next year's assembly line. The independence and responsibility of these teams make them an additional vehicle for skill enhancement and upward mobility.

The net result of these varied routes to advancement is an organization that offers a higher level of mobility than GM. While many workers stay in their team member positions, others have found opportunities unavailable at GM-Fremont. Said one former line worker, who became an engineer, "Compared to GM, NUMMI is much more of a meritocracy. Look at us, coming from where we did, and seeing how far we've been allowed and encouraged to come. At GM, we were confined to semi-skilled manual work for life."

The climate within the local union has evolved in ways that both reflect and reinforce the changes in the plant. Although the factional wars within the union were legendary during GM-Fremont days, NUMMI started operation with the strong backing of the local and regional UAW leadership, and 92 percent of the work force endorsed the first contract.

Within two years, however, the union had split again, and a dissenting People's Caucus was formed in opposition to the ruling Administration Caucus. The People's Caucus was concerned that the Administration Caucus had become too cozy with management and had not been fighting aggressively enough to protect workers' rights in cases such as injuries, transfers, or overloaded jobs. The Administration Caucus, in response, saw the People's Caucus as naysayers with few positive proposals who merely criticized and wished to return to the "good old days" of union-management conflict.

In the elections of 1991, the People's Caucus won the presidency of the union local as well as most of the other elected offices. Of the Administration Caucus incumbents, only veteran Bargaining Committee chairman George Nano won reelection, and his winning margin was small. (Soon after the election, the new union president Charlie Curry broke with the People's Caucus and began to work closely with the Administration Caucus.)

The relationship between the two caucuses is contentious and possibly counterproductive. By 1993 the local was somewhat paralyzed by its internal conflicts—many union committees were not meeting, and long-time members were bitter about the high level of acrimony at union meetings.

Neither caucus has defined a completely satisfactory role in the new labor-management climate. The Administration Caucus has become comfortable as an early participant in discussions about the policies that affect the plant's overall direction, decisions that management at most plants makes without union input. The caucus has been less successful in convincing a majority of its members that it will defend their interests in all cases.

When opportunities for dialogue between labor and management leaders increase, the union makes more important decisions. Thus the union needs to be informed about what members want, and members need to understand the issues over which the union is bargaining. When dialogue and participation increase between union and management, the need for dialogue and participation between the union leadership and the rank and file also increase. The Administration Caucus's proponents of union-management cooperation do not have a model of such internal democracy; instead, Bargaining Committee Chairman Nano proposes that members trust him to bargain on their behalf and elect a replacement if they do not like the job he is doing.

The People's Caucus has done a better job of convincing the work force that it will defend their rights. At the same time, it has failed to outline how it will take advantage of the possible benefits of labor-management cooperation, such as the ability to influence decisions concerning new technology or management policies.

Employee Involvement at a Typical GM Plant

Throughout the 1980s quality circles and other employee involvement programs proliferated throughout GM. Unfortunately, with important exceptions such as the Saturn plant, the majority of these programs had minimal results. In this sense, GM is a microcosm of the U.S.

experience with employee involvement: widespread experimentation, but few successes.

The typical GM plant began its shop-floor employee involvement efforts in the 1970s with quality of worklife (QWL) union-management committees, followed in the early 1980s with quality circles.[13] Typically, plant managers had heard good things about quality circles from other managers and the business press, and they were pressured from central headquarters to adopt this management innovation.

Managers recruited volunteers in each department with instructions to meet on a weekly basis to discuss problems relating to working conditions, quality, safety, and productivity. Employees were suspicious. GM had always designed jobs to minimize employees' discretion, and the company had never listened to their ideas. Employees were not sure that GM was serious about listening now.

In spite of these handicaps, quality circles were often successful at first. Many employees had been in the company for years and had accumulated a host of suggestions. Some, as simple as rotating a machine by 90 degrees to make it more accessible, increased production substantially at almost no cost. Employees were pleased to be listened to, after years of having no way to communicate their ideas.

In time, however, problems began cropping up. Employees complained that managers carefully listened to suggestions that cut costs but ignored suggestions for improving safety or making work easier. In addition, when management used employees' ideas to increase efficiency, nothing was given in exchange. At the same time, employees began contrasting the theoretically democratic process in the quality circles with the continuing autocratic approach that most supervisors took on the job. After they ran through their initial set of suggestions, these employees felt little incentive to offer new ones. Some groups spent increasing time on individual grievances.

Supervisors felt threatened by the process; each new idea became an implicit criticism of how they managed their area. Supervisors longed to be treated by their bosses the way they were expected to treat their subordinates.

The UAW often opposed quality circles because they can divert worker loyalty from the union. Managers were enthusiastic about employee involvement for the same reason. Furthermore, management frequently introduced quality circles with other Japanese-style innovations, such as reductions in the number of job titles. Union leaders worried that the new flexibility in assigning jobs to workers would be abused by management, fears that managers did little to assuage.

In most cases, employees gradually lost interest. Those who had supported the plan most enthusiastically at first became most disillusioned. After three years, virtually all the quality circles were no longer meeting, and plant managers were looking for new shortcuts to increasing productivity.

Union-management cooperation remains the buzzword of almost all GM plants, but the reality is far short of the level at NUMMI or Saturn. The management at a GM plant in 1993, for example, announced the introduction of an andon cord to permit workers to stop the production line. Two weeks later, the union president remained uninformed of the change. When he found out about the proposed change, however, he was very interested in negotiating protections for workers who used the andon cord to stop the line.

The 1993 Model Change

During the change from the 1992 to the 1993 model, NUMMI completely revamped its production process in a matter of weeks; a traditional U.S. automobile plant requires several months. NUMMI used employee involvement to facilitate the change. However, in times of maximum stress, employee involvement was not enough to avoid conflict over the trade-off between safety and productivity.

For generations, American manufacturers have been modifying their cars on an annual cycle. The vast majority of these changes are purely cosmetic: a higher fin, a deeper dashboard, a sleeker hood. Only every decade or so do car companies introduce a new model that requires profound modifications in the vehicles and the way they are manufactured. Until then, the basic design of the model—and the manufacturing technology underlying it—remains essentially the same. Major model changes are rare largely because six months or more are required to regain full productivity and up to a year to regain former quality levels.

Japanese auto companies have accelerated the processes of both design and technological change. Major model changes, which occur every four years, tend to be dramatic, incorporating more new technologies than at the U.S. Big Three. Thus a new-model Honda Accord or Toyota Corolla differs significantly from its predecessor.[14] Japanese firms have had to become much more nimble in managing plant changeovers. Their success has been extraordinary; whereas the typical Big Three plant takes six months to resume normal production levels after a major model change, Toyota typically takes less than three months. Moreover, in Big Three plants, quality degrades considerably at the start of production and returns to normal after a period lasting anywhere from six months to more than a year, while at Toyota the goal is to maintain or improve on the prior model's quality level right from the start of production.

The key to the Japanese success is the close cooperation of designers, manufacturing engineers, suppliers, and production workers in planning the new car and its production process. NUMMI became involved more than two years before the start of production of the 1993 model. Already at this stage engineers from NUMMI and its suppliers were visiting Japan to work with Toyota's designers.

The early involvement of assembly plants in the design process is fundamental to the Toyota Production System. Simultaneous engineering works in contrast to the standard American system, in which the design department traditionally "threw the drawings over the wall" to the engineering department, which then converted the new design to engineering specifications. The engineering department in turn threw these specifications over the wall to the manufacturing staff at division headquarters, who designed the equipment and line configuration. The staff finally passed on its plans to the plant engineers, who installed equipment on the factory floor and organized the specific assembly tasks. After a long break during which the equipment was installed, workers returned to their new jobs and were expected to do them basically as conceived for the rest of the model's life.

The advantages of early interactions among design, engineering, and production are numerous. For example, in their visit almost two years before the start of production, a NUMMI engineer and a Toyota colleague found that the bumper did not fit into the designated channel on the body of the car. By finding the problem early, the engineers were able to solve it at minimal cost. Had the drawing been released to manufacturing, rectifying the errors on the shop floor would have been much more expensive and might have delayed the start of production.

The 1993 model changeover introduced several key changes in the work process. First, NUMMI began assembling two distinct models on the line instead of just one. In previous years, although the models bore different labels—Nova or Geo for GM and Corolla for Toyota—the cars were basically identical. Starting with the 1993 model, the Toyota model remained a Corolla, but GM introduced the Geo Prizm, largely based on the Toyota Sprinter, which was sold by Chevrolet dealers.

Assembling two models simultaneously on a single line required major changes in the organization of the shop floor. Because the two models no longer used identical parts, some work stations needed to be expanded. Instead of stocking one front grill at a work station, for example, the new line needed to have two sets of grills that were each installed differently. The interior of the Prizm, which was designed by GM, required a unique set of parts as well.

Second, two major changes were made in the assembly of the doors and instrument panel. The most dramatic was the addition of a second conveyor for "doors-off" assembly. Until 1992 the body of each car was welded together, painted, and then sent to final assembly. During assembly, the doors became obstacles, workers had to maneuver around them to get inside the car, and they had to bend in awkward positions to install wires and other components on the inside of the doors. As a result, the paint on the doors was constantly being bumped and scraped. In the doors-off process, after a car was painted, the doors were removed and installed on a secondary line. This secondary line threaded its way along the ceiling and converged with the original car at the end of assembly.

The other major change in assembly involved the instrument panel, or dashboard. In previous models, workers assembled the speedometer, temperature controls, and so forth within the car itself. The jobs were notoriously cramped and difficult, which showed in the relative frequency of defects. With the 1993 model, NUMMI introduced an innovation borrowed from the Takaoka, Japan, plant—workers on a miniassembly line put together the entire instrument panel and install it as a single unit.

These two changes were expensive—$14 million for the doors-off process alone. Nonetheless, the doors-off process and instrument panel subassembly brought clear benefits in increased quality because they made certain tasks easier and helped prevent scratches to the paint. In addition, by relieving workers of operating within the cramped space of the vehicle and working around the doors, the changes reduced physical strains.

The Pilot Team

Unlike GM's top-down procedure, NUMMI, when changing models, tried to bring together the knowledge of Japanese and American workers, suppliers, and design and manufacturing engineers.

The pilot team was the key organizational mechanism in NUMMI's model change process. The pilot team bore responsibility for designing rough-cut standardized work sheets and training workers in their new jobs. An elite group of team leaders, the pilot team grew and shrank depending on the workload of each model change. Exemplary workers joined the team for months or even years, usually returning to the shop floor when a project ended.

At the beginning of 1992 the pilot team consisted of eight members, only three of whom had worked on the previous major model change in 1988. By the spring of 1992 the pilot team had added sixteen members, all of them first-time pilot team members. The high proportion of new members was partly because many former pilot team members were working on the truck line start-up, which had been launched in 1991. In addition, a number of the 1988 pilot team members had been promoted to group leader. Finally, NUMMI management had deliberately added newcomers, consistent with its philosophy of spreading out experiences and learning instead of concentrating them in a few people.

Initial 1992 pilot team training was minimal. All pilot team members had received some training in standardized work when they were promoted to team leader. Later on, they received a few days of additional training covering, for example, work design and ergonomics. (Ergonomics is the applied science of designing the work environment to minimize physical discomfort or injury.) Most training was on-the-job—reading books describing the jobs; learning to write up engineering change requests; and determining the pilot team's role in the big picture of engineers, designers, suppliers, and assembly. By and large, however, the pilot team had to be enterprising and independent and figure things out themselves.

LEARNING FROM JAPAN. Early in the process, the pilot team traveled to Japan. (Some members made multiple trips.) Toyota's Takaoka plant had begun production of the new model Corolla in 1991. NUMMI based most of its large-scale changes, such as doors-off assembly and the instrument panel subassembly line, on the innovations already up and running at Takaoka.

The trips to Japan also gave the pilot team a chance to see the minor kaizens that the Japanese had introduced. Pilot team members knew what the problem jobs were and some difficulties that would arise with the new model. As a result, they worked the assembly line in Japan to see how their counterparts had designed it.

The Toyota design engineers in Japan continued the kaizen process with the help of the Americans. For the Prizm, which was a modification of the Toyota Sprinter but with a different interior, the pilot team was the first to build the complete car. Although some engineers were more attached to their designs than others, most were pleased to incorporate the suggestions of the pilot team into how to make the car easier to manufacture. For example, one small lever that helped attach the door latch was a bit too short to be reached easily. When a pilot team member suggested that the lever be extended a half inch, the change was made. It was a minor alteration, but one that saved a few seconds for each car and made the task easier to perform.

The trip to Japan helped the pilot team kaizen the assembly line design as well as better train their fellow team members. For example, when returning from Japan, the pilot team brought a large binder containing pictures of individual parts and explanations of how they should be installed. The pilot team turned the book into detailed work instructions, making modifications for the production of two cars on one line. The team also had to design the appropriate equipment for each job, including hoists and balancers to hold heavy equipment and parts, trays for each size or combination of parts, and tables to subassemble certain parts.

NUMMI tried to involve everyone in the kaizen process. Early on, the company dismantled a Honda Civic and lined up Corolla and Civic parts. Suppliers, team members, and office workers were free to examine the parts and share their ideas. One worker noticed that the flat deck under the rear window was held on by six clips in the NUMMI design and by only three clips in the Civic design. As a result, NUMMI changed to four clips because, as one engineer noted, the part was unlikely to blow away.

BUILDING A PILOT VEHICLE. In June 1992, only two months before the start of production, the pilot team built the first cars from parts that had been assembled on the suppliers' assembly lines. (Previous pilot vehicles had been built with custom-made parts.) Unfortunately, although a number of modifications had been made since earlier pilot runs, many parts were still not fitting. With only a few weeks before production was scheduled to begin, the pilot team realized it needed more time, which it did not have.

NUMMI had increased the number of parts it bought in North America, and many suppliers were having difficulties achieving the NUMMI quality levels. Unlike GM-Fremont, NUMMI had no inspection of incoming parts and required that suppliers provide essentially perfect parts.

Even NUMMI's experienced North American suppliers had problems performing such a quick model change. A GM supplier might build up its inventory from the normal four-week supply to eight weeks and then have a cushion of those eight weeks plus the several months the GM plant was closed to retool and fine-tune its production process. With just-in-time deliveries, however, NUMMI suppliers could not build up a buffer, and NUMMI was closed only one week.

TRAINING FOR THE NEW MODEL. While some problems that arose after the start of production could be traced to supplier relations, others were caused by inadequate training of the team members. Training began early in the process; the pilot team trained group and team leaders, then team members. Training group leaders first was important, because they were responsible for a substantial part of the design of the standardized work process for their groups. Thus some group leader training began as much as a year before the start of production. Although the goal was eighty hours of training per team leader, sixty to seventy hours was more typical. This pattern of less-than-ideal training levels was repeated for team members.

The first workers came up to the pilot room more than six months before the start of production. The goal for team members was to have ten hours of training to learn a primary job, and most workers also were to be trained to do a secondary job. In one group with above-average training, for example, most team members received twelve hours of training per job, with most of the training taking place after the regular scheduled workday, on overtime. However, no team members in this group were fully trained on a second job by the start of production, though some were by the time the line had ramped up to full production.

Unfortunately, most groups were not as well prepared. Some team members did not show up for scheduled after-hours training, and not all group leaders were energetic in promoting the training to their groups. As a result, at the start of production, few team members knew more than one job. This situation was in sharp contrast with NUMMI's stated goal of enabling all workers to rotate among all the jobs performed by their team.

Absenteeism, while low by GM standards, was still above NUMMI's target rate. The result was lower training. When a team member was absent, the team leader had to substitute; ideally, the team leader would be substituting for a worker who wanted to attend training. In the worst case, pilot team members had to substitute on the line, slowing down training even further.

Although cutting back on training reduced the scope for kaizens, some valuable improvements still came from the workers. For example, members of one team complained that they had to stretch to get to a section of the car on which they needed to work. In response, the pilot team introduced a platform to help address ergonomic complaints. Team members felt the initial work platform was too low, and in the process of preparing for the new model change, it was raised from six to eight inches and then raised again to ten inches.

In another case, one team member installed the starter and several additional parts. He suggested that the starter be assembled outside the vehicle and that the entire subassembly be installed as one piece into the car. This arrangement permitted him easier access and made the job safer and faster. As one pilot team member put it, "That's the key: getting people to work with you. And they will as long as they know they have influence over their jobs."

The Changeover

GM model changes required plant closures of up to twelve weeks. Workers would be laid off and would receive unemployment benefits, often with supplements approximating full pay. At NUMMI, the plant was closed for only a week. A year in advance, workers had been warned that they would be required to use a week of their vacation during this period

When NUMMI opened, the team members returned to new jobs and a slower pace of work. Instead of producing four hundred cars a day, they began with four or five a day, trying to attain a sixty-second cycle time per vehicle but stopping after each assembly was complete to identify the sticking points.

The primary goal of the first week was training. Although most workers had had some training before the start of production, few had achieved the goal of ten hours set by the pilot team. Thus the main task was walking through the job: putting on a part, removing it, and putting it on again.

After training, the main goal in the first days of production was experimentation and kaizen—in addition to learning their jobs, workers were expected to improve them. During the first days of constructing the new model, nearly every worker made suggestions for increasing quality, productivity, or safety. In addition, engineers, the pilot team, suppliers, and workers in the skilled trades helped team members kaizen their jobs. For example, the new 1993 model had airbags for the first time. When team members installed an airbag, they also entered the serial number of the bag into a computer that linked the airbag with the vehicle identification number of the car. One team member explained how her team had a problem with typographical errors. Ten to fifteen cars were returned each day because a team member typed in an incorrect airbag number. Team members suggested that an engineer reprogram the computer so that it would reject impossible serial numbers, such as those with the wrong number of digits. This simple change immediately reduced the defect rate to one per day.

A difficult job was installing the wiring harness—the bundle of wires that connect the electrical systems of the car. The pilot team had seen a trick in Japan: Wiring harnesses about to be installed were placed in a warm air chamber to make them more pliable. When the wiring harness turned out to be difficult to install, NUMMI set up a similar warming system a few months after the start of production.

Typical kaizens involved moving machinery and carts that held parts, installing signs for safety and for job instruction, and placing railings to prevent accidents. Some kaizens involved suppliers as well. One part had to be wrapped around a rear pillar just behind and to the side of a rear passenger's head. Initially, the material was so stiff that the job took twice the allotted ten seconds. During the first months, the problem was communicated to the supplier, which switched to a more pliable material. As one pilot team member explained, a "night and day difference [was brought about] just from change in materials to make [the parts] more flexible." After the supplier began using the new material, the job took the allotted time.

An important set of kaizens involved rebalancing work within a team and between teams. If one job was overloaded and another underloaded, team members switched tasks between the jobs to equalize the work.

As the production process began to work more smoothly, production volumes grew. Output went from one car an hour to one car every ten minutes—a car followed by nine empty slots. Each time the line pace increased, new problems became apparent. Jobs that were easy at low volumes became difficult at higher rates or were determined to be overloaded.

For example, the doors on the Prizm presented a workability problem that could not have been seen until cars were being produced on the assembly line. At Takaoka, to install the doors on the Sprinter, Toyota's counterpart to the Prizm, the team member needed to pull a number of rubber and glass pieces tight before fastening them together. In Japan, this procedure posed no problem; the team member could pull hard because the Sprinter door was attached to the car. On the Prizm, however, the door was unattached.

This minor difference led to a series of kaizens. Engineers worked with suppliers to tune the parts, so less pulling was needed. The work procedures were changed slightly, so workers pulled at a different part of the door. The rubber parts were moistened so they would be more pliable. In this fashion, the workability problem was slowly eliminated from the assembly line.

The performance results of all kaizens were impressive. Although the line ramp-up fell about one week behind schedule during the first three months, planned productivity was quickly reached, and quality did not take a dip as it did after the previous model change.

The result was an assembly line with many parents: the Japanese engineers, managers, pilot team, and workers who set up the Japanese line and the NUMMI engineers, managers, pilot team, and workers who kaizened the NUMMI line in thousands of ways. The direct involvement of the workers was doubly important. They contributed valuable technical expertise, and as one pilot team member put it, "They're the ones who set it up, who fine-tuned it. So they're a whole lot more likely to buy into it."

Ergonomics

The 1993 model change at NUMMI was not an unmitigated success. Six months after the change, the California state Occupational Safety and Health Administration (Cal-OSHA) responded to a complaint against NUMMI by the UAW and issued a strongly worded citation:

Ergonomic hazards were not adequately evaluated when the 1993 major model change was planned and implemented on the Corolla/Prizm passenger car assembly line. . . . In many cases, the nature of particular tasks—repetitiveness, high necessary force from postures with high static loading—predict ergonomic problems from first principles.[15]

Some observers have cautioned that the intense work pace of Japanese manufacturing may cause serious health problems.[16] Other, more critical observers, have denounced Japanese manufacturing management techniques as "management by stress."[17]

The Cal-OSHA citation referred to problems that began during the start of production in August 1992. Line workers and management quickly discovered that they were facing formidable problems with workability. Many parts of the car simply did not fit together. Some parts could not be installed, and others did not align with adjacent parts. Gaps formed between pieces of the interior, and cars rattled when they were driven. It was a "tough launch," said Vice President of Manufacturing Gary Convis.

Several factors contributed to the parts problem. First, many of the suppliers had never before worked with NUMMI. Second, some parts had been altered on the line in Japan, but not on the written specifications. "Most parts were to spec, but the cars were still hard to build," said Alex Nikashin, assistant manager in quality control engineering. Third, the pilot team that set up the changeover was relatively inexperienced. "The engineers and pilot team members didn't see the magnitude of the problem," said Convis. "In part it was due to a lack of experience. Their focus was on product specs. When we finally uncovered the problems in pilot production, the engineers were stretched too thin to resolve them all in a timely fashion."

The result was serious quality problems; the poor fit overall reduced the cars' reliability. In addition, productivity fell. Parts that should have taken ten seconds to snap into place were taking twenty or thirty seconds. With a cycle time of sixty seconds, that difference could require that the line be stopped repeatedly.

The ill-fitting parts created a second set of problems related to workers' health and safety. When parts did not fit well, workers forced them in place by pushing, wrenching, and jerking. During the changeover, management and union officials alike reported seeing workers pounding parts with the palms of their hands. "People were using their hands as hammers, their body parts as though they were tools," said Bargaining Chairman Nano. This activity exposed workers to key risk factors for such ergonomic disorders as tendinitis and carpal tunnel syndrome.

Within weeks, ergonomic complaints soared. "When there are problems in the factory, team members will pull you over as you walk down the aisles," reported Joe Enos, the UAW safety representative. "Usually I get someone telling me about troubles every week or two. Then, there were three or four every time I went out on the floor. My barometer is how far I can walk into the plant without getting called over. [After the model changeover] I couldn't walk more than a few feet. It was terrible."

The ergonomic effects of the workability problems were compounded by the suspension of job rotation during the model changeover. Rotation would have reduced the injury rate as workers moved to jobs that used different muscles and off jobs that were particularly likely to cause injury. At the same time, however, rotation would have reduced productivity and quality, because workers were not fully trained on all jobs performed by their teams. NUMMI's plan was to increase rotation to a second job within the team only when all members of the team knew their primary job.

According to Convis, the unanticipated workability problems set off a vicious cycle. As the ergonomic problems worsened, absenteeism grew. Pinched for labor power, team leaders had to work as replacements instead of substituting for team members being cross-trained on their secondary jobs. The delay in cross-training in turn made rotation more difficult. As a result, team members had to work long hours on what were often physically stressful jobs, which led to more ergonomic problems and more absences.

The result was a spike in ergonomic injuries and illnesses. According to Cal-OSHA, after the model change a 12 percent increase was reported in the number of workers recorded on the company's logs who missed work because of health and safety problems. By October the company had used up its reserve group of thirty-two workers and had to hire additional employees.

Union Safety Representative Enos described the changeover from a different perspective than did Convis:

We got some promises that they would do something, that the problems would soon get fixed. But in the meantime people were still getting hurt. The problems weren't getting fixed as quickly as they should have. Not because the company wasn't trying. But there were two problems: people were getting hurt and there was a parts problem. The people getting hurt was caused by lack of rotation. To me, the smart move would be to rotate people to cut down the injuries. We don't have control over the parts, but we do have control over people getting hurt. You'd think they would have dealt with that. Unfortunately they didn't.

Enos concurred that the lack of rotation exacerbated the ergonomic problems. He claimed that the disorders were even occurring at 25 percent of normal line speed. Although the injuries signaled serious trouble, he said, management refused to deviate from the planned path of line acceleration. As the number of cars per hour increased, injuries continued to rise.

NUMMI reacted by focusing on the root cause: workability. That is, the company assumed that with well-designed parts and jobs, the parts would fit together easily and the jobs would not require stressful pushing or reaching. This approach deemphasized short-term measures such as job rotation that promoted safety at the expense of quality or productivity; instead, NUMMI management looked for long-term solutions that would benefit both safety and productivity or quality. Unfortunately, the result was a jump in injuries and the need for the union to call on outside regulators to bring about an ergonomic evaluation.

Cal-OSHA was unimpressed by NUMMI's responses to the problems. The citation noted, "Serious employee injuries due to repetitive stress, as well as employee symptoms of impending stress injury[had] increased alarmingly." In addition, NUMMI did not respond quickly enough to correct the "numerous ergonomic hazards on the 1993 Model Corolla/Prizm assembly line."

Only after the Cal-OSHA citation did NUMMI implement an ergonomic evaluation for the new assembly line. Even after the evaluation identified a number of problem jobs, several months passed before a majority of the fixes were implemented. Job rotation was still not fully reintroduced a year after the start of production.

The rhetoric of employee involvement at NUMMI often suggests that fundamental conflict over the pace of work was eliminated. The OSHA citation proves that management and workers remain with somewhat divergent interests, even in a highly cooperative setting. The pilot team setting up the 1993 assembly line had minimal ergonomics training; the company was unresponsive to union complaints concerning ergonomic issues in the first months after the model change; and the Safety Department was consistently understaffed—it had no full-time ergonomist, for example.

Secretary of Labor Robert B. Reich in 1993 raised some controversy by stating, "The jury is still out on whether the traditional union is necessary for the new workplace."[18] The OSHA citation and a related dispute over ergonomics after the 1993 model change at NUMMI show a quintessential "new workplace" with a union performing a traditional role of using its bargaining power to promote workers' goals. At least in this case, the combination of a confrontational role with the bargaining power provided by OSHA regulations was useful in enhancing workers' safety.

Effects of NUMMI on GM

The importance of human resources is evident at other General Motors plants. When GM installed robotics at the Hamtramck plant in Detroit, Michigan, where Cadillacs are made, it made the mistake of automating obsolete production methods.[19] In 1986, one year after the plant opened, the technology at Hamtramck was so unreliable that only about half the cars were being produced per hour that were supposed to be. Echoing earlier statements about GM-Fremont, the *Economist* referred to Hamtramck as the "most troubled car plant in America." As described in the *Economist,*

> the production lines ground to a halt for hours while technicians tried to debug software. When they did work, the robots often began dismembering each other, smashing cars, spraying paint everywhere or even fitting the wrong equipment. Automatic guided vehicles [which had been] installed to ferry parts around the factory, sometimes simply refused to move. What was meant to be a showcase plant turned into a nightmare.[20]

GM's expectations were not met. The high-technology Hamtramck plant was failing, while the medium-technology NUMMI plant was achieving the quality and productivity targets that billions of dollars had failed to buy. But within four years, an impressive GM-UAW commitment to employee involvement turned the Hamtramck plant around. The robots were retired, and workers were trained in quality and process controls. As a result, Cadillac was awarded the prestigious Malcolm Baldrige National Quality Award in 1990. The Hamtramck facility was recognized as one of America's best plants by *Industry Week* magazine in 1991.

The lesson for GM was that the way workers are trained and how work is organized, not the machines that are purchased, are the real keys to competitive car making. Unfortunately, the lesson disseminates slowly. The typical General Motors plant has nowhere near the level of employee involvement of NUMMI, Saturn, or GM-Hamtramck.

The experience at NUMMI shows both the power of employee involvement and its problems. No amount of involvement can fully resolve conflicts over the pace of work. And disseminating employee involvement is not easy, even within a single large corporation.

3

Employee Support

*Q: What did Pope John XXIII tell the journalist who asked him
how many people work at the Vatican?
A: "About half."*

—ITALIAN EDITION OF TRIVIAL PURSUIT

More than two centuries ago, Scottish economist Adam Smith outlined
the efficiency benefits of a detailed division of labor, in which each
worker performed the same task repeatedly. Implicit in his model of pin
manufacturing was a hierarchy—the same hierarchy that evolved into the
almost complete division between thinking and doing at GM-Fremont.

Smith also outlined the problems with a detailed division of labor; for
example, a person who again and again executes "a few very simple
operations . . . generally becomes as stupid and ignorant as it is possible
for a human creature to become."[1] Debate continued for many generations about the conditions under which managers can afford to hire only
employees' hands, not their heads as well.

The fundamental problem of management is to convince employees
that they will benefit by working hard and sharing ideas. If workers
share their ideas with a noncooperative management, management will
merely raise the expected level of output; the result is that workers will
end up working harder for lower wages. Conversely, if managers give
autonomy and rewards to workers who restrict output, profits will
plummet. One likely outcome is that managers will not trust workers,
will not expect workers to contribute ideas, and will not permit workers
to innovate when they have ideas. The dilemma can be resolved only if
managers and workers learn to trust each other. Workers will only work

36

hard and share ideas if managers follow through on their promises of rewards for good ideas and efforts.

Elaborate theoretical explanations have been put forth for the virtues and weaknesses of participation.[2] Although employee involvement can raise productivity, satisfaction, and product quality, it may not always work. Given the many potential costs of participation, the evidence of participation's effects on productivity is, unsurprisingly, mixed. Each cost corresponds to a management practice that must be in place for involvement to succeed (see boxes on advantages and disadvantages of employee involvement and on difficulties in measuring the relationship between participation and performance).[3]

No magic formula exists for creating successful employee involvement. Nevertheless, organizations striving to tap into the resources of their work force must build support from employees, managers, unions (when present), and business partners. Three preconditions are required to build employee support and capability for involvement to succeed.[4] First, workers need to be involved and given some responsibility for organizational change and their daily work. Employees need mechanisms through which their suggestions can be evaluated and implemented. If jobs are narrowly defined and rigid, workers have less opportunity to make suggestions. The methods used for creating employee involvement range from active suggestion systems to self-directed work teams. What they have in common is that they give employees the ability to propose changes in work methods, the product, the choice of technology, other matters that affect performance, and the quality of worklife. Second, employees must be motivated to make improvements. While the incentive mechanisms in high-involvement organizations vary widely, the objective is to share the rewards gained from new ideas. Many organizations link pay and rewards to performance and new skills. In addition, most high-involvement organizations find it important to ensure that ideas generated do not result in adverse actions such as layoffs or dismissals. Third, workers must be capable of making improvements. Their knowledge and skills are developed through training and continuous learning, and their contributions are made possible through information sharing.

Employee Empowerment

For employees to be empowered, the company must provide means for employees to participate both at the shop or office floor and at higher levels in the organization.

Advantages and Disadvantages of Employee Involvement

The following summarizes many theories of how employee involvement can raise productivity, satisfaction, and product quality, stressing the reasons that employee participation may not always work.

Possible Advantage of Participation	Possible Disadvantage of Participation
Participation may result in better decisions. Workers often have information that higher management lacks. Furthermore, participation permits a variety of different views to be aired.	Workers may be less informed than managers, and the premises upon which they make their decisions may be different. The rewards motivating workers to share their ideas may be larger than the value of the ideas themselves.[1]
People are more likely to implement decisions they have made themselves.[2] They know better what is expected of them, and helping make a decision commits one to it.[3] Participation may lower the disutility of effort, by providing intrinsic motivation.[4]	Once becoming committed to a decision, employees may be reluctant to change it.
The process of participation may satisfy such nonpecuniary needs as creativity, achievement, and the desire for respect.	Not everyone has strong desires for creativity and achievement, or they satisfy these sufficiently off the job.
Participation may improve communication and cooperation; workers communicate with each other instead of requiring all communications to flow through management, thus saving management time.	Participation is time consuming, and if decisions are made by groups, reaction to changing environments may be particularly slow.
Participative workers supervise themselves, thus reducing the need for managers and so cutting overhead labor costs. Participation teaches workers new skills and helps train and identify leaders.	Retraining of employees and managers can be expensive.

Participation enhances people's sense of power and dignity, thus reducing the need to show power through fighting management and restricting production.

Once a precedent of participation is established, withdrawal of the right to participate becomes difficult.

Participation increases loyalty and identification with the organization. If participation and rewards take place in a group setting, the group may pressure individuals to conform to decisions.[5]

Cohesive, participative groups may unite against management to restrict production and prevent change.

When union and management leaders jointly participate to solve problems on a nonadversarial basis, the improved relationship may spill over to improve union-management relations.

Sharing information with unions raises their bargaining power, so companies may lose.[6] Cooperating with management may lower unions' legitimacy with members, so they may lose as well.

Participation frequently results in the setting of goals. Goal setting is often an effective motivational technique, particularly when workers set their own goals.[7]

Goals workers set for themselves may be low.

Note: This draws on David I. Levine and George Strauss, "Employee Participation and Involvement," in Commission on Workforce Quality and Labor Market Efficiency, *Investing in People: A Strategy to Address America's Workforce Crisis,* background papers, vol. 2, paper 35b (Department of Labor, September 1989), pp. 1893–948.

1. Michael C. Jensen and William H. Meckling, "Rights and Production Functions: An Application to Labor-Managed Firms and Codetermination," *Journal of Business,* vol. 52 (October 1979), pp. 469–506.

2. L. W. Porter, Edward E. Lawler III, and J. Richard Hackman, *Behavior in Organizations* (McGraw-Hill, 1975).

3. Barry Staw and Jerry Ross, "Commitment to a Policy Decision: A Multitheoretical Perspective," *Administrative Science Quarterly,* vol. 23 (1978), pp. 40–64.

4. Barry Staw, "Intrinsic and Extrinsic Motivation," in Harold J. Leavitt and others, eds., *Readings in Managerial Psychology,* 3d ed. (University of Chicago Press, 1980).

5. George Strauss, "Managerial Practices," in J. Richard Hackman and J. Lloyd Suttle, eds., *Improving Life at Work: Behavioral Science Approaches to Organizational Change* (Santa Monica, Calif.: Goodyear Publishing, 1977), pp. 297–363.

6. Morris M. Kleiner and Marvin L. Bouillon, "Information Sharing of Sensitive Business Data with Employees," *Industrial Relations,* vol. 30 (Fall 1991), pp. 480–91.

7. Gary P. Latham, Miriam Erez, and Edwin A. Locke, "Resolving Scientific Disputes by the Joint Design of Crucial Experiments by the Antagonists: Application to the Erez-Latham Dispute Regarding Participation in Goal Setting," *Journal of Applied Psychology,* vol. 73 (November 1988), pp. 753–72.

Measuring the Links between Participation and Performance

When you cannot express it in numbers, your knowledge is of a meager and unsatisfactory kind.

—Lord Kelvin

Determining the true effect of work practices such as employee involvement on productivity is difficult. Measurement problems can lead researchers to find no relationship when one does exist or vice versa.

Factors That Understate the Participation-Performance Relationship

Factors That Overstate the Participation-Performance Relationship

Measuring work practices such as participation is difficult because plans differ according to the level of participation (frontline employees versus representatives), the number of people involved, the topics covered, the power the employees have on each topic, and the gap between official and actual involvement and empowerment. Measuring most forms of performance, such as productivity or worker satisfaction, also is problematic. The measurement of both work practices and performance typically leads to the estimated effect of a work practice being less than the true effect.

Successful participatory schemes are more likely to be reported in the empirical literature than are failures. For example, Richard A. Guzzo, Richard D. Jette, and Raymond A. Katzell found in their meta-analysis of studies of changes in work organizations that studies with better designs (for example, experiments with true control groups) revealed smaller effects than studies with other designs (for example, before-after comparisons).[1] The latter forms of research are less rigorous and expensive, and they are probably rarely published when not successful.

Many samples of organizations are small, making the detection of any effect difficult. Work practices are most useful in combination (for example, participation plus gainsharing plus training). If the researcher does not specify the interrelationships correctly, a true relationship may not appear. The effects are particularly difficult to detect in small samples, because testing for all possible combinations is hard.

Most samples of companies that adopt a work practice will disproportionately include those who find it most useful. Thus any correlation between work practice and performance does not predict what would happen to additional companies that adopt that work practice. Because companies differ, no single true effect of a work practice can be measured.

Failing to control for relevant aspects of the environment or context can lead to understatement of the importance of employee involvement. For example, if unionized companies are likely to adopt high-involvement practices when the company is in trouble, then employee involvement will become correlated with troubled companies.

Failing to control for relevant aspects of the environment can lead to overstatement of the importance of employee involvement. Prosperous companies could (for example, because of a technological advantage) share their good fortune with workers via employee involvement or profit sharing and also have high productivity and profits. In this case, employee involvement would falsely appear to raise performance.

Mismeasurement of the lags between the up-front costs of implementing a new program (training, for example) and the benefits biases researchers against finding any true effects.

Note: In response to Lord Kelvin, economist Frank Knight reportedly said, "Yes, and when you *can* express it in numbers your knowledge is of a meager and unsatisfactory kind."

1. Richard A. Guzzo, Richard D. Jette, and Raymond A. Katzell, "The Effects of Psychologically Based Intervention Programs on Worker Productivity: A Meta-Analysis," *Personnel Psychology,* vol. 38 (Summer 1985), pp. 295-91.

Direct Participation

Successful employee involvement requires that workers have substantive involvement, not the superficial ability to make suggestions (but not be listened to) or to make decisions (but not about anything that matters). Employee involvement may pertain to many topics, including how employees do their job, how safe the jobs are, and how pleasant the working conditions are. What these topics have in common is that they focus on matters of importance to the work force. This simple lesson is frequently ignored in American efforts to implement programs calling themselves employee involvement. Not surprisingly, lack of employee empowerment is associated with high failure rates among such programs.

CONSULTATIVE PARTICIPATION. Consultative participation involves direct participatory arrangements with little or no formal influence. Typically, employees are allowed to give their opinions, but final decisions are made by management. The focus most often is on workplace organization and other shop-floor and personnel issues important to workers and about which they often have significant information not readily available to management. While worker suggestions are solicited, workers are not permitted to decide how to solve problems, and often they do not even implement the suggestions that are accepted by management.

In the United States, the quality circles (QCs) fad of the early 1980s provided strong evidence on the effectiveness of purely consultative participation. Quality circles at their peak were implemented by perhaps half of all large U.S. employers, although typically only in a minority of workplaces and including only 25 percent of the work force at each workplace. QCs usually consist of small voluntary groups of employees from the same work area who meet on a fairly regular basis to identify and solve quality, productivity, and other problems. Frequently, members of QCs receive special training in such subjects as group dynamics and problem solving. Despite their name, QCs often deal with subjects other than quality—for example, work flow, productivity, safety, and employee welfare.

Numerous studies have examined consultative participation, in which workers have little power. M. L. Marks and others, for example, examined the effects of QCs in a manufacturing plant. The study compared the productivity of employees who volunteered to participate in the QC program with the productivity of nonparticipants over a twenty-four-month period. While the two groups had similar demographic characteristics and almost identical initial work records, the productivity of the nonparticipants increased by less than 10 percent, while that of the participants increased by more than 20 percent during the course of the study.[5]

Although a number of studies indicated that QCs had positive impacts, the preponderance of evidence does not suggest positive long-term effects from consultative participation. Maryellen Kelley, for example, found that productivity was lower at nonunion metal-working establishments (plants or offices) with worker-management problem-solving committees (typically quality circles) than at similar establishments without committees. William N. Cooke reached similar conclusions in his study of Michigan manufacturing: Introducing teams in nonunion settings (typically with only consultative power) had minimal impact on productivity.[6] Both studies indicated that in union settings, when workers in teams had rights to due process, implicit gainsharing via the bargaining process, and representative participation, productivity was higher in factories with teams.

The most important evidence on the long-run effects of QCs comes from studies that do not directly measure their performance, but measure their longevity. Most studies revealed that the half-life of QCs was less than three years.[7] Anecdotal evidence suggests that virtually all QCs of the mid-1980s are no longer functioning; most have closed down, a minority have evolved into more substantive forms of involvement.

Evidence repeatedly showed that managers liked QCs because they gave workers the impression that someone was listening to them. In one survey, the most common benefit of QCs reported by managers was that they permitted the supervisors to explain managerial actions to the workers.[8] Until managers believe their subordinates have valuable ideas and are willing to substantially empower workers, few improvements in quality will result, and few employee involvement programs will flourish.

The studies of consultative participation, in short, support a general consensus that purely advisory shop-floor arrangements are not likely to achieve sustainable improvements in productivity. Such improvements require work reorganization and a broadening of employee participation in decisionmaking.[9]

SUBSTANTIVE PARTICIPATION. Substantive participation in work and workplace decisions includes formal, direct participation schemes, such as work teams. Usually substantive participatory arrangements concentrate on the same kinds of issues as consultative arrangements, but workers have more influence. (Intermediate levels of power also exist, such as where workers' suggestions are implemented unless management specifically justifies its negative response. Sometimes, management is required to explain what changes would make the suggestions acceptable.)

Several early studies examined short-term empowerment, often as experiments. These results were typically positive.[10] Several other studies suggested that more participation—in the form of more channels for participation and coverage of a broader range of issues—leads to higher productivity. A study by Daniel Mitchell and others constructed an index of the number of issues over which participation was involved. Regression results indicated that the participation index was positively related to the productivity of both clerical and production workers.[11]

Two 1980 studies by John R. Cable and Felix R. FitzRoy examined a group of West German "industrial partnership" firms that provided both profit sharing and participatory rights for their workers. Cable and FitzRoy constructed an index of participation based on managers' perceptions of worker participation in various areas. The index rises as the extent of worker participation increases from no participation to purely advisory participation to active influence and as the number of issues on which workers participate expands. The regression results indicated that as the participation index rises, value-added rises (holding constant the amounts of labor and capital). Cable and FitzRoy also split their sample into companies with above- and below-average levels of employee involvement. On average, the high-involvement companies outperformed the low-participation firms by 15 percent, 177 percent, and 33 percent in output per worker, output per unit of capital, and profitability (rate of return on capital employed), repectively.[12]

More recent research has often focused on work teams. Although the role of teams varies, in many cases workers in work teams are given wide discretion to organize their tasks and operate with very little supervision. Typically, these groups make their own work assignments and determine their own work methods, subject to overall workflow requirements.

Work teams have been given responsibility for developing relations with vendors, determining which operations can be handled individually and which by the group as a whole, setting work pace (perhaps fast in the morning and slow in the afternoon), training new employees, and keeping financial records. Sometimes team members serve in roles normally reserved for staff personnel or supervisors: chairing the plant safety committee, redesigning work equipment, or troubleshooting customers' problems. At some locations, the job of supervisor is rotated among members of the group. At GM's Saturn plant, "councilors" (first-line supervisors) are elected by their subordinates.

Even in companies with substantive participation, empirical research indicated that productivity increases do not follow automatically. For example, a 1989 study by John F. Krafcik on the automobile industry suggested that team production techniques, which are an integral part of the Japanese automobile production system, have a positive effect on productivity in Japanese plants. But these plants also have several other unique features of Japanese industrial relations, and the studies did not distinguish the effects of work teams from the effects of the other factors on productivity performance.[13]

In contrast, econometric work on a U.S. auto plant by Harry C. Katz, Thomas A. Kochan, and Jeffrey Keefe in 1988 distinguished the productivity effects of work teams from the productivity effects of other forms of substantive and consultative participation in technology and work group decisions. The results suggested that team production techniques, by themselves, lower labor productivity and quality, while substantive participation in work groups when coupled with technology-related decisions increases labor productivity and product quality. The statistical association between the measures of participation and plant performance, however, are weak (many of the estimated coefficients are not statistically significant at even the 10 percent level).[14]

These results and the findings of other empirical studies by Katz and his colleagues suggested that team production techniques, like QCs, accomplish little unless they are integrated with broader changes in the company's industrial relations environment, including changes that facilitate greater employee participation in higher-level decisionmaking. This conclusion is buttressed by qualitative case study evidence indicating that team production produces sizable improvements in both organizational performance and the quality of working life when accompanied by such organizational changes as increased worker participation in business strategy decisions, job-security programs, and group pay reward structures.[15] Broader organizational changes appear to be essential to the long-term viability and performance of substantive employee participation.

Maryellen Kelley's study of machine tools operators provided evidence that substantive involvement is more important than consultative involvement.[16] She found that workers who program their own machine tools have substantially higher productivity, even though in nonunion settings having a quality circle or similar committee has a negative effect on productivity.[17]

Anthony Carnevale and his colleagues studied 239 organizations that identified themselves as restructuring. They found that more extensive use of teams and higher skill variety are correlated with higher quality and lower absenteeism.[18]

Other studies focused not on work practices, but on employees' perceptions of empowerment and commitment. For example, Daniel Denison and Gary S. Hansen and Birger Wenerfelt examined companies that had employees, within a single section or division, fill out a questionnaire known as the "Survey of Organizations." They found that companies whose workers reported more participative cultures had a higher return on investment and sales and a higher return on assets than the industries as a whole.[19]

Representative Participation

Successful cases of employee involvement often provide representative participation to complement direct participation. Typical institutions include union-management committees, workers' representatives on the board of directors, and works councils.

Representative forms of participation are important for resolving disputes that occur at a lower level; for example, when a work group feels a suggestion will increase safety, but the supervisor disagrees. At NUMMI, for example, a union-management safety committee meets to discuss problems that are not settled on the shop floor. Representative forms of participation are also important when issues span multiple work groups. Finally, these forms of participation can provide benefits to all workers that no single worker has an incentive to provide. For example, on average no single worker will find it worth his or her time to ensure that management is telling the truth in its financial statement, even if that statement is the basis of gainsharing. An elected representative, however, will be able to check the numbers and provide reassurance to all employees.

Overall, the available empirical literature suggests that various forms of representative participation can improve performance when they are part of a package of participatory policies. Taken alone, they may improve labor-management relations, but they have little effect on productivity. This section focuses on codetermination and works councils; union labor-management committees, the most common form of representative participation in the United States, are discussed in the following chapter.

MEMBERSHIP ON COMPANY BOARDS OF DIRECTORS. Union representatives have served on the boards of Chrysler and several financially troubled airline, steel, and trucking companies. In addition, employee directors (not always selected by the union) have been involved in a considerable number of employee stock ownership plans (ESOPs) and worker buyouts. As has been the experience in other countries, employee directors in the United States have not been very important.[20] They have been handicapped by rules keeping board deliberations confidential, thus restricting communication with constituents. Directors from the shop floor lack the technical expertise to make contributions in areas such as finance. Regardless of the employee director's skill, management can usually keep issues that matter the most to employees off the board's agenda.

In any case, boards, which meet as infrequently as once a quarter, usually exert little influence.

Workers on the board may be more important when board membership serves as only one of several channels for employee participation and only one of several distinctive features of the company's industrial relations system. For example, in a 1987 study on British retail cooperatives, Derek C. Jones found that the presence of worker representatives on the board of directors had a positive but modest effect on productivity.[21]

The ineffectiveness of codetermination has been verified in empirical studies of West German codetermination laws requiring worker representatives on company boards of directors. Jan Svejnar concluded that the introduction of codetermination had either no significant productivity effect or a mildly negative one. In 1976 Germany passed a law requiring most large employers to increase from one-third employee representation to equal numbers of employee and stockholder representatives. Felix R. FitzRoy and Kornelius Kraft found that between 1976 and 1983 companies subject to this law enjoyed significantly less productivity growth than did smaller companies not subject to it. They pointed out that part of the result was plausibly because of the influence of employee directors in slowing layoffs. If this was the case, then the slower measured productivity growth represented a private cost to the owners, but not a social cost, because the workers were more productive at the companies than they would have been if unemployed.[22]

WORK COUNCILS. All continental nations of western Europe require large employers to have employee representation councils. The councils typically have the right to be informed about the financial situation of the company and to discuss certain employment-related matters such as training and layoffs. In some countries, works councils have the authority to veto some employment-related decisions. In Sweden, for example, no layoffs can occur without the concurrence of the works council.

Most researchers have found minimal effects on productivity for mandated works councils.[23] At the same time, case study evidence suggests that works councils can often serve a useful role in moving information up and down the organization and in improving the quality of decisionmaking. In addition, works councils create a problem-solving atmosphere, and managers prefer dealing with works councils to unions for problem solving.

As with codetermination, works councils may be more important when coupled with other forms of involvement. A 1991 econometric study by Motohiro Morishima examined the productivity effects of joint consultation committees, a form of representative participation common in Japan. These committees are corporate- and plant-level bodies that deal with business strategies and plans pertinent to the entire organization. The committees serve two major functions: sharing of business information with employees and prior consultation by the management with employees on upcoming business decisions. Morishima's econometric results indicated a strong and sizable positive association between an index of information sharing and firm profitability, employee productivity, and labor costs. An important point about the Japanese case is that "information sharing complements other aspects of the Japanese enterprise-level industrial relations system."[24]

Employee Motivation

What benefit has man from his toil under the sun?

—ECCLESIASTES

Traditional reward systems focus on individual achievement and the skills used at the current job. New forms of work require new forms of rewarding the cooperation and learning that underlie high-involvement workplaces. In addition, employees must be reassured that their ideas will not lead to layoffs or punishments such as dismissals.

Sharing Gains

Some kind of sharing of rewards from involvement is a key element of almost all participatory systems. (Profit sharing, which is usually based on the accounting profits of the enterprise, is differentiated here from gainsharing, which is usually based on cost reductions at a particular department, plant, or office.)

Financial sharing can occur without participation and vice versa, but both theory and evidence suggest that the two are likely to go together in successful participatory systems. In the short run, participation may be its own reward for many employees. In the long run, however, sustained, effective participation requires that employees be rewarded for the extra effort that participation entails and that they receive a share of any increased productivity or profits. Workers feel that it is unfair if their ideas generate cost savings and they do not share the benefits.

Group-based gainsharing provides workers with incentives to maintain norms of high effort, to monitor each other, and to discipline workers who are shirking. More positively, group-based pay gives workers incentives to cooperate and not to try to advance at the expense of their colleagues.

Just as participation can lead to demands for profit sharing, profit sharing can lead to demands for participation. In a company with profit sharing, workers' incomes depend upon the management's decisions, and workers want to have a say in these decisions.[25] Moreover, growing empirical evidence indicates a positive interaction between profit sharing and participation, implying that the combination is more potent than the sum of its parts.[26] According to a 1991 study, "the available evidence is strongly suggestive that for employee ownership, including profit-sharing and ESOP programs, to have a strong impact on performance, it needs to be accompanied by provisions for worker participation in decision making."[27]

GAINSHARING AND TOTAL QUALITY MANAGEMENT. Changes in reward systems have often been neglected by advocates of total quality management (TQM). For example, in many workplaces, the main effect of the quality movement has been that, in addition to their regular work, employees must fill in statistical process control (SPC) charts that track when errors occur. With little employee motivation, few of these charts are completed as they should be. When workers must fill in SPC charts but are not empowered, SPC is little more than a speed-up of the pace of work. Furthermore, without the cooperation of the employees in analyzing the data they collect, SPC loses most of its potential for improvements.

Quality consultants are aware that SPC can be perceived as a speed-up. Quality guru Joseph M. Juran, for example, warned managers that unless workers have substantial training and participation they will view the introduction of control charts as an unofficial tightening of specifications leading to more work.[28] That is, workers will perceive the new quality emphasis as an attempt to make them work harder.

Juran noted that upper management will experience the same problem. With the new emphasis on quality, top managers will need to measure the quality achievements of their divisions, attend more cross-functional meetings, and so forth. Juran advocated that high-level managers' pay should rise substantially when they achieve their quality goals. These bonuses will eliminate high-level managers' concerns about a speed-up of their jobs and motivate them to perform the extra quality-oriented tasks. Juran ignored the possibility of (or need for) rewarding workers for doing extra work to achieve their quality goals, however.

In contrast to many total quality consultants' recommendations, successful TQM efforts, such as at NUMMI, provide a number of gainsharing mechanisms. Most directly, NUMMI's workers' pay is tied to increases in productivity and to performance based on productivity and indicators of the quality of their cars. In addition, individuals and groups receive modest rewards for their suggestions. Finally, the presence of a union implies gainsharing exists over the long term; if NUMMI prospers, the union will bargain for a share of the profits. All of these incentives help motivate employees to share their ideas and enforce norms of high effort within the factory.

Several studies have found that high-involvement companies are more likely to have gainsharing. For example, in the 1987 survey of the Fortune 1000, gainsharing, where pay is based on plant or departmental performance, is roughly twice as prevalent in companies with above-average employee involvement than in companies with below-average involvement.[29] A 1991 survey of steel plants revealed a wider gap. More than half of the companies with work teams had multiple incentives based on a department's performance, while only 11 percent of those without work teams had nontraditional incentives.[30]

The gap is smaller for profit sharing, a companywide incentive. In the Fortune 1000, profit sharing is almost half again more likely in companies with above-average levels of employee involvement than in companies with below-average levels (36 percent versus 26 percent).[31] In a 1977 survey of the U.S. population, employees who reported having above-average autonomy at work also were about half again more likely to have profit sharing than those with below-average autonomy (23 percent versus 15 percent).[32] In a 1994 steel industry survey, profit sharing was only slightly more prevalent in plants with work teams (68 percent versus 64 percent).[33]

In his 1990 survey of publicly traded companies, Mark Huselid found that high-involvement companies also tended to have more use of profit sharing and incentive plans. Similarly, as a result of his 1990 survey, Paul Osterman reported that establishments with at least half the core work force involved in high-involvement practices were more likely to have profit sharing (48 percent versus 39 percent). Differences in incidence of gainsharing were not statistically significant.[34] Canadian establishments with semiautonomous work teams were more likely to have both profit sharing and gainsharing.[35]

In the 1987 survey of the Fortune 1000, companies that reported above-average success from employee involvement provided substantially higher levels of gainsharing and slightly higher profit sharing. Consistent with their emphasis on group-based rewards, they provided similar levels of individual incentives and merit pay. In the 1990 survey, companies that reported above-average success from employee involvement provided higher levels of profit sharing, gainsharing, and nonmonetary awards. They had similar levels of individual incentives, team incentives, and employee stock ownership.[36]

EMPLOYEE OWNERSHIP. Employee ownership occurs in two main forms in the United States: thousands of employee stock ownership plans, in which workers own a minority of the company's shares, and a much smaller number of companies that are majority owned by the work force. Although some of the employees at the majority-owned companies own their stock via an ESOP, the companies are referred to here as worker cooperatives.

Employee stock ownership has long been suspected to lead to higher productivity, as workers act as owners. Jeffrey Pfeffer noted, "It is probably no coincidence that all five of the companies . . . providing the best shareholder returns from 1972 to 1992 appear on the Employee Ownership 1000," a listing of one thousand companies in which employees own more than 4 percent of the stock of a corporation.[37] (The five companies are Southwest Airlines, Wal-Mart, Tyson Foods, Circuit City, and Plenum Publishing.) In spite of those impressive performances, most ESOPs have little or no employee participation and have no measurable effects on productivity. However, ESOP companies that provide employees with additional opportunities for participation in decision-making are significantly more likely to outperform conventionally owned companies than ESOP companies that do not. Furthermore, of the various forms of participation, those that reach closest to the shop floor have the biggest productivity effects, while stock voting rights or employee representation on company boards of directors have insignificant productivity effects.[38] These findings for ESOPs are consistent with the findings for conventionally owned companies.

As with representative participation, the Japanese experience with ESOPs is somewhat different. Perhaps because of extensive shop-floor consultation, in Japanese companies the net effect of introducing an ESOP was an almost 7 percent increase in productivity.[39]

Extensive empirical literature is available on the performance of worker-owned companies (cooperatives) in the United States and abroad.[40] At worker-owned companies, most studies concluded that the extent of employee ownership has a significant positive effect on the firm's productivity. Employee ownership is measured variously as the share of the firm's equity owned by employees or the share of the firm's employees who choose to become firm members by investing in a minimum number of shares. Richard J. Long and Bodil Thordarson found the productivity performance of worker-owned companies superior to that of conventionally owned companies that are otherwise similar. A study of the death rate of French cooperatives yielded indirect evidence of high effectiveness.[41] Death rates of cooperatives were only a fraction of the rate in similar conventional firms.

None of these studies directly measured the productivity effects of the participatory arrangements that usually accompany significant employee ownership or distinguished the effects from the productivity effects of employee ownership per se. Moreover, several of the studies, including the extensive econometric studies of the European producer co-ops, interpreted their ownership variables as proxies for the extent of employee participation in enterprise decisionmaking.[42] Such variables are imprecise and provide no information about the actual form and content of participation in the companies.

Several studies examined the effects of participation on productivity in worker-owned companies. These studies fairly consistently found that participation raises productivity in the worker cooperatives.[43]

Overall, the results of empirical research on employee-owned companies suggested that, within these companies, employee participation is positively associated with productivity. However, the companies almost always have several other characteristics that distinguish them from conventionally owned companies. For example, the European worker coops, which have been the subject of the most extensive empirical inquiry, typically have managements committed to employee ownership and representation, job security, compressed status and compensation differentials, and guaranteed worker rights. As a result, drawing general conclusions about the effects of employee participation on productivity from the experience of these companies is dangerous. The effects are likely much smaller in conventionally owned and organized companies without such characteristics.

Pay for Knowledge

Traditional workplaces reward people for the particular job they perform. Workers can lose pay or benefits when transferred to lower-skilled jobs, and they have no direct incentive to continuously improve their skills. Given these difficulties, many high-involvement companies have a pay-for-knowledge compensation system that rewards employees for each new skill acquired. These pay systems reward workers for learning multiple skills, which increases flexibility, enhances workers' ability to see the big picture and to suggest improvements, and encourages teamwork.[44]

An increasing proportion of American businesses have introduced knowledge-based pay systems. The proportion of the Fortune 1000 with pay-for-knowledge rose from 40 to 51 percent between 1987 and 1990, although most plans affected less than 20 percent of the labor force.[45] In his 1990 survey, Paul Osterman found that establishments with at least half the core work force involved in high-involvement practices were more likely to have pay for knowledge (36 percent versus 20 percent).[46] Canadian establishments with semi-autonomous work teams were also more likely to have pay for knowledge.[47] Companies in the Fortune 1000 that reported above-average success on employee involvement also have higher pay for knowledge.

Group Cohesiveness

Most participatory workplaces reduce pay and status differentials among employees, particularly between workers and managers, relative to nonparticipatory workplaces. Smaller differentials are associated with participation for three related reasons.

First, narrow differences in wages and status help develop an atmosphere of trust and confidence between workers and management, reinforcing the atmosphere of participation. Large differences in status can inhibit participation.[48] As employee involvement increases, management relies more on the good will and cooperation of employees. Employees often feel large wage differentials are unfair, and employees who feel disadvantaged are less supportive of the goals of the highly rewarded group.[49]

Second, bonuses based on group output give workers incentives to work for group goals and provide incentives for workers to monitor and discipline free riders. Narrow wage dispersion promotes cooperation, while large wage differences and competition for promotions can reduce cooperation, as workers try to win the bonus or promotion "tournament."[50]

Group-based pay, almost by definition, reduces individual pay differentials. According to Morton Deutsch, who has been studying the relationship between egalitarianism and productivity for more than forty years, when "efficiency requires efficient cooperation, almost any movement towards a democratic egalitarian structure increases effectiveness." Numerous laboratory experiments have found that narrow wage dispersion increases worker cohesiveness and increases productivity.[51]

Third, participation may extend into the realm of compensation. To the extent that the median employee exerts influence on the firm's compensation policy, pressure likely will exist to reduce high-end wages, thereby compressing wage differentials.

Regardless of the theoretical rationale, in practice, most participatory workplaces—including worker-owned companies in the United States and abroad, large Japanese companies, and successful participatory companies in the United States—tend to pay relatively egalitarian wages and to reduce status differences, largely to induce cohesiveness within the work force. For example, NUMMI has only a single parking lot and cafeteria, and managers are more likely to wear the company uniform than a suit. Personnel research supporting the importance of equality includes works by John F. Witte and Katrina Berman on U.S. participatory companies; Keith Bradley and Alan Gelb on foreign cooperatives; and William Ouchi, Thomas Rohlen, and Ezra Vogel on Japanese companies both at home and abroad. Edward E. Lawler III and Michael Beer and others recommended that participatory employers rely heavily on group-based compensation and narrow wage differentials.[52]

Policies to promote cohesiveness are more common at high-involvement companies. One commonly used mechanism to reduce status differences is to eliminate time clocks and put all workers on salary. Use of all-salary pay is more prevalent at companies with high levels of employee involvement than at companies with low levels of employee involvement, according to the 1987 survey of the Fortune 1000.[53] Similarly, at companies undergoing workplace transformation, extensive use of teams is correlated with an all-salaried pay system.[54] Consistent with a greater emphasis on cohesiveness, in an Indiana sample of manufacturing plants, workers reported a higher average level of cohesiveness at plants where autonomy or quality circle membership was high.[55]

Policies to promote cohesiveness are more common at successful high-involvement companies. In the 1990 survey of the Fortune 1000, companies with high reported success with their employee involvement had substantially higher levels of all-salaried work force.[56]

A sample of business units provides indirect evidence to support this contention. Business units with less inequality (both within management ranks and between management and workers) reported higher quality levels.[57] Product quality is the performance characteristic most responsive to employee effort and initiative as well as the focus of recent TQM-inspired employee involvement efforts.

Employment Security

Most high-involvement workplaces have implicit or explicit long-term employment contracts with their workers, contracts that stress reciprocal commitments and management's pledge to minimize the need for layoffs. Successful participatory systems usually avoid laying off workers for several related reasons. (Economic crises can prod management, workers, and unions to initiate participatory experiments. Nevertheless, employment stability reduces the costs of maintaining participation.)

Most directly, workers are unlikely to cooperate in increasing efficiency if they fear that by so doing they jeopardize their employment. Guarantees of job security reduce fears that higher productivity will lead to layoffs. Conversely, the fear of layoffs has inhibited the success of participation in several cases.[58]

Workers with job security expect to remain at their jobs for many years and are more likely to forgo short-term gains (for example, shirking) to build a more effective organization. Participation works only if employees share their ideas and if managers reward workers for increased productivity. In the short run, the rational strategy is for workers to hide productivity-improving techniques to enjoy more on-the-job leisure. Similarly, the company's short-run rational strategy is to deny that productivity has increased to avoid raising pay. Only a long perspective can convince both players to cooperate.

To the extent that participation relies upon work group cooperation and employees monitoring one another, long-term employment relations are essential. The longer an employee expects to be in a work group, the more effective are group-based rewards and social approval as motivators.

Participatory employers often make large investments in the selection, socialization, and training of workers. From the firm's point of view, long-term employment relations recover the higher investment in human resources that usually accompanies participation. Conversely, training in a variety of jobs and skills lowers the costs of long-term employment relations, because workers can be shifted to more critical tasks. Moreover, the process of training shows a commitment to workers that may increase their trust in managers' promises to avoid layoffs.

The case study literature on labor-managed companies provides evidence that participatory workplaces rarely lay off worker-members (although temporary workers are laid off). Fairness considerations constrain these companies from reducing the work force via layoffs. More generally, layoffs are inconsistent with the sense of membership and community that participatory companies try to instill.

Numerous examples exist of companies that provide high levels of employment security as part of a package of policies to ensure the success of participation.[59] In the United States, Hewlett-Packard and NUMMI have had policies of avoiding layoffs. During the early 1980s Hewlett-Packard adopted hiring freezes, shortened work weeks, and ordered the elimination of perquisites, for example, while other companies were engaging in mass layoffs.[60] During the mid-1980s NUMMI sent its entire work force into retraining during a time when, as one union official put it, General Motors (the previous owners of the plant) "would have closed the second shift."[61]

The relationship between participation and avoiding layoffs appears to be causal, not merely correlational. Evidence comes from IBM, for many decades the preeminent U.S. employer that avoided layoffs. For example, during the 1972–75 slowdown, IBM transferred seventeen thousand workers, completely retraining seven thousand of them.[62] A typical comment by an IBM executive:

"Our people, by using their minds as well as their hands, have cut two-thirds of the hours that go into manufacturing our product. . . . That achievement would have been impossible without productive and committed employees. And much of their commitment stems from the security they know is theirs through our practice of full employment."[63]

Declining market share in the early 1990s induced IBM to begin its first set of layoffs. Morale has plummeted at the company, and anecdotal evidence suggests employee loyalty and participation are substantially lower as well.

No-layoff policies are also common in other successful examples of worker participation, such as the Mondragon worker cooperative network in Spain, as well as in large companies in Japan.[64]

Rhino Foods

Rhino Foods is a fifty-employee specialty dessert manufacturer in Burlington, Vermont. In the spring of 1993, efficiency improvements, resulting in part from the company's employee-driven productivity program, and an unexpected drop in orders threatened to displace workers. Shunning layoffs, Ted Castle, president and founder of Rhino, brought the problem to the whole company and asked for volunteers to find a solution. The twenty-six volunteers developed a list of ten solutions. The top one was an employee exchange program between Rhino and other companies in the area with a need for workers. Rhino sent employees to companies such as Ben and Jerry's and Gardener's Supply as contract workers, broadening the employees' experience and building commitment for the entire work force.

Note: This example was drawn from Department of Labor, Office of the American Workplace, *Road to High-Performance Workplaces* (1994).

The most direct evidence that downturns in demand hurt participatory efforts is found in the survey of the 1987 Fortune 1000 data survey. "Worsened business conditions" was cited as a barrier to employee involvement efforts by 45 percent of the respondents, with 14 percent claiming that it was a barrier to a "great" or "very great" extent. Furthermore, short-term performance pressures (which worsen during downturns when performance is low) were cited as a barrier by 87 percent of the respondents and as "great" or "very great" by 43 percent.[65]

Policies to avoid layoffs are more common at high-involvement companies. According to a 1982 survey, Indiana manufacturing plants with quality circles and with workers reporting high levels of autonomy also had more workers agreeing that "My job security is good."[66] In his 1990 survey of publicly traded companies, Mark Huselid found that high-involvement companies also tended to have more promotion from within.[67]

Companies with above-average levels of employee involvement also had above-average levels of employment security policies in the 1987 survey of the Fortune 1000. This relationship was not replicated in the 1990 survey. In both the 1987 and 1990 surveys, companies that reported above-average success with employee involvement also reported higher proportions of their work forces were covered by policies to provide employment security.[68] In a 1992 survey of U.S. workplaces, companies with work teams were only half as likely to have experienced layoffs as those with no teams (although no difference was found in the incidence of formal policies to avoid layoffs).[69]

The lack of relationship between formal employment security policies and high-involvement practices may be the result of the recent rise of reengineering, in which job redesign is explicitly tied to downsizing. The tensions between asking workers to "work smarter" and laying off their colleagues, when "smarter" workers reduce labor requirements, are not emphasized in the literature prescribing reengineering.[70]

Guaranteed Individual Rights

Participatory systems usually have rules and procedures to safeguard employee rights. To participate effectively, people need "the assurance that they will not be penalized for their participation. Such acts as criticizing existing procedures or opposing proposed policy changes could invite reprisals from management."[71] Personnel systems governed by the rule of law are perceived as more legitimate and fair than systems in which decisions are at the discretion of managers.[72]

Empirically, the rule of law is found in most high-commitment work organizations, typically implemented with a formal grievance or complaint resolution system.[73] Paul Bernstein found guaranteed rights in essentially all of the successful participatory companies he studied. He concluded that such rights are a necessary component of workplace democratization.

Guaranteed rights increase workers' trust in the company. Several studies indicated how high-trust environments depend on employee perceptions of due process and facilitate employee participation, better performance, creativity, and communication.[74]

Guaranteed individual rights are an important part of long-term employment relations, because workers have an alternative to quitting if they are unhappy about one aspect of their jobs. Richard Freeman and James Medoff surveyed the evidence relating individual rights and performance. They concluded that union workers with guaranteed individual rights have higher productivity and are less likely to quit than are other workers.[75]

The most crucial right for most employees is knowing that they will not be dismissed for their critical ideas but will only be fired when the company can show good cause. In contrast to "just-cause" dismissal policies, the "at-will" dismissal policies at most U.S. companies mean that employment can be terminated at any time "for good cause, for bad cause, or even for cause morally wrong."[76]

When companies guarantee individual rights, traditional motivators such as fear of dismissal become less effective. However, in most successful participatory companies, workers are motivated by group rewards, peer pressure, and so forth—not by traditional fear of punishment. The evidence suggests that the gains in perceived fairness and in workers' willingness to participate outweigh the losses for participatory companies. High-commitment companies such as Hewlett-Packard have voluntarily adopted just cause and established many other employee rights, implying that the company anticipates net benefits from constraining managerial actions.

In his 1990 survey of publicly traded companies, Mark Huselid found that high-involvement companies also tended to have more employees with access to a formal grievance or complaint resolution procedure.[77]

Employee Capability

Even if workers are empowered and motivated, to make improvements they need to have ability. At high-involvement plants, their knowledge and skills are developed through training and continuous learning, and their contributions are made possible through information sharing.

High Levels of Training

Participatory companies invest much more in their workers than the average U.S. employer. At Saturn, for example, new hires go through 350 to 700 hours of training, even though they are long-time auto workers.[78] Training involves problem solving, quality tools, and understanding the auto industry and labor history. Because Saturn is founded on a philosophy of consensus decisionmaking—but just about everyone hates meetings—a large portion of the training is focused on effective skills in working in groups. Saturn workers are also trained in a number of different jobs, which improves their understanding of the production process and their ability to discover and implement improvements.

Consistent with this high level of training, Saturn workers receive a constant stream of information on how the plant is performing, the status of the automobile industry, and how their department performance compares with its goals. Saturn workers also receive on-the-job training in a variety of jobs as they rotate throughout their work group.

The participatory company's investment in human resources goes far beyond the initial training. Selection costs are typically far higher, because dismissals so rarely occur. Socialization is also a major investment in new hires—reaching its ultimate expression in "boot camps" found at some Japanese companies, where new recruits undergo strenuous physical exercises in which they learn to rely on each other.[79]

High level of training is not special to Saturn. As high-involvement employers rely more heavily on decisionmaking by employees, those employees need many skills to have the ability to succeed. Both formal classroom training and training on the job (via job rotation and cross-training) are common at high-involvement enterprises.

Numerous studies found very high rates of return on training. At the same time, evidence is available that training by itself is not effective in raising productivity substantially.[80]

Some of the most convincing studies of the role of training involve detailed cross-national comparative case studies within a particular industry.[81] These studies consistently found that U.S. and British employers train less than their German and Japanese counterparts. For example, newly hired auto assembly workers receive 310 hours of training in Japan and 280 hours of training in Japanese-managed plants located in the United States, but only 48 hours of training at traditional American plants. Moreover, employees at traditional plants have substantially lower autonomy. The net result is substantially lower productivity and quality.

High levels of training are more common at high-involvement companies. In the 1990 Fortune 1000 survey, companies that reported above-average success from employee involvement provided substantially higher levels of training in leadership skills, job skills training, and team-building skills, while they provided marginally higher levels of decisionmaking and problem-solving skills and in quality and statistical analysis and skills for understanding business.[82]

Similarly, in the Indiana survey of manufacturing plants, on-the-job and off-the-job training are both higher at plants where autonomy or quality circle membership are above average.[83] The 1992 survey of steel plants showed that companies with work teams are much more likely to have training in problem solving, high overall training, and sharing of financial information, while the use of teams is correlated with high levels of multilevel training at companies undergoing restructuring.[84]

In his 1990 survey, Paul Osterman found that establishments with at least half the core work force involved in high-involvement practices had higher levels of training (38 percent of workers in off-the-job training versus 22 percent) and cross-training (53 percent versus 31 percent). In his 1990 survey of publicly traded companies, Mark Huselid found that high-involvement companies also tended to have more hours of training per employee. At companies undergoing workplace transformation, higher intensity of training correlated with higher rates of on-time delivery and quality.[85]

High levels of training are more common at successful high-involvement companies. In the 1987 Fortune 1000 survey, companies that reported above-average success from employee involvement provided higher levels of training in decisionmaking and problem-solving skills and in quality and statistical analysis, although they provided only marginally higher levels of training in leadership skills, skills for understanding business, and team-building skills. In the 1990 Fortune 1000 survey, companies that reported above-average success from employee involvement provided substantially higher levels of training in leadership skills, job skills training, and team-building skills. They provided marginally higher levels of training in decisionmaking and problem-solving skills, quality and statistical analysis, and skills for understanding business.[86]

Sharing Information

The absence of information limits employees from participating in the business's mission and outcomes. High-involvement companies tend to provide their employees with more information on the progress of the company, new technology, and the big picture of the enterprise.

Employees who understand management priorities and budgetary constraints can make better decisions concerning training issues, customer service problems, quality, product design, and work process improvements. For this strategy to be effective, workers should receive training in how to interpret and apply the information they receive. Information that addresses the operating results of the employees' team or unit will be more useful than overall corporate operating results. Although having employees see and understand the big picture is important, information related directly to their work will allow them to make necessary improvement to increase productivity, or it can serve as feedback for improvements already implemented.

The 1987 Fortune 1000 survey revealed that high-involvement employers share more information on the business unit's operating results, fellow employees' pay, competitors' relative performance, planned new technology, and the company's plans, goals, and overall operating results. A 1990 follow-up showed that the gap had widened.[87]

Companies that reported above-average success from employee involvement also provided their employees with more information on the business unit's operating results, fellow employees' pay, competitors' relative performance, and planned new technology. They provided similar levels of information on the company's plans, goals, and overall operating results. In his 1990 survey of publicly traded companies, Mark Huselid found that high-involvement companies also tended to have employee attitude surveys and formal information-sharing programs (for example, a newsletter). Similarly, in Casey Ichniowski, Kathryn Shaw, and Giovanni Prennushi's study of steel lines, companies with teams are more likely to receive financial information on a regular basis.[88]

4

Managerial, Union, and Business Partner Support

Policies that enhance the ability and willingness of employees to participate effectively in their place of employment, although critical, are not sufficient for employee involvement to succeed. A company must maintain support of its managers, unions (where present), and business partners such as suppliers and customers.

Managerial Support

> *Ninety-five percent of American managers today say the right thing. Five percent actually do it.*
>
> —JAMES O'TOOLE

Most directly, employee involvement requires changes in companies' management systems, both for low- and midlevel managers and for top-level executives.

Lower- and Midmanagement Support

Many middle- and lower-level managers resist and sometimes sabotage employee involvement.[1] For frontline employees, one of the main advantages of participation is the greater freedom to use their own discretion, instead of having bosses hovering over them. This same freedom may be threatening to supervisors and managers.

Participation challenges supervisors' authority and status. Employees are encouraged to make decisions on their own. Discussions may reveal managers' mistakes. Autonomous work teams are encouraged to contact staff people and suppliers directly, thus bypassing line managers.

63

In addition, first-line supervisors often feel discriminated against. Quality circles have often been described as "something the top tells the middle to do to the bottom." Supervisors are forced into a system that typically they had no part in designing. In many cases they are forced to share their power, but they do not see their bosses sharing theirs.

In extreme cases, supervisors' jobs may be threatened. Job redesign can lead to the elimination of one or more levels of management, as occurred at Ford's Sharonville plant.[2]

Finally, American management has always stressed the division between managers (who know and plan) and employees (who execute). As justification of this division, an ideology emerged that stresses employees' incompetence to participate in decisionmaking. Many first-line supervisors are firmly convinced that quality circles have nothing to teach them.[3] If managers are forced to listen to their subordinates, they are often uncertain as to what they are supposed to do, which is very threatening. Yet participation is unlikely to take root if it is confined to an occasional committee meeting, while day-to-day workplace relations between employees and their supervisors remain autocratic.

Managerial attitudes such as these may threaten participation's success. Research suggests, for example, that the success of the Scanlon Plan, which combines gainsharing with a formal employee involvement program, is directly related to the degree to which managers believe that their subordinates are capable of making worthwhile suggestions.[4] When trust is lacking (for example, when the supervisor views participation merely as a morale builder), the parties may go through the motions of "counterfeit participation," and the desired payoff in productivity and satisfaction is unlikely to be obtained.[5]

A variety of approaches can reduce management opposition. First, managers must realize power is not "zero sum": Increases in employee discretion need not come at the expense of lower management.[6] When the parties are at loggerheads, neither side has much power. Effective participation can increase everybody's power.

In a similar vein, managers need to quit doing some of their old tasks before taking on new coaching and training duties. Thus an important step in implementing high-involvement management is to identify tasks managers perform that are not needed. Managers will appreciate the new work system more if one of its goals is to make their lives easier by, for example, reducing the number of unread reports they must create.

Managers are more likely to feel comfortable in the new system if they have had a voice in its design. Retraining managers in the training,

---

Chrysler and AT&T

A number of companies are creating new systems to measure nonfinancial performance such as quality and investment in human resources. Chrysler, for example, links its chief executive officer's pay to customer satisfaction ratings. American Telephone & Telegraph (AT&T) has begun tying lower-level executives' pay not only to financial measures such as economic value added (EVA, profits minus the cost of capital) but also to customer value added (CVA, measured with customer satisfaction) and people value added (PVA, measured with employee satisfaction). AT&T, as with many other companies, also assesses each department on its progress toward achieving a high-involvement workplace—in AT&T's case, using the Malcolm Baldrige National Quality Award's criteria to evaluate its total quality program.[1]

1. John J. Kendrick, "AT&T Universal Card Services," *Quality*, vol. 32 (January 1993), pp. 27–28.

---

leadership, coordination, and planning skills upon which participation relies is essential. Managers will also be more likely to support participation if they share in the organization's profits and if part of their performance rating is based on their subordinates' successful involvement.

If job redesign leads to a reduction in the number of managers, those who become redundant should be transferred within the organization. Management, as well as employees, needs job security if participation is to work.

Top Management Support

Successful implementation of participation requires that top management give the program continuing support. This may require wholesale modifications in the overall organizational culture. As Howard Love, president of National Steel, said, introducing shop-floor participation in his company involved changing "an old-line hierarchical organization into a more participative company from the executive suite to the shop floor."[7] Top management must decentralize power, so that managers as well as workers gain authority.

Changing a long-established organization may be difficult, though the success of Toyota at NUMMI suggests it is possible. In any case, participation may be easier to introduce in completely new organizations not encumbered by the heritage of past practices.

Most important, managers must be committed to a long-term vision of the enterprise, which must include skilled workers and decentralized power. A crucial component is that employees, customers, and suppliers are stakeholders of the company; thus management decisions must take into account the interests of these partners as well as the interests of the owners.

The empirical evidence supports the key role of top executive support. In the 1987 Fortune 1000 survey, companies with above-average levels of employee involvement tended to have higher support from the chairman of the board and other top executives. More important, companies that reported above-average success with employee involvement also reported higher support from the chairman of the board and other top executives. On a five-point scale of support, companies with more involvement and more successful involvement reported support ranging from 3.3 to more than 3.5; low-involvement and less successful companies had mean support ranging from 2.7 to 3.0.[8]

Union Support

We want more school houses and less jails; more books and less arsenals; more learning and less vice; more constant work and less crime; more leisure and less greed; more justice and less revenge; in fact, more of the opportunities to cultivate our better natures.

—SAMUEL GOMPERS

Establishing and maintaining union support for employee involvement is both crucial and difficult. Understanding the role of the union in the high-involvement workplace requires knowing about the three bases of union power in the traditional U.S. workplace and how employee involvement challenges each of them.

The first source of union power is an ideology based on worker solidarity, united against management. In the traditional setting, managers make all investment, technological, and production-related decisions; thus unions are left free to fight for workers' interests with minimal regard for productivity. In an extreme case of management-worker conflict, such as at GM-Fremont, the union fought the dismissal of workers who were caught stealing or were routinely incapacitated by drugs or alcohol.

Employee involvement challenges solidarity based on opposing management by emphasizing labor-management cooperation. Cooperation in dispute resolution puts union leaders in a quandary. Even if joint problem solving leads to more fair outcomes on average, in any given grievance the affected worker wants the union to be a strong advocate, not a fair judge. Furthermore, many gainsharing and bonus plans reduce solidarity by turning workers against their slower colleagues. In addition, some autonomous work teams determine pay and discipline—blurring the sharp line between managers and workers that unions have sought to maintain.

The second source of power is a detailed contract that limits managerial favoritism. Employee involvement, by contrast, leads to flexibility, which opens up possibilities of managerial favoritism and playing workers off against each other. Moreover, the contract is often disregarded when workers make suggestions that contradict it. In addition, in a high-involvement workplace, new nonunion forms of employee representation often compete with the union as mechanisms to resolve problems. These alternative sources of power are often threatening for the union leadership.

The third source of union power is the set of detailed work rules that permit workers to "work to rule" as a form of job protest; that is, workers precisely follow all rules when they want to slow down work and punish management. Employee involvement's flexibility removes this source of bargaining power. Workers often offer their good ideas, leading to management demands for a faster pace of work. In many cases, managers embrace the additional flexibility of weakened work rules and increased ability to reassign workers, but they do not deliver substantive participation as a quid pro quo. The result is often unhappy workers with fewer job rights and a distaste for participation.

Tensions between unions and employee involvement are augmented when the threat of plant closures is one force motivating managers to propose employee involvement. Many workers come to participate and share their ideas because they fear that their plant or office will close down otherwise. Critics claim that employee involvement introduced under the threat of job loss is hardly "involvement." In defense of employee involvement, the threat of plant closure is present for workers whether or not their jobs include involvement; employee involvement merely makes it more likely that surviving jobs are more interesting (although they may have less slack time). This point does not address critics' claim that an economic system based on the threat of job loss to motivate employees has a built-in element of stress and injustice. Furthermore, no amount of cooperation at the workplace or the corporate level eliminates the struggles workers may have with owners at the industry, national, or international level over the appropriate amount of wages and profits.

To maintain union support in the long run, employee involvement must not eliminate the role of the union leadership, reduce union solidarity, or lower the union's bargaining power. Thus strong pressures exist to extend the scope of participation beyond the shop-floor level, if for no other reason than union officials are permitted to become involved in the participative process. At NUMMI, for example, the union participates in committees that resolve disputes that occur at a lower level; for example, when a work group feels a suggestion will increase safety, but the supervisor disagrees. Labor-management committees are also important when issues span multiple work groups. Finally, these forms of participation can provide benefits to all workers that no single worker has an incentive to provide.

As with management support, participation is more likely to enjoy union support at low levels if it is also supported by higher-level union officials, as is increasingly the policy of both the AFL-CIO and many national union leaders.[9] Companies that implement participation at one plant while fighting unionization at another will often run into difficulties with higher levels of the union hierarchy.

The union is understandably less likely to resist if it is an equal partner in designing the participative program, as is occurring increasingly. Employee involvement must be implemented with carefully crafted agreements, so that workers have no incentive to punish their peers, such as those who emphasize safety or quality at the expense of productivity and short-run bonuses.

Finally, successful employee involvement in the long run requires that the workers' collective bargaining power not decline. Critics of employee involvement are correct when describing how the typical employee involvement plan does little to truly empower workers.[10] At the same time, low-power employee involvement programs are not long-lived, given that workers are rarely repeatedly fooled. If employee involvement is only a cover for a speed-up, the flow of new ideas usually dries up. In almost all cases, sustained employee involvement is coupled with reduced managerial oversight and increased reliance on workers' suggestions and creativity. The result is a workplace where productivity will decline immediately if workers protest or even if they passively fail to share their ideas. Management's reliance on workers for continuous improvement can strengthen workers' bargaining power. For employee involvement to be sustained, this increased bargaining power must be coupled with implicit or explicit gainsharing with workers.

Empirically, QCs introduced in unionized settings are more likely to last than those in nonunion plants for at least two possible reasons: (1) unions may screen out badly designed plans; and (2) unionized employees may be less afraid to express their opinions, even if they are critical of management.[11] Guarantees of job security and gainsharing are significant as means of reducing employee resistance. These promises become more credible if the union is in a position to guarantee them.

Because of the advantages to worker representatives, some nonunion employers in the United States and abroad (especially Japan) have introduced forms of representative participation. They include American counterparts of works councils, in which workers elect representatives and employees to sit on appeals committees for grievances and dismissals. Some of the forms of representative participation have been judged illegal in the United States.[12]

Union involvement is more common at successful high-involvement companies. In the 1987 Fortune 1000 survey, unionized companies that reported above-average success with employee involvement also reported higher union participation in the employee involvement effort. Companies with more union participation also reported that their employee involvement program was more successful in improving union-management relations, in increasing employee trust in management, and in decentralizing power.[13]

Other studies supported the positive effects of union involvement with employee involvement. Maryellen Kelley and Bennett Harrison also found that worker-management committees raise productivity in unionized establishments, but not in nonunion ones. Kelley and Harrison's measure of committees was ambiguous, encompassing both direct participation such as quality circles and representative participation such as union-management quality of worklife committees. One possible interpretation of their findings is that the combination of quality circles and union-management committees is effective, while QCs alone have negative effects. Similarly, William N. Cooke concluded that teams are more useful in raising productivity in union than in nonunion settings.[14]

Business Partner Support

Paralleling the change in employment relations, many high-involvement organizations made modifications in their customer and supplier relations, turning customers and suppliers into business partners. A new business partner model emerged. At NUMMI, as at other examples of successful quality programs, "The organization establishes a partnership with suppliers and customers to assure continuous improvement in the quality of the end products and services."[15]

In contrast, in the days of GM-Fremont, GM's relationships with outside suppliers were adversarial and were held at arm's length. If one supplier had rising costs or declining quality, GM quickly switched to another supplier. To maintain a credible threat to terminate a relationship, GM employed many suppliers per part and negotiated only short-term contracts. To facilitate comparison among prospective suppliers, GM did virtually all of the design.

In all of these respects, GM was like most of the organizations in the American public and private sectors. Purchasing decisions were based on the outcome of a competitive process for supplier selection. On the one hand, this strategy maximized GM's bargaining power and made monitoring the purchasing agents easy. On the other hand, it cut GM off from suppliers' ideas about product design and limited suppliers' willingness to invest in equipment and skills that were useful only for GM products.[16] The result was a cumbersome purchasing bureaucracy that maintained comparability among suppliers while stifling communication between suppliers and the purchaser's engineers (because that might lead to favoritism). Taking an example from another big purchaser, the military specifications for chocolate-chip cookies run to sixteen pages of tiny, single-spaced type.[17]

Supplier Relations at NUMMI

Partly to promote close supplier relations and partly to avoid protectionist pressures, NUMMI has rapidly increased the proportion of its parts that are made in North America. Unfortunately, few North American suppliers had ever dealt with the Toyota Production System.

Toyota and NUMMI engineers initially worked closely with seventy North American suppliers. In some cases, the company responsible for supplying Toyota in Japan helped its North American counterpart establish a lean production process. During the production start-up period, NUMMI found three times as many defects in North American–supplied parts as in Japanese-supplied parts. But between 1985 and 1989 North American suppliers improved steadily to achieve quality, delivery, and cost levels comparable to their Japanese competitor.[18]

The NUMMI production system leads suppliers, like workers, to continuously work to improve the production process. While GM would often have a dozen or more suppliers producing a single part, NUMMI has one source for each major component. GM's strategy maximizes bargaining power but requires GM to perform all design work in-house.[19]

When a supplier was late in delivering parts or did not deliver sufficient quality, GM threatened to cut off purchases. NUMMI works closely with the supplier to discover the root cause of any problem that arises. As with just-in-time production, just-in-time deliveries from suppliers increase opportunities for learning—each blip in production leads to a stoppage of the assembly line. The procedure greatly increases incentives for understanding root causes of problems and preventing recurrences. As part of the process, engineers (and even production workers) often move back and forth between NUMMI and its suppliers.

During start-up of a new model year, engineers from the supplier work in the NUMMI plant, just as they worked with the Toyota design team during the previous year. The goal is to jointly optimize, eliminating operations that are expensive for the supplier but add little or no value to the product. For example, one NUMMI supplier discovered it was painting the surface of a piece that, when installed, could never be seen by a consumer. When a supplier better understands the use of a part, operations that are not cost effective are eliminated. Similarly, the automakers better understand the cost of their design decisions, permitting future models to be built more cheaply. Under the old arm's-length regime, suppliers did not want to share information with purchasers. They feared that if the automaker knew how much a part cost, then the price would be lowered to that level.

New forms of supplier relations have spread throughout the United States since the mid-1980s. One indicator of the magnitude of the change is that the percentage of U.S. auto suppliers that provide detailed information about their production process to their customers has doubled over the last ten years, from 38 percent to 80 percent.[20] The basis for this change has been mounting evidence that long-term, information-rich relationships between suppliers and customers lead to faster product development, increased flexibility, and higher quality. For example, Kim Clark estimated that supplier contributions accounted for one-third of the Japanese automakers' advantage over their U.S. counterparts in total engineering hours required to develop a new car.[21] In the mid-1980s defect rates of parts supplied by Japanese companies were one-tenth the rate of those supplied by U.S. companies.[22] In the United States, suppliers with long-term contracts are significantly more likely to invest in computer-controlled equipment—investments that increase productivity, quality, and flexibility.[23] In all of these long-term relations, quality and innovation count as much as or more than price in determining sales.

The contracts between purchaser and supplier are mostly implicit. Michael Smitka described the arrangement as "governance by trust."[24] For example, if the supplier experiences a problem with cost or quality, the automaker will attempt to work things out before switching to another supplier—perhaps by sending its own personnel to help resolve a supplier's production problems. The high degree of trust engendered by such a process means that complete contingent contracts are not necessary. Instead, the parties continuously renegotiate their agreements. Each side is confident that if it loses a little bit (compared with its expectations) in one instance, it will come out ahead in the next.

This commitment leads both sides to make many investments whose value depends on the relationship continuing. Suppliers make large, fixed investments in areas such as quality-control training and in maintaining a product-design staff. The parties also invest in mechanisms for information flow. Intensive communication over the course of a long-term relationship means that the parties come to understand each other's products and processes very well. Typically, a Japanese automaker will not design a part that it requires for a new model. Instead, it will specify exterior dimensions and performance characteristics, then allow a specialist supplier to design the part to best match its process.[25]

Problems with Just-in-Time Delivery

Just-in-time deliveries from suppliers to automakers put pressure on suppliers to be perfect. When JIT is coupled with successful problem solving, suppliers rapidly learn about their own production problems. When JIT is not coupled with successful problem solving, suppliers hold on to inventory buffers instead of the purchaser, leading to no net savings on inventory cost. (Inventory shifting is common at GM suppliers.)[26] NUMMI, for example, works with its suppliers to integrate JIT delivery with JIT production and to reduce set-up times on its suppliers' machines.

Integration of JIT delivery and production poses difficulties for U.S. auto suppliers. They dislike modifying their production process for a single customer, particularly one known to be as fickle as GM. Most important, suppliers distrust GM engineers investigating their production process. They fear losing their trade secrets and anticipate that sharing true cost information will remove their bargaining power. To counteract these worries, NUMMI depends on only one or two sources for each of its major components. For example, because of the subtle interactions between a stamping press and the chemical composition of steel, NUMMI requires two years to switch suppliers for its rolled steel. GM prided itself on being able to change most suppliers within a matter of weeks.

Worker and Supplier Participation

A linkage between supplier and employee participation can be expected for several reasons.[27]

First, the process of continuous improvement is more effective if good communication flows from the supplier's shop floor to the manufacturer's marketing department and on to the consumer. For example, in 1991 Honda of America found that its customers wanted a continuously variable heater control, instead of the initial design that allowed the vent to be only on or off. A team of engineers and operators at Honda's supplier realized that they could achieve variability with the existing design if they could tighten the tolerances enough so that the plastic louvers could come to rest anywhere in their range of motion, not just at their endpoints. Implementing the change, however, meant modifying the production process at five or six places. Operators contributed many of the suggestions to reduce variability by understanding the different steps in the manufacturing process. The supplier's high level of employee participation made supplier participation work, and Honda was able to implement the change quickly and with minimal cost of redesign and new tooling.

Continuous improvement requires that employees' ideas be spread to suppliers. For example, when Honda of America introduced a new paint system, more than one thousand suggestions were made by Honda to its paint supplier.

In addition, worker participation can improve processes as well as products. The U.S.-Japan quality gap in automobile parts is both a cause and an effect of Japanese companies' widespread use of JIT techniques, which, as described at NUMMI, increase incentives for and ability of suppliers and workers to understand the root causes of problems and prevent recurrences.[28] Employee participation can be crucial in permitting problems to be solved quickly so the line will begin running again, even with minimal inventory buffers.

Close business partner relations can make employee involvement more effective because suppliers' workers, by visiting the plant and witnessing the production process, see the big picture of what they are doing. Suppliers also can help troubleshoot problems at the customer's site, promoting closer relations.

Finally, both forms of participation require significant and similar changes in management vision. The company must move from a low-trust environment to a more cooperative system based on high levels of communication, skills, and relationship-specific investments, supported by a foundation of trust and commitment to a long-term relationship.[29]

Close supplier relations are more common at high-involvement companies. Employee involvement efforts are substantially more common in companies with long-term customer contracts. According to a 1989 survey, auto suppliers with contracts one standard deviation above average in length had 10 percent more of their work force in quality circles or related employee involvement groups than did suppliers with contracts one standard deviation shorter than average (56 percent versus 46 percent). (By contrast, a supplier's report of the difficulty its main customer would face in switching to another supplier was not correlated with employee involvement.) For reasons that are unclear, this relationship disappeared in preliminary analyses of a 1992 follow-up: Auto suppliers with close relations to their customers (that is, the Big Three and Japanese producers) were no longer more likely to have high levels of employee involvement. Automobile suppliers, however, who had close relations with their suppliers were more likely to have high levels of employee involvement.[30] In a separate study of machine tools users, Maryellen Kelley, Bennett Harrison, and Cathleen McGrath found that group problem solving and gainsharing are more common at companies with collaborative ties (for example, mutual technology assistance, joint product design and development) to subcontractors and customers.[31]

Companies with high levels of employee involvement also have more employees in units that undertake collaboration with suppliers in quality efforts, although the companies report similar proportions of employees with direct exposure to customers, according to the 1990 Fortune 1000 survey. In the 1992 survey of steel plants, companies with work teams were three times as likely to have frontline employees visit customers as were those with no teams. At companies undergoing workplace restructuring, collaboration with suppliers is positively correlated with team structure, skill variety, and having multilevel participation.[32]

Close supplier relations are more common at successful high-involvement companies. Companies that report success with employee involvement have more employees in units that undertake collaboration with suppliers in quality efforts, although the companies report similar proportions of employees with direct exposure to customers, according to the 1990 Fortune 1000 survey. Similarly, at companies undergoing workplace restructuring, collaboration with suppliers is positively correlated with higher quality and lower accident rates.[33]

The Importance of Integration

A systematic approach to employee involvement is substantially more likely to bring sustained success than an individual element, such as a quality circle, a training program, or a small employee-stock ownership plan.

The Power of Integration

Numerous studies have addressed the effects of employee involvement on productivity and other measures of corporate performance.[34] A multiyear study of steel finishing lines is one of the best and yielded results representative of the larger literature.[35] The authors used statistical techniques to identify four distinct human resource management systems. For example, production lines that adopted System 1 used much more innovative practices than System 4, while Systems 2 and 3 fell between the extremes.

Work practices	*System 1*	*System 4*
Problem-solving training	Common	Uncommon
Worker-management discussions	Frequent	Infrequent
Use of problem-solving teams	Often	Seldom
Job classifications	Few	Many
Gainsharing compensations	Used	Not used
Selection procedures	Extensive	Minimal
Employment security	High	Low

The presence of more innovative systems was associated with significantly higher productivity. The highly innovative System 1 plants ran 98 percent of the scheduled time, while the untransformed System 4 plants ran 88 percent of the scheduled time. Systems 2 and 3 were in between. System 4 plants lagged in product quality as well as productivity. In a separate study, Jeffrey B. Arthur concluded that high-involvement plants not only excel in quality and productivity but also enjoy lower turnover.[36]

Chaparral Steel

Chaparral Steel, a joint venture of Texas Industries and Co-Steel, was created in 1973 to produce a wide range of products at a low cost. To do this, the company began with only four layers of management. Decisionmaking authority was placed where it would be most effective, and traditional job barriers were eliminated. All 935 employees are considered part of the sales department and are authorized to handle any quality, billing, credit, or shipping request. The plant has been redesigned so that all sales functions are located in one customer service center, which is easily accessible to all employees. Every employee is salaried. Pay is based on individual performance, company profits, and skills learned. Chaparral has a compulsory annual educational sabbatical program that requires employees to visit customers, premier companies, and universities worldwide to learn new processes and technologies. As a result, Chaparral's production employees were able to produce and test a new casting technique that drastically cut costs and cycle time. Chaparral has achieved the fastest per-ton production time in the world. The high-performance management practices fit well with Chaparral's strategy of selling high-quality products with rapid delivery. Operating with such efficiency, Chaparral could invest $65.4 million in capital expenditures and repay $58.4 million of debt over a three-year period without issuing any additional debt.

Note: This example was drawn from Department of Labor, Office of the American Workplace, *Road to High-Performance Workplaces* (1994).

The results are not unique to the steel industry. A worldwide study of the automobile industry found that a coordinated change to an involvement-oriented human resource system can simultaneously improve workers' autonomy, product quality, and productivity.[37] Similar results were reported in the electrical components industry and with flexible manufacturing systems.[38] Although most of the famous cases are in manufacturing, the basic set of human resource policies giving all employees the ability, incentive, and power to constantly improve their workplace and the product also appears relevant in service industries as varied as airlines, insurance companies, and department stores.[39]

Industry-specific studies have the advantage of measuring performance fairly accurately, because they focus on specific operations common to different sites. However, they suffer from concerns about generalizing to other industries and technologies. A few studies have linked financial performance to human resource practices, but most have suffered from problems of small sample sizes and unusual samples.

The largest of these data sets was created by Mark Huselid, who surveyed 850 publicly held companies.[40] He found that human resource policies cluster. Companies with high participation in employee involvement programs tended to have a high proportion of workers in formal information-sharing programs. More of the workers are administered attitude surveys and have access to profit-sharing or gainsharing plans as well as to a formal grievance or complaint resolution procedure. The workers also received more training. Huselid also discovered that high-involvement companies have above-average promotion from within, use of formal job analysis, and administration of formal employment tests before hiring.

In Huselid's sample, high-involvement work practices predicted organizational performance. He found that a one standard deviation increase in his measure of high-performance work practices correlated with a reduction in turnover of more than 1 percentage point (for example, from 14 percent to 13 percent per year). It also correlated with 16 percent higher sales per employee (controlling for capital per worker and research and development spending), raised annual cash flow by $3,800 per employee, and raised the market value of the company by more than $18,000 per employee.

Casey Ichniowski studied sixty-five nonunion manufacturing companies and found, consistent with Huselid's results, that those with more flexible job design and training had substantially higher stock market value and productivity than did other companies. Unfortunately, Ichniowski's sample size was small, consisting of only about 2 percent of the initial population of enterprises surveyed.[41]

Sample selection problems also arose in a result reported by the Department of Labor: Companies that appeared in the 1984 edition of *100 Best Companies to Work for in America* had significantly higher stock market returns from 1985 to 1992 than did most companies (15 percent a year for the sixty-three publicly traded companies listed in the book versus 12 percent for the Frank Russell average of 3,000 companies' stock prices).[42] The companies were selected based on nominations, site visits, and interviews with employees. They ranked high on pay and benefits, career opportunities, job security, perceived openness and fairness, and friendliness.

Different sample selection problems affected a detailed study of more than six thousand work groups in thirty-four companies.[43] To enter the sample, companies had to volunteer access to their employees. The study concluded that an emphasis on workplace cooperation and the involvement of employees in decisionmaking were both positively correlated with return on investment and return on sales over five years following the survey. (Performance measures were standardized by industry.) The financial measures took up to three years to show improvement. Dennis Kravetz conducted a similar study of 150 large companies and found similar positive results, with similar problems of interpretation.[44]

Following a different methodology, Barry Macy and Hiroaki Izumi presented evidence drawn from a number of companies by aggregating results from 131 different studies.[45] Each individual study focused on one or a few cases and measured the effects of introducing employee involvement on productivity, quality, or other outcomes compared with the preintervention levels or to a control group. The individual studies typically found beneficial effects from employee involvement; companies with more interventions generally had larger increases in productivity or quality. Tempering the conclusion is that descriptions of individual cases are more likely to be written up when they are successful.

Total Quality Management

A final set of evidence on the power of an integrated approach comes from evaluations of total quality management (TQM) programs. While not all TQM programs contain much employee involvement, most successful cases of TQM do empower employees.[46]

While TQM has been credited with much of Japan's manufacturing success, an integrated approach has also been effective in American-run workplaces. A General Accounting Office (GAO) analysis of U.S. companies that won the Baldrige award for their quality programs concluded:

> Companies that adopted quality management practices experienced an overall improvement in corporate performance. In nearly all cases, companies that used total quality management practices achieved better employee relations, higher productivity, greater customer satisfaction, increased market share, and improved profitability.[47]

A large number of cases of successful TQM are found in the public as well as the private sector.[48] In Madison, Wisconsin, for example, the very first quality team improved preventive maintenance on the vehicle pool and saved the city $700,000. Since then, teams have spread throughout the city government, from administrative offices to cops on the beat.[49]

Unfortunately, at many private and public sector workplaces in the United States, TQM is implemented in ways that do not empower employees. For example, Ken Stockbridge, a GAO expert on TQM, told of a county government quality team that required ten meetings over ten weeks to choose a name for the group.[50] Even worse, in many programs, workers are not rewarded for their efforts or ideas, and both middle managers and unions often resist the new programs because they are seen as poorly conceived and threatening. At its worst, TQM becomes a management speed-up that makes workers work harder but does not lead to sustained improvements in the quality of products.[51] Thus many TQM efforts show only modest success.

Because of TQM's relatively recent implementation on a large scale, empirical analyses with large samples remain rare. One of the largest samples comes from a 1991 GAO survey of more than twenty-eight hundred federal government installations.[52] Two-thirds of the respondents claimed to have some quality program in action, but most programs were less than two years old. As expected, given the newness of the typical program, only 3 percent of respondents claimed that their installation had achieved "long-term institutionalization"—integration of TQM into all aspects of the organization's operation. All of this 3 percent reported that TQM had a positive impact on customer service, efficiency, customer satisfaction, and timeliness.

Barbara Flynn and Roger Schroeder surveyed U.S. plants in the machinery, electronics, and transportation components industries.[53] They found that plants high in use of teams are also high in training, information sharing, gainsharing, and worker-management cohesiveness. Moreover, these companies are high in measures of TQM practices such as just-in-time production, systematic preventive maintenance as well as in worker commitment and cohesiveness. Perhaps most important, companies with these practices enjoyed higher product quality. (Unfortunately, the sample selection included "world-class" plants. To the extent these respondents were chosen based on knowledge of their high performance, the correlations reported may overstate the effects of management practices.)

In the long run, a high-involvement work organization appears to translate into stock returns as well as high quality and productivity. Sherry Jarrell and George Easton, for example, used a search of companies' annual reports to reveal those with TQM efforts. Follow-up phone calls identified which companies were fairly thorough in their implementation of TQM; that is, those that would score above approximately five hundred (out of a maximum of one thousand) on the Baldrige award evaluation. They found that the companies had 15 percent excess returns over the five years after the start of the TQM program.[54] No excess returns were evident over the first three years, which was consistent with the stock market failing to observe the quality of the investment in the TQM program until it was already paying off financially.

Similar results are found for companies that won independently administered quality awards, according to a study conducted by Kevin Hendricks and Vinod Singhal.[55] The companies achieved stock market returns greater than those of similar companies—only about 0.6 percent in the narrow window of a few days around announcement of the award but more than 6 percent in the years leading up to the award (and after the implementation of the quality program). Both the Jarrell and Easton and the Hendricks and Singhal studies suffer from modest sample sizes— a limitation that will be alleviated as their research continues and as more companies have mature TQM programs.

Thomas Heller identified companies with TQM programs from their annual reports and from his meetings with top management. Heller, an independent stock market analyst, used the maturity of a TQM program as a leading indicator of corporate stock returns. He found that a portfolio of such companies that was matched to achieve risk similar to the S&P 500 had excess returns of several percentage points per year.[56]

The recent introduction of most American quality programs makes all conclusions tentative. Researchers also have had difficulty discriminating between typical TQM programs and those that are best practice. In addition, several of the studies were possibly biased in their sample based on positive financial results. Nevertheless, so far all research on the relation between mature TQM programs and corporate performance demonstrates that well-designed TQM programs can increase productivity, quality, and returns to shareholders. These well-designed programs, in turn, rely on, for example, employee involvement, training, and rewards for employees who innovate.

Conclusion

In 1990 Laura D'Andrea Tyson and I summarized forty-three empirical studies on the relationship between employee involvement and productivity:

Motorola

Motorola is recognized as a world leader in quality. Its quality improvement system is based on a program of Management by Measurement. Using the Statistical Process Measurement to keep track of defect rates, Motorola has set ambitious goals of Six Sigma–level quality (3.4 defects/million possibilities for occurrence) and drastic total cycle time reduction. To achieve these goals, Motorola benchmarks production practices from a wide array of manufacturers and trains every employee, regardless of assignment, in statistical techniques. The company also promotes teamwork. For instance, simultaneous engineering is used in product design and development. Defects at Motorola are down 80 percent. Based on two systematic studies, Motorola estimates that it saved $962 million in inspection and rework costs. The company also estimates that it earns $30 for every $1 invested in quality training.

Note: This example is drawn from Department of Labor, Office of the American Workplace, *Road to High-Performance Workplaces* (1994).

There is usually a positive, often small, effect of participation on productivity, sometimes a zero or statistically insignificant effect, and almost never a negative effect. . . . Participation is more likely to produce a significant, long-lasting increase in productivity when it involves decisions that extend to the shopfloor and when it involves substantive rather than consultative arrangements.[57]

Several dozen new studies have been conducted since then, several of which have particularly strong research designs and data quality.[58] Their conclusions reinforce the earlier findings: A small-scale employee involvement plan, just as a small amount of training or a modest change in pay systems, may have some beneficial effects, particularly in the short run. Furthermore, a system of high involvement, strong rewards, and high levels of skill and information, integrated with a corporate strategy that relies on frontline employees' ideas and creativity, is capable of impressive improvements in organizational performance.

The positive effects of a high-involvement system do not appear to be restricted to management goals such as quality and productivity. High-ivolvement companies tend to have lower turnover, and most studies found higher job satisfaction as well.[59] A smaller number of studies examined wages, and again the relationship was generally positive.[60] The effects are typically stronger and more likely to be long-lasting when companies create a high-involvement system instead of adding a single profit sharing, involvement, or training program.

Deep cultural change accompanies the policies and practices of successful high-involvement companies. Despite their important differences, most successful high-involvement companies share one fundamental feature that explains their similarities. According to Masahiko Aoki, "The body of employees is, together with the body of shareholders, explicitly or implicitly recognized as a constituent of the firm, and its interests are considered in the formation of managerial policy."[61] More broadly, employee, managerial, union, and business partner support is maintained by increasing each group's ability to contribute to the organization and by providing incentives for each group to work for the organization's long-term success.

5

Profits and Employee Involvement

The empirical literature strongly suggests that employee participation, correctly done, has positive effects on productivity. The question then arises, Why are workplaces with substantive involvement so rare? A number of economists have concluded that the relatively low incidence of participatory arrangements implies that such arrangements are inefficient. Their reasoning is that if participation were a good idea, then the free market would select for companies with employee involvement.[1]

However, the market may provide less employee involvement than is socially optimal. Numerous arguments suggest that the free market will not lead to the profit-maximizing level of employee involvement.

One set of obstacles is many managers' preference for a quiet life in which they retain high amounts of control and confront minimal change. Thus these managers will resist many forms of employee involvement, even when that involvement would raise profits.

A related set of problems occurs in financial markets, where owners and investors are concerned about whether managers are abusing the funds entrusted to them. Owners and investors prefer investments that are easy to observe. Because the investments that support employee involvement are hard to monitor, the market will often yield an inefficiently low level of employee involvement. Although many owners would like more employee involvement, current incentive systems for managers lead to a lower level of involvement than would maximize profits.

Fortunately, owners and investors can take a number of actions to improve the measurement of how well managers are investing for the long term. Improved corporate governance—the system of stockholders, banks, boards of directors, and management—can increase invest-ments that lead to long-run profitability.

In analyzing how markets may be biased against efficient employee involvement, two fictitious nonunion auto plants are used. The first plant, IMMUN (Integrated Motor Manufacturing Uniting Neighbors), has a highly participatory work organization. It has the characteristics neces-sary for successful participation: empowering workers by modifying the compensation system to reward innovation and build cohesiveness; maintaining high levels of trust, training, employment security, and guaranteed rights; and building support of managers, unions, and suppli-ers. IMMUN's competitor in the auto industry is Motors Gigantium (MG), which has a traditional labor relations system.

Organizational Inertia

All you need in life is ignorance and confidence, and then success is sure.

—MARK TWAIN

The most obvious source of delay in implementing a new work orga-nization is organizational inertia. MG managers have a set of procedures for everything from new product development to selecting secretaries. The manuals and rules on these procedures run into thousands of pages, and making revisions is a massive undertaking. In addition, MG managers are promoted based on their success at following the rules, so they have little desire to change them. Given these forces of inertia, MG managers, like most managers, have been slow to implement new methods of doing just about anything.[2]

Even when few issues of power or compensation arise, the im-plementation of improved methods takes time. In one well-studied ex-ample, the dissemination of hybrid breeds of corn that were substantially more productive and resilient than older species of corn took twenty years to reach half of the farmers who would eventually adopt the new breeds.[3] The modest pace of adoption occurred even with the presence of the Department of Agriculture's Agricultural Exten-sion Program, which was intended to disseminate precisely this sort of innovation.

In a second example, General Motors and Du Pont in the 1920s introduced the divisionalized "M-form" of organization, in which semi-autonomous operating divisions are administered from a central headquarters. This organizational innovation took approximately thirty-five years for half of the large corporations that would eventually adopt the structure to do so, even though early adopters enjoyed higher profits.[4]

The diffusion of high-involvement workplaces is slowed further by the systemwide nature of the changes that are required.[5] Organizations, like other evolutionary systems, are relatively good at adapting slowly and making incremental changes. Unfortunately, if a training program in group process is only useful when accompanied by a work organization that empowers groups, and neither will succeed without group-based pay, then incremental change of one policy at a time will never arrive at the efficient work organization. Instead, the pattern dominant in the United States will emerge: an experimental pay system here, a quality improvement team there, and perhaps a new training program somewhere else.

In short, organizations adapt slowly, and the adaptation to systemic changes is slower still. Thus potentially productive work organizations are not implemented quickly. At the same time, government policies that promote efficient innovations can increase productivity and profitability.

Managerial Opportunism

The best of all monopoly profits is the quiet life.

—JOHN HICKS

Adoption of employee involvement is slowed by more than inertia: Managers usually do not want to reduce their power and discretion. Managing a McDonald's cook who is easily replaceable is less stressful than overseeing an emotional French chef who must always be mollified. Unfortunately for managers, empowering workers implies that decisions must be discussed and modified to take their point of view into account—diminishing the quietness of managerial life.[6]

Edward E. Lawler III, an expert on high-involvement management, claimed,

> The major reason why more U.S. organizations have not changed to high-involvement management is the failure of senior management to provide leadership in this area. . . .
> Major change in the way an organization is managed can take ten years to produce significant advantages and many senior managers are

not in their jobs that long. Perhaps more important, senior managers often are very comfortable with the power, authority, and rewards that are associated with their positions and do not want to risk losing them. In addition, these managers have fine-tuned their skills over decades so that they will be effective in a traditional top-down organization.

A change to high-involvement management requires that senior managers learn new skills and that they give up some of the special perquisites and financial rewards.[7]

Employee involvement also diminishes several privileges that many managers enjoy.[8] If owners had infinite information, they could simply give managers orders to follow and not have to pay high salaries. Managers, however, know things that owners do not. As a result, owners must compensate them to take actions that raise profits. When workers communicate directly with owners, for example, via a works council or representation on the board of directors, managers lose some of their perquisites and power. (Some unions have taken advantage of the information that they have to embarrass managers in "corporate campaigns," in which the union brings facts to the attention of owners, directors, and bankers of the enterprise.) In addition, managers in a rigid hierarchy can take credit for employees' ideas. This scenario does not play out as often when workers are empowered to implement their own suggestions. Problems of managerial opportunism are not solved by the owners' ability to replace managers, because the new managers have similar incentives to retain an inefficiently high level of centralization.

In unionized settings, union leaders also are encouraged to keep the traditional system. They have often risen to power based on confrontation with management. New styles of interacting require new skills and new risks, which many union leaders are unwilling to face.

If inertia were the only factor impeding full deployment of employee involvement, the effects would not persist indefinitely. Over time, more efficient high-involvement workplaces would replace high-inertia workplaces. In fact, this is occurring. As a business school joke goes, "America will surely have an automobile industry in twenty years; it may just be that it is all foreign owned."

Capital Markets

> *Where large sums of money are concerned, it is advisable to trust nobody.*
>
> —AGATHA CHRISTIE

Both MG and IMMUN face imperfect capital markets. In perfect markets, all investments with positive present values are undertaken. When information is imperfect, however, little investment is made in hard-to-monitor projects. Three conditions are needed for underinvestment to occur: Managers must care about stock prices in the short run as well as the long run, stock prices must respond to short-run accounting measures, and managers must see the investments better than the market can.[9]

Managers care about short-run stock prices for several related reasons. First, many shareholders intend to sell in the short run. To satisfy current shareholders, managers undertake policies that hurt long-run shareholder value. Shareholder horizons are much shorter in the United States than in Japan and Germany. More important, money managers are evaluated based on short-run returns (the last year or two is typical). The threat of takeovers reinforces managers' concern with short-run stock price, because undervalued companies are often targets, leading to the dismissal of incumbent managers.[10] Finally, managers' compensation relies typically on short-run stock prices, not long-run value creation.

A large number of studies found that stock prices do respond to short-run accounting measures, particularly earnings and cashflow.[11]

Kenneth A. Froot and his colleagues summarized: "There is a wealth of empirical evidence supporting the existence of an information gap," which allows managers to see investments better than markets can.[12] The basis of the information gap is that outside stakeholders rely almost entirely on the financial results reported in quarterly accounting statements. Financial results have a variety of limitations.[13] First, they are a lagging indicator of performance and are generally available only at the end of a long series of earlier actions and events. Second, accounting measures are often poor predictors of future financial results. Finally, financial results provide little guidance about what actions might be appropriate in improving future performance. What stakeholders need are nonfinancial measures that are leading indicators of future financial results and that suggest clear and immediate management actions.

Absent such nonfinancial leading indicators, the presence of an information gap implies that banks, stockholders, and the central headquarters of multidivisional companies prefer investments in tangible assets. They discount managers' claims that current earnings are low because the company is investing in intangibles such as training, building good reputations with workers, or research. Outsider stakeholders fear that managers are using the resources to cover up their own incompetence, purchasing on-the-job amenities and leisure, or increasing current reported performance at the expense of investments that pay off in the future.[14]

Exacerbating the information gap is that an appropriate accounting is not being made for some financial investments, such as training expenditures. As Eric G. Flamholz, a leading expert on human resource accounting, explained,

> It is obvious that a manager can liquidate a physical asset and generate cash that is reflected as improved profit. This kind of mismanagement would be evident in a conventional accounting system. A manager can likewise depreciate a customer asset and improve profit in the short run by, for example, cutting back on quality. Or a manager can destroy organizational assets and improve profit in the short run through the simple expedient of withholding merit increases or driving employees harder.[15]

Some argue that accounting measures of training would be misleading, because they do not take into consideration whether the training was a good investment. The complaint is valid, but it is equally valid for other forms of investment such as research and development (R&D) and new factories. Both R&D and new factories, for example, can be (and often are) poorly designed or implemented. In addition, both are difficult to measure, and ascertaining the correct depreciation rates is hard. Nevertheless, the market gives some weight to accounting measures of R&D investment. For example, companies that increase reported R&D have higher stock prices than similar companies that merely maintain R&D.[16] However, when a company raises its training expenditures, it reports only the short-run decrease in earnings, not the increase in human assets.

The information gap persists partly because stock market analysts are judged primarily on short-run results. Expensive investment in research on fundamentals is not worthwhile. In addition, at the large brokerage houses, which sponsor most analysts, analysts are rewarded largely for the trading that results from their research.[17] Thus they prefer putting their energies into predicting short-run returns, to beat the market. The short horizons of analysts, in turn, are supported by the short horizons of most fund managers. Even if the assets they invest belong to a pension with liabilities due in many decades, fund managers are almost always judged and compensated for short-run results. As two researchers on pension plans in 1991 noted, "The papers on an analyst's desk do not include many five-year financial reports or ten-year business plans."[18]

Few analysts have the training or inclination to focus on human resources, or even on management practices more broadly defined. The two hundred pages of sample tests and answers for the three-year program to become a chartered financial analyst, for example, contain precisely two sentences on assets that are not measured on financial statements.[19]

In addition, virtually no analysts describe human resource investments in their reports. In a recent Dilbert cartoon, the boss stated, "I've been saying for years that 'Employees are our most valuable asset.' It turns out that I was wrong. Money is our most valuable asset. Employees are ninth." An employee replied, "I'm afraid to ask what came in eighth." The boss answered, "Carbon paper." In a survey of nineteen corporate financial and nonfinancial performance measures that managers feel are valuable to report to financial markets, employee satisfaction, turnover, and training expenditures came in seventeenth, eighteenth, and nineteenth, respectively.[20] These measures of investment in human resources not only lag behind financial measures such as earnings (first) and capital expenditures (fourteenth), but also corporate ethics statements (sixteenth). The measures of human resources were also at or near the bottom of importance for financial analysts and portfolio managers.

As one chief executive officer (CEO) of a large company said,

When I brief Wall Street analysts on our current earnings, sale projections, downsizing program, and capital spending plans, they busily punch these numbers right into their laptops as I speak. When I start telling them about our plans to invest in training and reform the workplace, they sit back in their chairs and their eyes glaze over.[21]

The result is a self-fulfilling system: If almost everyone else cares primarily about stock prices in the short run, then a quick payoff can be had from research that beats the market in short-run predictions of, for example, earnings or cashflow. Conversely, minimal short-run payoff comes from information about long-term returns. Market analysts and money managers reinforce each other's tendency to focus on the short run.

Analysts value information about a company if they can compare it with other companies within the industry using a common definition.[22] In those rare instances when data on training are included in corporate reports, the focus, for example, is on the number of employees involved in, hours spent on, or dollars expended for training. Because definitions of training vary, analysts cannot meaningfully compare isolated cases. What is needed is a common language for evaluating nontraditional measures of performance and investments.

Debt holders have less information than equity holders, the owners of stock. In the United States, bankruptcy rules provide that debtors often receive full repayment. The rules encourage debt holders to demand full repayment. They constrain management with rigid covenants that protect against large down-side losses, and deter managers from undertaking hard-to-monitor investments.[23] In Japan and Germany, by contrast, debt holders are often equity holders, leading to sharing of both bankruptcy risks and the benefits of good payoffs. As a result, debt holders are better informed about managers' actions and can replace managers or modify strategies without the need for bankruptcy. A better flow of information permits managers to undertake investments that hurt current financial ratios but have a positive expected value.

Evidence exists that U.S. managers routinely forgo good investments that do not pay off in the short run; moreover, this behavior is far more likely in the United States than abroad. A researcher compared fifty-four profit-center managers of an American company with twenty-eight profit-center managers from Toshiba. Three-fourths of the Japanese managers responded "Never" when asked, "In the past year, how frequently have you (or someone within your profit center) pulled profits from future periods into the current period by deferring a needed expenditure?" The typical U.S. manager said, "Occasionally," with more stating "Frequently" than "Never."[24]

Information problems arise within organizations as well as within the capital market. That is, divisional managers may sometimes bypass good investments to increase current reported earnings. A 1993 survey of seventy-five large U.S. companies found that all of the CEOs examined financial data from operating divisions but only half saw measures of customer satisfaction and only a third saw internal measures of quality.[25] When the top executives are judged primarily on short-run financial performance, the corporation as a whole focuses on these measures.

The lack of interest in long-term performance or leading indicators is reflected in compensation practices. At 163 large U.S. companies analyzed by the compensation consulting firm Towers Perrin, only 1 percent of division managers' total compensation was based on long-term divisional measures, while two-thirds was from salary and bonus based on short-term divisional results. "As a consequence of this system, the divisional executive tries to maximize current operating profits even at the expense of the long-term competitiveness of the business."[26]

Because of these biases, corporate procedures are typically tilted in favor of investment in hardware such as machines and structures.[27] For example, most companies make little attempt to evaluate projects in terms of their "invisible" consequences on worker commitment or their expected impact on product quality. Instead, most large American corporations evaluate new investment projects almost solely on their ability to replace direct labor. For example, a number of new technologies integrate computers with the manufacturing process to increase product quality, flexibility, and the speed of innovation. Nevertheless, the vast majority of managers in large manufacturing companies report that to justify the purchase of new technology they must be able to show how it will "cut heads."[28] Increased quality was a potential justification in only 35 percent of the firms, and the effect was typically small.

Furthermore, most companies evaluate projects based on a single estimate of the present value of the returns from an investment. They do not consider that some investments are more flexible than others.[29] For example, employees at Mazda's U.S. plant receive more than twice the training of workers at a traditional U.S. auto plant. With their skills, the Mazda workers helped design an assembly line that can build cars for both Japan and the United States. (In Japan, as in Great Britain, people drive on the left; the steering wheel is on the right side of the car.) The ability to change the mix of left- and right-hand drive does not increase the capacity of the plant to produce more cars. Even though the flexibility increases the expected utilization and profitability of the plant, traditional cost-benefit analysis will undervalue the worker training.

Lessons for Investors

> *Paul and Milton, two famous economists, were walking along. Paul saw a $100 bill lying on the sidewalk. He exclaimed, "Look, there is a $100 bill!" Milton turned to his colleague and replied with derision, "No, there isn't. If there were a $100 bill on the sidewalk, somebody would have picked it up."*
>
> —A CLASSIC ECONOMIST JOKE

Long-term investments can make a difference.[30] Unfortunately, most shareholders look to the short term, as, even worse, do most institutional investors. About 75 percent of trades on the New York Stock

Exchange are by institutional investors trying to beat the market, to be above average.

However, the performance of most institutional investors is not above average. Pension funds holding large companies have total returns below a simple index of the S&P 500 because they have high trading costs. Similar results are found for funds in different sectors of the market—most have total returns below that of a similar index fund. As the chairman of the Vanguard Group noted, "An overwhelming body of data confirm that, on a long-term basis, the average investment advisor has been unable to outperform the stock market."[31]

That indexes beat actively managed funds is not a historical accident, but an unavoidable truism. Because all investors collectively own the entire stock market, active investors as a group and passive investors (who usually hold an index of stocks) as a group both match the gross return on the market. For example, from 1971 to 1990 the average pension equity fund and the average mutual fund achieved returns very close to that of the market as a whole. The difference is that actively managed funds paid expenses (typically in the range of 1.5–2 percent per year) for fund advisory fees, operating expenses, and transaction costs.[32] The market led the average actively managed fund by a substantial amount, year after year. Because fund returns are roughly uncorrelated year to year, looking over longer time periods of five or ten years, the proportion of actively managed funds losing to index funds increases.[33] The costs of this trading are enormous: "In 1987 $25 billion was spent in trading stocks, an amount equal to one-sixth of corporate profits and 40 percent of all dividends paid out that year."[34] When institutions own most of the market (pension funds alone own more than half the blue chips), trading with each other cannot ensure high returns for most funds.

Corporate Governance

Because pensions and other institutions make up a large proportion of the market, an improved system of corporate governance, which moves beyond reliance on accounting numbers, is needed. Accounting numbers are fundamentally backward-looking and incomplete.

The issue of long-run shareholder value arises when companies invest for the long run. As Harvard Business School's Michael Porter noted, "Value resides in a company's activities, its stock of scientific and technical knowledge, its skill base, its reputation with various constituencies, and its market position."[35] Good corporate governance, although not a guarantee of high future profits, is needed to reward managers for investing in assets that are not measured on financial statements. Poor corporate governance, by contrast, implies that managers will not be rewarded for the long-term investments that lead to sustained profitability.

In recent years, leading pension fund managers, business school researchers, and members of corporate boards of directors have begun examining how good corporate governance can help solve the problem of underinvestment in human resources. Establishing a system of corporate governance that leads to the profit-maximizing level of investment in human resources and high-involvement work practices is in investors' interest. This level is almost surely higher than the current level.

Ultimately, good corporate governance is in management's interests. For example, corporations are moving away from arm's-length relations with suppliers based solely on price. Supplier relations are increasingly based on high levels of information flow, high levels of trust, joint problem solving, and long-term relationships.[36] In the mid-1980s Ford required top-management approval to sign a contract with a supplier of more than a year. In 1994 Ford required top-management approval to sign a contract with a supplier of less than a year. High-commitment supplier relations reduce Ford's bargaining power. Ford, like many other large companies, is finding that the increased productivity and quality resulting from better communication outweighs the loss in bargaining power.

Similarly, more and more U.S. corporations are building relationships with their suppliers of capital, as well as their suppliers of equipment and components. Just as in Japan and Germany, companies are finding that if their suppliers of capital are well informed about their efforts to invest for the long run, they will be more likely to forgive the temporarily lower earnings that accompany these investments.

Top managers can take a number of steps to lengthen their investors' horizons. First, top managers must solve the incentive problems within the organization. Few divisional managers are rewarded for long-term improvements in the performance of their operation. Managers must decide what divisional measures indicate ability to produce value in the long term and set goals for each of these measures. Top management must then link the leading indicators of financial performance to pay. "To reinforce the long-term strategy, annual incentives can be linked to the accomplishments of measurable quality, service, innovation, and productivity targets."[37]

Managers must also communicate their long-term investments to outside stakeholders. Few organizations report their trends in quality, customer satisfaction, or human resource development to financial market stakeholders—even fewer report them relative to competitors. How can stock market analysts, for example, evaluate the quality of management if they cannot see what management is doing to build long-term value?

Boards of Directors

In the effort to build high-trust relations with investors, managers can benefit by having a credible and independent board. Only a credible board can certify to shareholders that management is investing for the long run according to an agreed-on strategic plan, regardless of low current earnings.

To fulfill this role, a board must be strong and well informed so that it can ensure that managers are investing in the long-run profitability of the enterprise. Boards must be able to reward managers who are building up an organization to maximize long-run shareholder value and penalize executives who are depreciating the nonfinancial assets of the company to increase current earnings.

While no magic recipe exists for forming effective boards, strong boards in general have the following characteristics: a high proportion of independent directors, regular meetings by the independent directors to evaluate the CEO, high qualifications for board members (including a diversity of viewpoints), attendance by directors at almost all meetings, self-evaluations to determine how well the board is adding value to the corporation; information packets provided to directors in a timely fashion, and access by directors to internal data without CEO approval. In some leading-edge companies, such as ALCOA, boards are being connected to the internal E-mail and management information system, which radically alters their ability to follow the company's internal operations.

General Motors' board in 1994 adopted a set of practices that reduces managers' independence in the short run. However, if the new policies build investors' trust that the company is well managed, then in the long run they enhance managers' ability to raise capital and follow independent strategic plans.[38]

Perhaps most important, to certify to shareholders that management is on track, boards cannot be satisfied with financial measures that show where the company has been. Instead, they must supplement these measures with nonfinancial measures that provide leading indicators of where the company is headed. A variety of authorities have presented arguments for nonfinancial measures of performance, including management writers, pension fund managers, total quality management consultants, and experts on management accounting.[39] The Competitiveness Policy Council, for example, recommended that nonfinancial analyses and measures of performance be used by corporations and shareholders to evaluate properly the long-term performance of management.[40] These factors go beyond traditional financial measures of performance and include customer relations measures such as customer satisfaction and market share; internal operations measures such as quality and productivity; human resources issues such as training, information sharing, and empowerment; and product development measures such as R&D expenditures and the proportion of sales from new products.

One or more of these measures may not apply in some industries, while in other industries additional headings may be important. Moreover, the specific measures for each category will vary by sector. In many cases, trends in these measures are more informative if they are presented relative to competitors and to world-class standards.

A balanced set of financial and nonfinancial measures reflects the company's strengths and weaknesses and acts as a leading indicator of future financial performance. Without putting too much emphasis on particular categories, if no outside board member knows trends for any of the nonfinancial metrics, then how well he or she can evaluate the plans and performance of management is unclear.

In addition, boards should encourage managers to compare their management systems with others, both those within their industry and those that exhibit the best practices. Several private outfits offer companies the opportunity to compare their management processes with those of others, while maintaining anonymity for respondents. Stakeholders should not only encourage the collection of comparative data, but also ask managers to explain divergences from the best practices and how they intend to reach world-class levels of continuous improvement, quality, and employee involvement. The board must periodically follow up the plan and compare it with financial and nonfinancial performance measures.

The existence of better measurement and better compensation systems suggests that short-term perspectives within companies are avoidable. A number of experiments and case studies show that providing managers with information about human resources investment, for example, improves the quality of their decisions.[41]

In addition, boards must link nonfinancial measures of performance to top managers' pay. Chrysler ties its CEO's pay to customer satisfaction ratings. AT&T requires all divisions to engage in quality audits that measure investment in human resources, while managerial rewards and evaluations are based partly on employee and customer satisfaction. More top executives and boards must follow these examples of rewarding managers for the nonfinancial returns they create that will lead to financial returns after they have moved on, as well as for the financial returns that occur while they are at the helm.

Pensions

Responsible fiduciaries cannot and should not micromanage the many companies in which they invest. But, in a system of good corporate governance, someone must be tracking management practices on some basis other than publicly available financial yardsticks. At a minimum, investors should hold directors and managers responsible for the policies they implement. Responsible fiduciaries should have some knowledge that, at companies in which they have major holdings, at least the boards they elect are well informed and competent monitors of the company's long-run investments.

Many pensions have policies for proxy voting, and many also purchase advice from consultants and rating services on which proxies raise shareholder value. In the future, many pensions should form policies for director elections and perhaps purchase advice on which directors raise shareholder value.

Pensions should make their standards for corporate governance clear. For example, the Council of Institutional Investors—an organization of large pension funds, largely in the public sector—has a "Shareholder Bill of Rights." Similarly, the nation's largest pension, TIAA-CREF, has a *Policy Statement on Corporate Governance.*[42] Both of these documents should be expanded to include standards for the structure and conduct of boards of directors. Other pensions should adopt their own standards as well.

As part of their investment strategy, responsible fiduciaries should evaluate the possibility of corporate governance interventions as alternatives to buying, selling, or passively holding stocks. Corporate governance interventions include meeting with the CEO or with outside directors, proposing shareholder proxies, and meeting with other large investors to pressure poorly managed corporations. Evaluating the feasibility of such actions does not imply that they will be implemented.

Evidence exists that corporate governance interventions can work. The Wilshire Associates studied the results of the California Public Employees Retirement System's (CalPERS) interventions into corporate governance. Since 1990 CalPERS has targeted twenty-four companies with very poor financial results (lagging the S&P 500 by more than 80 percent in the five years preceding the intervention) that also had poor corporate governance. In the years following CalPERS's first communication about its corporate governance concerns, the targeted stocks out-performed the S&P 500 by 109 percent.[43]

Regardless of pressure put on boards, enormous barriers remain to independent boards of directors. As a result, large owners such as pension plans should monitor the quality of management directly. CalPERS, for example, recently announced that it will incorporate measures of how well organizations are investing in human resources in their corporate governance plans.[44] In some cases, large investors may find it sensible to require companies to collect and disseminate benchmarks of leading indicators. For example, a company that has declining levels of training expenditures and employee satisfaction coupled with rising turnover appears to be depreciating its human assets. Even if financial performance looks healthy today, such a company is likely to have worse financial performance in the near future.

Ultimately, some company will undoubtedly begin to collect comparable human resource information across enterprises, just as compensation consultants currently collect cross-company data on pay, benefits, and (for executives) bonus plans. Companies typically can compare their performance with the average of similar companies in their industry or region, while anonymity is maintained for other respondents. In the near future, managers and boards of directors should engage similar consultants to obtain comparative data on human resource practices and outcomes. Measurements of investments in human resources will never replace measurements of financial performance, but they can provide valuable leading indicators of future operating results.

Financial market stakeholders rarely observe whether managers are investing in human resources. In spite of analysts' lack of concern, human resource investments do matter for productivity and financial performance. Thus investments in high-involvement management are not properly valued by the stock market, leading to systematic underinvestment in these assets.

Important for investors, stock market returns at companies that invest in human resource assets will on average be predictably above average.[45] Portfolio managers, analysts, and lenders would be well advised to investigate the human resource investment of their companies as well as other investments such as plant, equipment, and R&D.

6

Market Failures and Employee Involvement

Free markets are biased against high-involvement employers such as IMMUN for a number of reasons. Some difficulties arise from bargaining problems within the organization. In addition, conditions in the product, labor, and capital markets affect IMMUN's viability. Finally, IMMUN provides benefits to the political system but is hindered by the legal system. Thus even when companies provide the profit-maximizing level of employee involvement, a higher level of employee involvement could lead to more satisfying jobs and to higher productivity.

Bargaining Problems

Bargaining problems within a company can lead to inefficiently low levels of employee involvement.[1] Even if employee involvement raises total output at IMMUN, MG may have higher profits because its workers have lower bargaining power.

When MG introduces a low level of employee involvement (specifically, quality circles), productivity increases a little bit; as employee involvement rises from none to low, total surplus produced increases from 100 to 160 (see table 6-1). The total surplus produced is the revenue of the enterprise minus the cost of raw materials, interest on the company's debt, and workers' market wages. As employee involvement rises, worker bargaining power also rises. Worker bargaining power is the proportion of the total surplus that workers can collectively win. IMMUN, with its high level of employee involvement, is the most productive possibility; total surplus is 200. At the same time, worker bargaining power is also fairly high (50 percent), so profits are

TABLE 6-1. *Relationship between Profit Maximization and Employee Involvement*

Employee involvement	Total surplus produced (thousands of dollars)	Worker bargaining power (percent of surplus)	Profits (millions of dollars)	Workers' share of surplus (millions of dollars)
None (MG before quality circles)	100	0	100	0
Low (MG with quality circles)	160	25	120	40
High (IMMUN)	200	50	100	100
Very High	160	75	40	120

Note: Total surplus produced is what the company can give to workers and management; that is, sales minus the costs of goods sold, valuing workers' time at their market wage. The profits, or owners' share of surplus, is larger when workers' bargaining power falls and when total surplus produced grows. Workers' share of surplus is larger when workers' bargaining power increases and when total surplus produced grows. Both workers and owners have a shared interest in a large surplus. However, owners prefer taking a larger share of a smaller surplus.

Profits = total surplus produced x (1 - worker bargaining power). Workers' share of surplus = total surplus produced x worker bargaining power, which equals the amount of wages paid above the market wage.

only 100. Profits are maximized at MG with a low level of employee involvement—120. They are greater than at IMMUN, even though the total productivity at MG is only 160, less than at IMMUN. If workers are given too much power, total surplus may decline. In this situation, workers may pay too little attention to owners' interests, such as maintaining machinery.

Product Market Conditions

The man who builds a factory builds a temple; the man who works there worships there.

—CALVIN COOLIDGE

The variability of product market demand, the level of monopoly power in the automobile market, and the reputations of related companies all affect the ability of IMMUN to survive.

Low Monopoly Power

The same bargaining problems that can cause companies to choose less efficient low-involvement strategies for workers can also cause them to choose low-involvement strategies for suppliers.[2]

IMMUN is a recent entrant into the automobile industry and has little monopoly power in the car market. It is interested in maximizing productivity above all else and chooses close supplier relations. Each of its parts is provided by a sole source, and the company invests heavily in choosing and training its suppliers. IMMUN requires years to switch to a new supplier, and its just-in-time production system is highly sensitive to the smallest glitch.

Close supplier relations create a highly efficient system. IMMUN's sales are $10 million higher than they would be if it had arm's-length supplier relations, with no additional costs to the supplier. The result is that IMMUN's suppliers have a lot of bargaining power, and IMMUN is left vulnerable to suppliers failing to ship essential components. Because of this threat, IMMUN must share half of its $10 million profit from the relationship (see table 6-2).

The nature of automobile production implies that the potential for legal, effective strikes always exists. Because of the complexity of producing a car and its five thousand parts, contracts with suppliers are necessarily incomplete. Because engineering changes are common, the part produced by the supplier is often not the same part specified in the contract. Kim Clark estimated the expense of shutting down production to be 1 million dollars per day.[3] Failure to deliver a part—or even a slow response to a problem—can have major repercussions and can be very effective. For example, the U.S. automakers' attempts to establish arm's-length relationships with suppliers were thwarted by antipollution laws requiring state-of-the-art technology. In the 1970s Ford's catalytic converter required a part available from only one supplier. This small firm's president quickly learned "the magic words in Detroit—'job stopper.' . . . If you said these magic words, doors opened up for anything you needed."[4]

MG could also raise total profits by $10 million if it had close supplier relations. Alternatively, MG can keep multiple suppliers per part, having each supplier produce exactly as MG instructs it. MG, unlike IMMUN, is an established company with substantial monopoly power in the automobile market, earning $20 million in monopoly profits. MG is unwilling to enter into close supplier relations for fear of losing bargaining power with its suppliers: Total productivity would rise by $10 million, but MG would keep only half of the total profits of $30 million ($20 million monopoly profits plus $10 million higher profits resulting from close supplier relations). Because half of $30 million is less than $20 million, MG chooses the inefficient arm's-length supplier relations.

TABLE 6-2. *Relationship between Profit Maximization Leads and Supplier Involvement*

	Monopoly profits from final product market (millions of dollars)	Surplus from close supplier relations (millions of dollars)	Supplier's bargaining power (percent)	Car maker's total profits (millions of dollars)
MG with arm's-length supplier relations	20	0	0	20
MG with close supplier relations	20	10	50	15
IMMUN with arm's-length supplier relations	0	0	0	0
IMMUN with close supplier relations	0	10	50	5

Note: Surplus from close supplier relations is the higher productivity resulting from joint problem solving.
Car maker's total profits = surplus from close supplier relations x (1 – supplier bargaining power).

Close supplier relations can be efficient but underprovided in a free market, when companies choose arm's-length relations to maximize their bargaining power with suppliers.

Declines in Product Demand

At both MG and IMMUN, nominal wages are set once per year.[5] MG lays off workers whenever demand for cars declines. IMMUN has long-term employment relations and a no-layoff policy. During downturns, IMMUN trains workers, enacts hiring freezes, transfers workers within the company, and strives to keep excess labor on the payroll.

MG's use of layoffs is relatively cheaper when recessions are frequent and deep, while IMMUN's no-layoff pledge and long-term employment relations are relatively cheaper when recessions are shallow or infrequent. As a consequence, IMMUN will flourish if its product market is characterized by lower probabilities of declines in demand; that is, the lower the variability of industry and aggregate demand and the higher the average growth rate of the industry and the economy.

Each company's decision about layoffs also affects the macroeconomy. Recessions are deeper when many businesses have layoffs (MG style).[6] Layoffs lead to lower spending on consumer goods by workers, resulting in further layoffs at stores in the area and eventually affecting consumer goods manufacturers around the world. Recessions are shallower when many companies avoid layoffs (IMMUN style). Because the costs of running participatory systems increase as the variability of product demand increases, policies that reduce this variability will encourage such systems.

Even without an explicit policy of avoiding layoffs, IMMUN would have more stable employment because its pay is more variable. The profit sharing and gainsharing at IMMUN imply that pay automatically declines when sales fall. This lower pay will help stabilize IMMUN's employment. Thus IMMUN's pay system, like its explicit employment security policy, helps to stabilize employment and make recessions less severe.[7]

National Quality Reputation

In a skit a generation ago, comedian Bob Hope pulled a pistol from his pocket and tried to fire it. The trigger clicked repeatedly, but the pistol did not fire. Hope inspected the pistol, then said with a sneer, "Made in Japan." At that time, "Made in Japan" meant cheap and shoddily produced, while "Made in America" stood for modern production techniques with the world's highest quality levels.

Japan's quality image has vastly improved in the intervening thirty years. Now "Made in Japan" is an advertising advantage for Dodge Colt, for example. The reputation of Japanese quality is so big that customers are willing to pay more than a thousand dollars extra to purchase an American-made Toyota Corolla instead of an almost identical Chevrolet Geo Prizm. (Both models are manufactured at the NUMMI plant.)

Bob Hope's skit in the 1960s and the high price of a Japanese-nameplate American-made car in the 1990s show the importance of a national quality reputation. Unfortunately, MG, like most American companies, produces relatively low-quality goods. This low quality penalizes IMMUN and hurts its ability to export, because other countries use MG's defect rate as a partial indicator of IMMUN's quality.

A Network of High-Involvement Companies

An enterprise will find eliminating inventory buffers and switching to just-in-time production costly if its suppliers are unreliable. Conversely, few suppliers will be willing to totally rearrange their production system solely to accommodate a single customer. Both are cases of network externalities, in which the cost of adopting a new workplace innovation depends on the number of other enterprises that have also made the switch. (Faxes are an important recent example of network externalities. The value of a fax rose rapidly when most businesses had fax machines.)

Network externalities are important, for example, in the U.S. textile industry. Some companies changed to a flexible team-based production system that can greatly decrease the time between the arrival of an order and the shipment of finished clothes. Unfortunately, this rapid response is valuable only when stores have made changes so they hold lower inventory and respond more rapidly to customers' desires. Because few stores have made the change, the incentive for textile producers to switch to flexible teams is low; because few producers can rapidly deliver, the incentive for stores to depend on rapid delivery is correspondingly low. The industry suffers because no coordinating mechanism operates to simultaneously increase workers' skills and customer choices while decreasing stores' delivery time.[8]

Labor Market Conditions

A man willing to work, and unable to find work, is perhaps the saddest sight that fortune's inequality exhibits under the sun.
—THOMAS CARLYLE

Labor market characteristics also affect the viability of employee involvement. Companies with employee involvement will be more successful when unemployment is low, wage differentials are narrow, dismissals are not allowed without showing just cause, and companies and workers capture all the rewards for training they pay for.

Low Unemployment

If all companies use participation, then low unemployment and tight labor markets are sustainable.[9] Because motivation does not depend upon the threat of dismissal, tight labor markets will not inevitably lead to declines in profits and investment coupled with increases in wages and turnover. While participation does not ensure full employment (other macroeconomic policies may be needed), participation may be necessary to sustain low levels of unemployment.[10]

MG's disciplinary system is based on fear of dismissal, and MG's costs of motivating workers are relatively low when unemployment is high. Whenever unemployment drops, however, MG suffers an increase in absenteeism and turnover and a decrease in productivity and quality. IMMUN's motivational system is based on participation, gainsharing, worker-worker monitoring, and so forth. When unemployment is low, IMMUN and other participatory firms gain in relative productivity.

If most firms have the same system as MG, the macroeconomy tends to generate a high average unemployment level. If unemployment temporarily drops to a low level, wages and costs increase and profits and investment decline, leading to lower labor demand.[11]

Theoretically, two stable macroeconomic outcomes are possible: an MG outcome, in which employers motivate workers with fear of dismissal and the average unemployment rate is high; and an IMMUN outcome, in which employers motivate with participation and the average unemployment rate is low. A new auto plant built in an economy with an MG macroeconomic outcome would find MG-style management profit maximizing—with many unemployed workers, no need exists to use participation to motivate. A new auto plant built in an economy with a IMMUN macroeconomic outcome would find IMMUN-style management profit maximizing—with low unemployment, the new company would be encouraged to use participation to motivate.

The choice of work organization by new companies partly depends on how tight the labor market is. When average unemployment rates are low for sustained periods of time, participatory work organizations become more attractive as ways to motivate and retain workers. For example, until the last few years, the Swedish government had consistently held the unemployment rate below 3 percent. Resignation rates and absenteeism in monotonous jobs in Sweden increased to the point that job redesign and increasing worker satisfaction became vital for any manager who wanted to maintain a stable, competent labor force. That is, at low unemployment, employers must make work intrinsically motivating to maintain productivity.

Narrow Wage Differentials

High-involvement companies' emphasis on equality of status favors their success when other organizations are also emphasizing equality; otherwise, high-involvement companies tend to lose their best employees.[12]

At MG, wage and status differentials are important motivators. In contrast, IMMUN reduces status and pay differentials to increase worker cohesiveness. No reserved parking places and no executive dining rooms, for example, are available. There are not even any "workers," only "associates." IMMUN also has lower wage differentials. Promotions are based largely on seniority, and promotions for star workers are less rapid than at MG. The policy promotes cooperation for group goals and reduces individual efforts for self-promotion. The extensive use of group-based pay, not individual incentives, also promotes cooperation and worker norms of high effort.

IMMUN's policies of narrowing differentials are implemented partly by increasing pay for the bottom of the wage distribution, paid for by the increase in productivity from participation. Thus low-end workers at IMMUN receive wages above the market rate. The wage is not taken into account by the market, because in a free market, only profitable firms survive. Therefore the market will supply inefficiently few firms paying wages above the market level to low-wage workers.[13] For example, assume that IMMUN increases cohesiveness by raising low-end wages by $1.10 per hour and productivity increases by $1.00 per hour. Productivity increases (that is, more output is produced with identical physical inputs), but profits fall by 10 cents per hour per low-wage worker. Because profits are lower, IMMUN will go out of business, even though productivity is higher than at other firms.

In addition to raising low-end wages, part of the narrowing in differentials occurs at the expense of high-wage workers. IMMUN has trouble keeping star and high-skill workers. If star and high-skill workers are essential for production, IMMUN's policy will be costly when employers with wide wage dispersion hire IMMUN's stars. However, if MG and all other firms had narrow wage and status differentials, IMMUN could keep its stars, and all firms could enjoy the efficiency gains of participation. Such an economywide outcome is not usually stable, though. Starting from a position in which all companies pay narrow wage differentials, MG can bid up the wages of star employees. The star employees will earn higher wages, and MG will make high profits. MG's policies will make paying narrow differentials difficult for all companies. Thus the gains of participation will be lost for all firms.

Universal Just Cause

IMMUN also suffers because its human resource policies are in many ways kinder than those of MG, and these policies sometimes attract employees who have high costs.[14] If all employers offered the same package of benefits, then IMMUN's costs would fall. For example, MG relies upon the threat of dismissal to motivate its workers and dismisses employees at will (that is, it does not need to demonstrate a reason to dismiss a worker). IMMUN has a just-cause dismissal policy, meaning that employees have a right to due process and IMMUN must have a reason for each dismissal. IMMUN management is concerned that its workers feel that personnel policies are fair and that an employee's criticisms will not lead to dismissal. IMMUN relies on internal motivation and worker-worker monitoring, not fear of dismissal; its dismissal rate is only 10 percent of MG's.

Because a just-cause policy is in place only at IMMUN, many of the less motivated workers at MG want to work there, especially those who are talented at exerting low effort without providing enough evidence to be dismissed. At IMMUN, they would enjoy a lengthy on-the-job vacation. Even if these talented shirkers are few in number, their concentration in IMMUN's applicant pool will vastly increase IMMUN's screening costs. If just-cause policies were universal, then these poorly motivated workers would be distributed evenly across all businesses, without concentrating their applications at IMMUN. Under these circumstances, the efficiency gains of just cause are more likely to outweigh the burden imposed by shirkers.

Externalities from just cause, therefore, are a second reason that two stable macroeconomic outcomes are possible. In an MG outcome, at-will dismissal policies are the rule, and the costs of introducing just-cause policies are very high for an individual employer. In an alternative IMMUN outcome, just-cause policies are the rule, and each employer finds that the benefits of just cause outweigh the costs.

Additional selection effects are in force. Companies with high-involvement management will have an especially high incentive to assist employees with difficulties, both because of their large investment in selecting, socializing, and training employees and because of the high-commitment culture they are trying to create.[15] Unfortunately, many other policies besides just cause and employment testing lead to selection effects and inefficiently punish nice employers. For example, firms can design acquired immune deficiency syndrome (AIDS) policies that reduce the incidence of AIDS in their work force, increase the productivity of employees who test positive for the AIDS virus, and reduce the productivity losses caused by coworker ignorance and panic related to being near such employees. Nevertheless, in 1987 fewer than 10 percent of American companies had an AIDS program or policy.[16]

One possible explanation for the lack of AIDS policies is that companies that create supportive environments for AIDS patients and that try to keep AIDS sufferers on the job longer will attract a high proportion of workers who are at risk for the disease. The Levi-Strauss Corporation, for example, is a leader in the field of AIDS policies. These policies have had the predicted selection effects, and Levi-Strauss has an above-average proportion of employees who have AIDS.[17] An identical argument applies to worker health policies such as employee assistance programs for employees who have substance abuse problems.

Child care and parental leave policies may also have undesirable selection effects if they lead to a disproportionate number of workers who have major nonwork responsibilities, are unwilling to relocate, and are unwilling to work nonstandard hours. If costs increase because of having a disproportionate share of such workers, then adverse selection effects may preclude a company from offering parental leaves, even if they were efficient benefits to offer the work force.

In the cases of AIDS policies and child care, as with many other policies with selection effects, government intervention can help. Using the same logic as in the just-cause example, government prohibitions of discrimination against those at risk for AIDS and government requirements for parental leave can potentially increase national income.

Employee Training

Substantial evidence exists that employers in the United States train less than their foreign competitors and less than is socially optimal.[18] Companies are often unwilling to pay for much training, because if the worker later quits, then the company is left with no return on its training investment. At the same time, workers are unwilling to pay for much training, because they are unsure of the value of the training at other employers, and they face the risk of being laid off.[19]

A number of commentators have suggested that the United States move toward the Japanese or German system of training, both of which appear to provide much higher levels of skill.[20] Unfortunately, neither system can be transferred to the United States. The Japanese system relies on employees remaining for most of their career at a single employer. An employer is willing to invest in training a worker, because the worker is unlikely to quit or be laid off. In Germany, strong union and industry federations pressure individual employers to train, even though some of the apprentices will later quit or be laid off. Both situations are unlike that of the United States, where turnover is high and strong union and industry federations are rare.

These problems are serious at IMMUN, which offers much higher levels of training than MG. Training involves problem solving, running meetings, quality tools, and understanding IMMUN's competitive position. IMMUN workers also receive on-the-job training in a variety of jobs as they rotate throughout their work group.

Unfortunately, IMMUN faces several serious difficulties with its training program. Because so many of the skills IMMUN workers receive are general skills that are useful at many employers, IMMUN fears that training will lead to turnover. Thus IMMUN must pay its trained workers more than they earned on their previous job. The high wages would not be a problem if IMMUN workers could buy their training, either with some form of tuition or with lower wages during their first years on the job. (For example, apprentices and medical residents receive low wages during the periods during which they both work and are trained.) Unfortunately, IMMUN workers are often unable or unwilling to buy their training in this fashion.

First, few can afford to pay tuition or to take the very low wages that are needed to pay for the full value of training. Most employees in the United States have virtually no liquid assets—almost 40 percent have none (other than their checking account).[21] Young workers, who have the greatest need to acquire training, are particularly likely to have no liquid assets.

Loans are another option. Unfortunately, the possibility of higher wages after receiving training makes poor collateral at most banks.

In addition, workers are unwilling to pay for training because many companies promise to provide training but do not deliver. Even MG, which gives minimal training, has some plants that advertise high levels of training for their nonunion workers. By doing so, they hope to trick workers into accepting lower wages; then, when MG provides little training, the company does not need to raise wages later in the workers' career. In addition, MG claims that its training is in general skills but provides mostly company-specific skills that are not valuable in the labor market. Fear of ending up at a deceptive employer makes it difficult for IMMUN to succeed in hiring workers at wages that implicitly pay for their training.[22]

IMMUN workers also suffer uncertainty over the value of the training. Workers fear that erroneous dismissals will lead to loss of both their job and their prepayment for training. "The financial returns to training are uncertain at the time the worker has to decide whether or not to invest in training. There is no insurance available for this uncertainty. As a result the investment in training will not be socially efficient: there is underinvestment in general training."[23] The problem is amplified at IMMUN, which provides just the combination of skills that it needs.

Even if each skill appears generally useful, the combination will be less valuable elsewhere.[24] Employers have difficulty properly evaluating the quality of training received on previous jobs. Workers will often receive little compensation for earlier training.

Furthermore, employers will be able to see the value of some general skills only after their new employee has been with them for a while. Highly trained workers cannot receive the full value of their training in the labor market.[25] This lack of reward may discourage employee investment in training.[26] The importance of this hypothesis is supported by the fact that both formal and informal training have similar effects on productivity, but only easy-to-measure formal training has much effect on wages.[27]

Capital Market Conditions

> One rule which woe betides the banker who fails to heed it . . .
> Never lend any money to anybody unless they don't need it.
> —OGDEN NASH

Just as the success of participation depends on product and labor market conditions, it also depends on capital market conditions. IMMUN faces the problem that capital markets are inherently biased against the hard-to-monitor human capital and trust that are prerequisites for participation. Profits would generally rise if employee involvement were implemented. Related problems exist that lead even companies that successfully maximize profits to underprovide employee involvement.

First, takeovers that result in companies reneging on their commitments eventually can lead to the deterioration of the trust needed for business to operate.[28] IMMUN's investment in human capital and in trust between managers and employees is made more expensive because other employers often break their promises. Such investment pays off only in the long term and only if the company's promises are credible. Every time a firm reneges on its promises, the faith that IMMUN workers have in their company's promises will be diminished. Takeovers, leveraged buyouts, mergers, and restructuring are often designed to yield short-run gains. Typically they lead to the rapid dismantling of human organizations and erosion of human capital. Takeovers with profits from reneging on promises to workers make it harder for remaining high-commitment strategies to work.[29]

Second, participation, long-term employment relations, and profit sharing dilute the decisionmaking and income rights usually accorded to the owners of a company. As a result, participatory firms face higher transactions costs for raising equity and loans. MG's owners have all rights to the profits of MG and have complete legal control over decisionmaking. IMMUN's owners share profits and decisionmaking rights with IMMUN employees. Therefore, all other things being equal, IMMUN will confront a higher cost of equity capital than MG. While IMMUN is disadvantaged in the equity market, it cannot survive solely on loans.[30] For both participatory and traditional enterprises, the cost of debt increases as the debt-equity ratio increases, because lenders are afraid of bankruptcy.[31] A business that tries to rely exclusively on debt finance will find the costs of funds higher than a business with partial equity financing. The higher the debt-equity ratio firms can support without encountering an increase in their capital cost, the more supportive are capital market conditions for participatory firms.

Third, the evolutionary perspective of many free-market proponents leads them to associate growth with efficiency; over time, the most efficient will grow faster and dominate the market.[32] Unfortunately, with imperfect capital markets, this optimistic long-term result is not assured. Because capital markets are biased against high-involvement employers, even if IMMUN is more productive than MG, capital market problems can lead to slower growth. For example, assume that with perfect capital markets IMMUN and other high-involvement companies would be 10 percent more productive than MG. Because of its productivity advantage, IMMUN would soon outgrow MG. With capital market imperfections, IMMUN will be somewhat undercapitalized. If its productivity advantage is reduced by 4 percent, IMMUN becomes only 6 percent more productive than MG. Meanwhile, the same capital market imperfections may also reduce the growth of IMMUN. If these restrictions on growth are severe enough, the less efficient MG may outgrow IMMUN. Less efficient enterprises with fewer difficulties raising capital may prevail over more efficient high-involvement enterprises.[33]

Despite the problems with capital markets, IMMUN can succeed. Suppose, for example, that IMMUN relies on investors, such as banks, pension funds, or other firms that have long-term interests in the company and extensive communication links with it. Further, assume that IMMUN borrows from banks with which it has close, continuous relationships. These investors, in turn, have detailed information about IMMUN and its investments over a substantial period of time. The result is that IMMUN will be able to finance its investments, including those in human capital and in corporate culture, at more favorable rates. Investors are likely to be more willing to share their income and control rights, because their information about IMMUN reduces their risks and monitoring costs.

However, if IMMUN relies on arm's-length relationships with investors, it will face a higher cost of capital. Stock market investors with limited access to information about the firm's performance will rely upon the information that can be effectively summarized in short-term fluctuations in its stock price. Banks will use the collateral price and the period of loan payoff as the main decision criteria. Investors will be much less willing to share their income and control rights with firm employees. Moreover, when IMMUN encounters financial difficulties, it may be forced by its creditors to cut back first on its human resource investments, even though doing so may quickly harm the trust and legitimacy on which its participatory system depends.

Capital market arrangements that allow higher debt-equity ratios without imposing a cost of capital penalty, that provide for long-term investment, and that broaden and improve the flow of information between a firm and its investors are likely to be relatively more favorable to participatory firms.[34] These arguments are important for understanding the borrowing practices of participatory American firms such as Hewlett-Packard. Hewlett-Packard has relied heavily on retained earnings and employee stock purchases and has avoided long-term debt. These policies are explicitly designed to facilitate investment in hard-to-observe human capital and R&D and to remove obstacles to the firm's job security policy.[35]

Political Environment

Democracy is the recurrent suspicion that more than half the people are right more than half the time.

—E. B. WHITE

A democracy will prosper only if its citizens have skills such as evaluating evidence, making decisions, and valuing one's own opinion, which are more likely to arise when they are strengthened at work.[36] Unfortunately, MG provides none of these skills. In the words of Adam Smith describing similar tasks two centuries ago, MG's style of work "makes men as dumb as men can be." In the words of more recent observers on the relationship between work organization and politics, "To take an extreme case, there may be no logical inconsistency between individuals being slaves in the economic sphere but voting citizens in the political sphere, but such a society is utterly implausible."[37]

IMMUN, unlike MG, teaches and reinforces in workers a number of skills that are essential for democracy. Most directly, workers are taught democratic procedures such as running efficient meetings. Perhaps more important, IMMUN workers are taught through experience that they are able to improve their surroundings. This lesson, more than any other, is a requirement for an effective and involved citizen. Robert Dahl nicely summed up this line of argument:

> Workplace democracy, it is sometimes claimed, will foster human development, enhance the sense of political efficacy, reduce alienation, create a solidarity community based on work, strengthen attachments to the general good of the community, weaken the pull of self-interest, produce a body of active and concerned public-spirited citizens within the enterprises, and stimulate greater participation and better citizenship in the government of the state itself.[38]

A number of empirical studies have shown that employees in jobs with autonomy and creativity become more involved in civic activities and feel more effective in the political process.[39]

IMMUN's empowerment will not only help its workers become more capable citizens, but also make them more concerned citizens. IMMUN workers, like MG workers, tend to live near their factory. Thus both sets of employees breathe and drink some of their factories' air and water pollution. MG pollutes the local environment to the limit allowed by law and sometimes a bit beyond. In addition, it lobbies to weaken antipollution laws to increase its profits. At IMMUN, worker pressure somewhat reduces pollution—not to the socially optimal level, but below the level that a company with no worker input would provide. Because of its workers' influence, IMMUN also provides more facilities and activities that benefit the entire community than does MG.[40]

MG workers toil on mind-numbing jobs that leave them alienated and unhappy, which costs their families and society as a whole. MG workers experience high levels of stress and high accident rates because of their low control at work.[41] Both stress and accidents leads to higher medical bills, paid partly by government insurance such as medicaid and disability insurance. MG workers are more likely to abuse their spouses and have much higher rates of alcohol and drug abuse. Many children of MG workers lose out as well, though in a subtler fashion. The authoritarian structure at work is echoed at home. Their parents focus on the importance of following instructions and obeying authority. Children of IMMUN employees are brought up in a fashion that emphasizes the skills their parents use at work: creative thinking, working together in a group, and problem solving.[42] While both sets of parents are trying to do what is best for their children, the children of IMMUN workers will likely have more of the skills needed to succeed at work and in society during their work lives.[43] Not surprisingly, a 1974 Department of Health, Education, and Welfare report compared the ill effects of an alienating management style on workers with the damage done by pollution to people and the environment.[44]

Legal Environment

The legal environment also is biased against IMMUN's work organization.[45] At IMMUN, committees of workers help make decisions about training, work schedules, and promotions. Section 8(a)(2) of the National Labor Relations Act makes it illegal for employers to discuss "conditions of employment" with company-sponsored committees of employees. Such a committee is an illegal "company union."

The situation would be no better if IMMUN were unionized. At IMMUN, workers make a number of decisions that are the province of management at MG. Work teams, for example, choose whom to hire, whom to promote to team leader, which machinery to upgrade, and the allocation of pay raises. Unfortunately, almost all of these activities are illegal, because U.S. labor law defines workers performing such tasks as managers and does not permit managers to be members of a union.

In addition, it might be illegal for union representatives to serve on IMMUN's board of directors, if the union has representatives on boards of competitors (as would be common with an industrial union such as the UAW or the United Steel Workers). Such overlapping directorates may face legal challenges as conflicts of interest. Even without such overlaps, worker directors on boards of directors have run afoul of laws requiring directors to act solely for the benefit of shareholders. (Directors sent by banks or other stakeholders with interests different from those of shareholders have not run afoul of the law.)

American businesses often complain that they operate in a litigious society and that the cost of litigation is increasingly burdensome. Unlike some complaints by managers, substantial evidence exists that the costs of doing business are being affected by changes in employment law and ensuing litigation.

"According to a 1988 estimate, lawsuits under statutes protecting employment rights account for the largest single group of civil filings in federal courts."[46] The number of court cases concerning just one class of employment litigation, wrongful discharge, doubled from 1982 to 1987. With the median wrongful discharge award around $150,000, a plaintiff win rate around two-thirds, and a defendant's lawyers' fees averaging around $83,000, employers' costs of employment litigation are rising rapidly.[47] The costs to employers are far more than the direct court costs and penalties. Like doctors practicing expensive defensive medicine to ward off malpractice suits, employers must change their management style to act defensively for fear of large settlements.

The case of wrongful discharge is just one example of how regulation in the United States is conflictual and legalistic.[48] A fundamental problem arises in a legalistic society: If one side has hired a lawyer, the other side must as well. Even if the most efficient outcome involves working together to solve joint problems and trying to find win-win solutions, each side fears the other will hire a lawyer and try to unilaterally win the case. In this situation, the most likely outcome is that each side will inefficiently invest many resources in defending its case, while neither side searches for joint gains.[49] Employee involvement and its accompanying internal problem-solving and dispute-resolution procedures can potentially reduce the cost of conflict.

Corporations in other nations tend to have a much less adversarial approach to regulation, and more regulation is oriented toward joint problem solving. For example, safety and health regulation in Japan is far from perfect. Nevertheless, when Japanese automobile assembly plants opened in the United States, both the Japanese and the U.S. managers preferred the problem-solving approach to safety regulation observed in Japan to the conflictual U.S. model. More important, even the U.S. regulators from the state OSHA preferred the Japanese style of regulation. For example, regulators were consulted on plans and asked for their feedback early, and problems were solved with minimal intervention from lawyers or formal regulatory proceedings.[50] Although comparisons are fraught with difficulty, accident and fatality rates appear to be relatively low both in Japanese factories in Japan and in Japanese-owned factories in the United States.[51]

7

Employee Involvement in Japan

We are very different from the rest of the world. Our only natural resource is the hard work of our people.

—JAPANESE EXECUTIVE

Substantive participation can raise productivity, but only if accompanied by business and public policies to encourage support from employees, management, unions, and business partners. Furthermore, the costs of needed business policies will vary according to the environment of the enterprise. The business environment in Japan has facilitated the growth of employee involvement in that nation.

Japanese Labor Relations

The labor-relations system characteristic of Japan's large companies has been the subject of extensive scrutiny, in part because of Japan's dramatic and persistent productivity gains and in part because of Japan's low unemployment rate. A vast and growing literature identified the distinguishing features of this system and speculated about its causes and effects.[1] Many conclusions drawn from the literature support the ideas presented here about the likely features of participatory systems and about the effects of product, labor, and capital markets on the development of such systems.

An estimated 30–40 percent of Japan's work force is employed in characteristically participatory companies. Most of these workers are employed in large Japanese companies (one thousand or more employees). The apparent positive correlation between firm size and participation may seem surprising at first. But sociological evidence from several organizations suggests that the management practices described here are more common in large firms than in small ones.[2] Furthermore, the product, labor, and capital market conditions facing Japan's large firms are particularly supportive of participatory arrangements.

Participation channels in Japanese businesses take three main forms: quality circles and team production at the shop-floor level, formal plant- or firm-level organizations for joint consultation between management and labor (including joint consultation committees), and the ringi system. Quality circles are widespread and are generally evaluated as successful in supporting real participation by workers in decisions about shop-floor organization. This success is attributed to the skill and knowledge of Japanese workers, resulting from frequent job rotation; substantive participation via team production methods; and extensive on-the-job training. Workers have the knowledge about shop-floor operations required to make meaningful suggestions, and they have the power to change work methods in accordance with their suggestions.

Formally, Japan does not mandate worker participation in management decisions in Japanese firms, but workers are extremely vocal about management issues, and joint consultation between labor unions and the company at the business and plant level is widespread. Through joint consultation committees, employees participate with management in forming high-level strategic plans and general company policies.[3] Unions also bargain on employment issues, such as wages and working conditions. The extensive communication between management and unions in Japanese businesses is helped by the many high-level firm managers who served as union leaders during their rise through the company.

The ringi system of decisionmaking within the managerial ranks promotes the flow of information through the company. The ringi system is a process whereby proposals originate with lower-echelon employees and are communicated to high-ranking officials for their approval after a long process of consensus-seeking discussion and modification in which virtually everyone affected is involved.[4] The ringi system combines a high degree of centralization of formal authority for plant- or company-level decisions in top executive positions with high levels of actual or informal participation of employees of widely differing rank.

Participation in decisionmaking in Japanese companies is supported by extensive profit sharing. On average, about one-third of the total annual compensation of employees is in the form of bonus payments.[5] Bonuses are mainly proportional to base-wage compensation for all employees, and only minor adjustments are made for individual performance. Although bonus payments vary with profits as would be expected in a profit-sharing system of compensation, both prosperous and declining enterprises pay some bonus; thus far less than one-third of compensation fluctuates proportionally with profits.[6] Companies also often set up group-level competitions, implying group gainsharing.[7]

Japanese firms rely heavily on job rotation and team production techniques. Such techniques allow workers to gain extensive on-the-job training, which adds to their skills and allows them to work up the internal job promotion ladder. In addition, team production methods make it easier for workers to monitor each other's effort. Such methods also allow a great deal of flexibility in the organization of individual work groups. Teams take advantage of this flexibility to organize production differently than in the United States.[8] Finally, team production methods serve an important integrating function, fostering participation, trust, and cohesiveness among team members.[9]

Cohesiveness is also encouraged by the compensation policy of Japanese firms. Individual compensation is tightly linked to employee seniority. As Kazuo Koike pointed out, the Japanese seniority system covers not only white-collar workers, for whom seniority and pay are positively related in most advanced industrial countries, but also blue-collar workers.[10] An implication of this compensation system is compression of wage and status differentials, especially between blue-collar workers and white-collar employees.[11]

Japanese companies are noted for their long-term employment commitment to their workers (at least their full-time male workers). This does not mean that Japanese firms never make layoffs, but layoffs are avoided, and the mechanisms for handling them when they are necessary have distinctive features. Japanese firms react differently to short-term cyclical reductions in product demand and to long-term reductions that are perceived to be permanent. During cyclical disturbances, Japanese companies use a number of mechanisms to maintain the employment of their regular employees, including hoarding of labor (often performing maintenance or training activities), layoffs of temporary (largely female) workers, a reduction in subcontracting of work to suppliers, transfers of workers from declining product lines to other product lines within the company with stable or increasing demand, and transfers of workers to other firms.[12]

Intrafirm transfers are facilitated by the union structure and the seniority pay scheme, which pose few barriers to the movement of workers from one job to another, even from one plant to another. Transfers are more feasible in large firms encompassing several product lines— hence one of the advantages of size in maintaining a participatory system. Most large Japanese firms either are members of so-called business alliances or work closely with a group of affiliates and subcontracting companies, which facilitates interfirm transfers. The networks of firms are held together in several ways, including mutual shareholding arrangements, long-term supply and customer relationships, and links to common banks and trading companies.

In the face of a sustained reduction in demand, all of these measures may prove insufficient to achieve the size of the employment adjustment required, and the company may be forced to cut the employment of its long-term work force. The firm then relies on attrition and special retirement allowances to encourage the early retirement of its senior workers. The company can often draw on resources from the government if it can demonstrate that its problems are symptomatic of a declining industry.[13]

The 1991–94 recession in Japan is sometimes used as evidence against the Japanese model, both because of poor macroeconomic performance and because of the supposed end of lifetime employment. In fact, the poor macroeconomic performance is the result of the doubling in value of the yen relative to the dollar, which makes Japanese exports very expensive overseas. The weaker export performance is not caused by lagging productivity growth or quality in Japanese enterprises. Similarly, although a few Japanese enterprises have resorted to layoffs of permanent employees, the vast majority of large companies are maintaining their core employees (although potential new hires, contract workers, and some subcontractors are suffering).[14]

Finally, large Japanese firms have just-cause dismissal policies as part of an elaborate structure of regulations that provide the foundation for organizational trust and union involvement.

External Conditions Affecting Employee Involvement

Japan's participatory firms arose in a high-growth environment, characterized by relatively small cyclical disturbances.[15] As a result of rapid, stable growth, the companies operated in tight labor markets in which they competed for the best available employees. These external conditions meant that it was in the individual firm's interest to build a labor-relations system that would attract and keep the best workers. Such conditions also lowered the costs of maintaining the system, especially the adjustment costs associated with cyclical declines in demand. And rapid growth allowed the firm to offer its workers quick promotion opportunities in return for their commitment to the firm's success. Slow growth would have been detrimental to the firm's seniority compensation system and its elaborate internal promotion ladder, both of which supported the commitment and cohesiveness of its permanent work force.

Most large Japanese firms opted for similar participatory systems, which meant that the cost to each company was lower than it would have been otherwise. In particular, the adverse selection problem associated with just-cause dismissal policies was less severe because the same policies were offered by other firms competing for workers. Nonetheless, the possibility of adverse selection is probably one reason that Japanese participatory firms engage in substantial screening of new employees. In this they are helped by the competitive tracking characteristic of Japan's educational system: The large firms recruit from the very best schools, and they draw from a labor pool that has already been significantly screened and has a high level of general educational attainment.

The compression of wage differentials in large Japanese firms is possible largely because their average compensation exceeds that of smaller firms. Frustrated good workers who believe that their relative pay and position should be higher cannot find attractive compensation opportunities outside the primary sector of the economy.

The best workers are not hired away by other large participatory firms that are willing to pay them more, for several reasons. First, the high investment in company-specific human capital made possible by long-term employment relations makes it difficult for outsiders to be as productive as insiders. Second, pay rises rapidly with seniority, so young workers are relatively cheap and older workers are relatively expensive. Furthermore, firms that hire new employees at high levels would reduce the number of promotions available for lower-seniority workers, thus reducing their motivation. And any new firm that tried to hire from existing firms would face problems establishing a reputation as a good employer. Finally, a cultural element discourages job changing for senior male employees, an element that may decline over time.

The capital market environment in which large Japanese firms operate has supported the development of their unique industrial relations system. As a result of close long-term relationships with their banks and institutional shareholders, large Japanese companies can sustain high debt-equity ratios without incurring a cost-of-capital penalty. In addition, external suppliers of capital have a variety of means to monitor the behavior of the firms to which they lend, including regular meetings between firm management and representatives of banks and other large companies who are significant institutional shareholders. Consequently, Japanese firms find obtaining external financing easier for long-term investment in intangibles such as human capital and research and development.

The extent and methods of control over company decisionmaking by external suppliers of finance appear to be significantly different in Japan from what they are in the United States. Most institutional investors in large Japanese firms are large Japanese banks and other large Japanese firms, often with close business ties in product or input markets. These institutional investors tend to have long-term associations with the firms in which they hold significant equity. Hostile takeovers are largely unheard of—indeed many observers see the system of reciprocal shareholding by large firms as a means to ward off takeovers.

Moreover, the income and control rights of large institutional investors—and of smaller private investors as well—appear to be much more limited than those of significant holders of equity in the U.S. capital market. In particular, the shareholders in large Japanese companies behave more like long-term investors and less like controllers.[16] Company boards of directors are composed almost entirely of inside members of the company, chosen by management. Many inside members are ex-officials of company unions. The directors appointed by shareholders are almost never a majority of the company board, nor are the directors truly outsiders, because they are usually appointed by the large banks and firms with which the company has extensive, ongoing financial and product relationships.

The close relationship between managers and a set of friendly investors insulates company management from external control to a considerable extent (as long as the company is not in crisis) and allows for significantly more participation by employees in company decisionmaking. The downside, as Masahiko Aoki and others have noted, is that a real possibility exists that managers, relatively free of control by external investors, will fail to take actions in the investors' interests. In such an environment, the neoclassical economists' assumption that the firm acts to maximize its value in the interests of its shareholders seems inappropriate. A more appropriate model, developed by Aoki, sees the Japanese firm as a quasi-permanent organization representing the interests of its stockholders and its employees. The behavior of the company is the outcome of a cooperative game between these two groups. The role of managers is to formulate the company's policy to lead to an outcome that maximizes the joint interests of workers and owners. The outcome should lie somewhere between value maximization in the interests of the firm's shareholders and income per worker maximization in the interests of the firm's employees.[17]

Capital market imperfections have also been less severe for Japanese than for American companies because of the methods by which participation was introduced. As Robert Cole emphasized, a key player in the dissemination of quality circles in Japan has been the Japanese Union of Scientists and Engineers (JUSE). JUSE is a highly respected professional association, with credibility in the business community. A firm that invests in JUSE-sponsored training for its members is making a more tangible, credible investment than a U.S. company that spends investor resources experimenting with participation. Finally, the costs of spreading knowledge are low while the benefits can be high. However, marketing knowledge is difficult because one buyer can so easily resell it. Thus the costs of disseminating knowledge about successful participation have been lowered because JUSE has acted as a clearinghouse.[18]

All aspects of the Japanese industrial relations system cannot be attributed to the characteristics of product, labor, and capital markets described in this book. Japan's history played a large role in shaping its industrial relations system. In addition, the Japanese model has numerous losers, including women, foreign workers, and workers trapped at the bottom of the secondary sector. Nevertheless, the success of Japan highlights how an economy with favorable product, labor, and capital market features can more easily develop participatory workplaces.

8

Public Policies

Reformers have the idea that change can be achieved by brute sanity.

—George Bernard Shaw

State and federal governments have hundreds of programs that affect workplaces. With little exaggeration, virtually everything that a corporation does is affected by the government. In addition to regulations governing, for example, safety and wages, the government subsidizes a number of actions explicitly (such as the research and development tax credit) and implicitly (such as ESOPs). More fundamentally, the government establishes the basic language and framework of business by creating accounting standards and by building or regulating the communications and transportation infrastructure. In short, the government influences each step of the operation of a business, from acquiring inputs (labor, capital, and supplies) to research, design, production, and distribution, as well as the staff functions of human resources, labor relations, accounting, information systems, and strategy.

However, many government agencies do not realize that their policies—from Securities and Exchange Commission (SEC) rules on the accounting treatment of training expenses to Consumer Product Safety Commission methods of regulating hazards—affect workplaces. Given this lack of understanding, a host of government policies function at loggerheads and impede the creation of high-involvement management. For example, the government spends billions of dollars in research that affects workplaces. Unfortunately, in many cases, the new technology is designed to lower the skill and autonomy of workers. Thus the innovations are likely to be both harmful to workers and less effective, because they will not capture the benefits of employees' ideas in implementing and improving the new workplace technologies. The U.S. accounting system treats investment in people as a cost, biasing managers away from human capital. The system of financial market regulation pushes managers to focus on the short run, while effective workplaces require investments for the long run.

More government policies are not needed. Instead, focusing the many government programs affecting workplaces toward promotion of the high-skill, high-involvement model can reduce costs of regulation while increasing the efficiency of the American workplace. The changes proposed here often merely remove barriers the government has inadvertently put in place. In a nutshell, the key is for all government policies that affect workplaces to help build an environment supportive of worker-management cooperation, long-run perspectives, and continuous improvement. Because enormous variations exist among American workers, companies, and markets, economywide mandates are not useful. The government, however, can implement a number of policies to reduce barriers and to encourage companies that are considering moving to high-involvement management style.

What the government does can be described in a few words: research, teaching, certification, regulation of market failures such as pollution, structuring the markets for labor and capital, and acting as an employer for approximately 20 percent of the work force. Each function is carried out in numerous agencies and departments of the federal, state, and local government. What is lacking is a consistent focus on encouraging high-involvement workplaces.

The first step toward building a coherent workplace policy must come from the top: The president must enunciate an overarching vision of the future American workplace. This vision must include a description of the role government will play as a facilitator (as opposed to a regulator) in creating the high-involvement workplace. To implement this vision, the president should request that all agencies be aware of their policies' effects on workplaces.

In addition, a cabinet-level committee should be formed to coordinate policies. The committee should be empowered to require any agency to explain the impact of its policies on workplaces and why any negative impacts cannot be avoided. The committee will also require a small staff, whose job is to consult with all stakeholders in the government and in private sector organizations to understand which government policies impede high-involvement workplaces.

A similar cabinet-level committee has been formed to coordinate science and technology policy across the government. This model should be extended to policies affecting workplaces. The technology committee has several subcommittees dealing with different aspects of technology such as national security and education. Similarly, the workplace committee should have separate subcommittees for each major theme, such as research, teaching, and structuring capital and labor markets.

The challenge of the coordinating committee is that each individual agency that deals with a given industry or sector usually focuses on the needs of that sector. Agencies are often captured by special interest groups for numerous reasons.[1] In most cases, most of the agency's employees have previously worked in that industry and will likely work in that industry after leaving government service (perhaps in a lucrative job, if they make many friends in the industry). Most employees of an agency emphasize promotion of their industry. (That is, people who care about farmers are likely to work for the Department of Agriculture; those who want a strong military, the Department of Defense; those who come from and care about Wall Street, the SEC.) In addition, members of Congress on a committee that oversees an agency receive substantial funding from companies in that industry. These members are often zealous about maintaining control over their sector. Lobbyists make trouble for the agency if their interests are not well represented, but broad-based groups such as consumers, workers, or citizens have little countervailing voice.

In short, whether well intentioned or acting out of self-interest, agency employees are far more likely to consider the narrow interests of a particular sector or industry than the general interest of workers. Agencies often view mandates to consider broader interests, whether the environment or workplace issues, as distractions and meddling from above. Ultimately, no simple change will solve the problem of powerful stakeholders disproportionately influencing government agencies. Nevertheless, the proposals to improve management within government and to empower workers throughout the economy can partially check the disproportionate power of organized interest groups.

Research

> *It ain't what he don't know that's so bad, but what he knows that just ain't so.*
>
> —ANONYMOUS

The majority of basic research in the United States is funded by the government. Much of this research relates to workplaces, which involves both the development of new technology and understanding how business can become more productive. It must be refocused to provide a more complete knowledge base for implementing high-involvement work practices.

Enhancing Skills

For more than a century, government has been a leader in developing new technologies. For example, development of numerically controlled machine tools was largely funded by the Air Force, in the hope that they would not require skilled machinists. The Air Force did not want to worry that the machinists might go on strike when it needed certain parts.[2] The desire to avoid reliance on workers' skills has not changed in the last generation. The Intelligent Welding Project of the Department of Commerce's National Institute of Standards and Technology (NIST), for example, is developing a system "to replace the eyes, ears, and know-how of a skilled welder."[3] The welding project is not an isolated example. The Commerce Department's Automated Manufacturing Research Facility is designed "for studying interfaces between production equipment and information systems."[4] The interface between operators and equipment or information systems is ignored. Similarly, Commerce's Computer-Aided Manufacturing System Engineering Project "would be used by engineers to design and implement future manufacturing systems" based on advanced tools for designing and evaluating "the performance of manufacturing processes, equipment and enterprises."[5] Again, workers have no role in the design or operation of these new work systems. Government-funded research must be reoriented away from developing skill-destroying technologies and toward providing the tools that are needed in high-involvement workplaces. The director of NIST, Arati Prabhakar, stated that "integrating technology and people is important for NIST." Nevertheless, NIST still has a long way to go because, as she noted, "technology organizations have traditionally not given much thought to the topic of integrating technology and people."[6]

Within manufacturing, major research projects are currently being undertaken by the Department of Defense's Technology Reinvestment Program, the Department of Energy, the Department of Commerce, the National Science Foundation, and a host of statewide programs. Most of these efforts focus almost exclusively on new technology and do not consider the role of frontline workers in operating the new technologies. This narrow research focus is maintained even though technology is typically more productive and jobs are more satisfying if the employees who use the technology have a role in designing it; the technology acts as a tool to increase employees' ability to be creative and continuously improve the process and product, not as a monitor that measures work effort; and the technology is integrated into the human resource system of the enterprise.[7]

Even within the applied social sciences, research is profit-oriented, often ignoring the gains and losses to workers. For example, organizational scholars largely stopped studying the determinants of worker satisfaction when satisfaction was shown to be a poor predictor of employee effort. The researchers then increased the research on worker satisfaction when satisfaction was determined to be a good predictor of turnover and absenteeism.[8] Employee satisfaction appears to be of interest not because employees matter but when it is thought to be useful to employers. In the future, government-funded research must take a more balanced approach toward meeting the needs of both owners and employees.

Improving the Efficiency of Employee Involvement

Because of the substantial research concluding that technological advances without accompanying human resource changes are not effective, government-funded research must incorporate elements of the high-involvement workplace. The federal government should subsidize an ambitious research program on the determinants of success of employee involvement and TQM. Employee involvement can work, and potentially enormous returns can result from improving understanding of what work organizations are more effective in particular settings.

As part of this research, the government should examine not just traditional management-initiated programs, but also the effects of employee representatives, ranging from safety committees (as mandated in the states of Washington and Oregon) to unions. The goal should be to understand and diffuse best practices within workplaces.

As a final step, the government must sponsor a continuing research effort on how its policies affect workplaces. Cross-agency coordination is hard, and agencies often have difficulty understanding how their decisions affect workplaces. The government should be funding outside research to monitor its actions to determine unintended consequences that raise the costs of high-involvement workplaces. (Related research should evaluate other unintended consequences of policies, such as harming the environment.)

Teaching

Why spend time learning when ignorance is instantaneous?
—HOBBES OF "CALVIN AND HOBBES"

Although people often associate teaching with schools, education takes place throughout their lives. Moreover, the government is involved at each step, from preschool to university and in continuing education on the job and between jobs. In addition, the government has a role in the education of union leaders, managers, and government employees, teaching them how to run high-involvement workplaces. Changes in schools, postschool training, and the training of decisionmakers can facilitate high-involvement workplaces.

Education at all levels must teach a few fundamental skills: problem solving, working in groups, and continuous learning. These must be taught—at different levels of sophistication—throughout citizens' lives.

Furthermore, any individual or group of employees, managers, union leaders, or other interested citizens needs easy access to the information that can improve the workplace. The Internet computer network provides a powerful platform for disseminating the information that is needed to make high-involvement workplaces succeed. Currently, roughly 20 percent of American workers and managers have access to the Internet directly. This proportion is growing exponentially and should reach more than 50 percent within a few years. In addition, almost all libraries and schools will be connected.

The Educational System

America's public education system is a natural starting point for discussing reform, because most schools are funded by the government. Furthermore, schools' topics and teaching methods are chosen largely by state and local governments, with some input and regulation by the federal government.

With their traditional focus on "talk and chalk," schools were well designed to teach future employees how to obey instructions and follow rules. In the future, the educational system must be geared toward providing workers with the skills for high-involvement workplaces. Many current reform efforts revolve around the importance of basic skills. While basic literacy and numeracy skills are crucial, more must be done. High-involvement workplaces require workers who are trained in teamwork, problem solving, and the tools for continuous learning.[9]

As part of preparing the work force for high-involvement settings, schools must promote norms of democracy and empowerment. The best way to learn about decisionmaking or working in groups is to make meaningful decisions and to work in groups. Students should learn in high-involvement settings (as appropriate to their level), with an emphasis on teaching them through experience that they are capable of problem solving and decisionmaking.

Schools in the United States have come under enormous pressure in recent decades for their failings. This new set of high-involvement skills is not an additional burden for schools, but an overarching focus that makes schools more interesting (because participation makes learning more engrossing) and relevant (because education is tied to job-related skills). The new focus will alleviate the difficulties schools have in everything from retention rates to school-to-work transitions.

The change in curricula must not stop at the twelfth grade. Engineers are taught virtually nothing about the benefits of designing workplaces with and for the people who work there. One of the more than two hundred engineering design texts reviewed by Harold Salzman and Robert Lund stated,

> The optimal performance of the element "man" in man-machine control system performance can be obtained only when the mechanical components of the system are designed so that human beings need only act as a simple amplifier.

Similarly, another text states that the primary objective is to eliminate workers and, when that is not possible, skill levels should normally be minimized.[10]

Most taxpayers probably do not want their tax dollars going to a publicly funded state university to teach engineers how to dumb-down jobs. Even more serious, having engineering students receive instruction that leads their products and processes to be less effective is counterproductive. Instead, students should be taught how to work with the ultimate users of technology. This approach raises the probability that engineers' ideas about technology will be effectively implemented.

Unfortunately, any changes in curriculum take time to implement. One important barrier is the training of teachers. Teachers' education and certification must be broadened to include these essential skills if workers are to be fully prepared in the twenty-first century.

The Training System

Most state-funded job training programs emphasize operating machines and tools, which is desired by businesses but does little to increase the long-term employability of workers.[11] State training programs should increase their emphasis on the problem-solving skills needed in high-involvement workplaces.

The Internet computer network provides a rich resource for training. The government should find and post a variety of training materials in the skills of the high-involvement workplace. A complete set of manuals would be compiled, with one or more for line employees, supervisors, managers, trainers, executives, and so forth. The line employees' manuals, for example, would introduce the high-involvement approach and begin with basic problem-solving skills such as problem identification, brainstorming, and the analysis of the root causes of problems. Later chapters would move on to more advanced skills such as running a meeting, statistical process control, and designing experiments. Variations could be provided for different settings (for example, assembly line versus employees who deal with customers). For all manuals, users would be encouraged to download them to their computer systems and customize the manuals for their workplaces.

Continuously updating and improving the manuals would be vital. Feedback from users in both the private and public sectors would keep the manuals relevant to managers' and employees' needs.

In a few years, technology will have advanced substantially. The government should begin planning now for when most users can access multimedia technologies from their personal computers. At that point, the government should provide complete training courses on-line, supplemented with lectures, videos, exercises and simulations, and other instructional materials. Using these materials, workers and work groups should be able to learn the principles of employee involvement in a setting similar to their workplace and using whatever media are best suited to their learning style.

Changing Norms

The government also should promote new norms of empowered workplaces for all citizens. In the 1930s President Franklin D. Roosevelt helped shape workplaces by stating, "If I went to work in a factory, the first thing I'd do would be to join a union." The current administration should promote a similar awareness campaign to inform workers of the potential of workplace reform.

For example, public service announcements could show employees describing briefly how they redesigned their workplaces. The point should be that even frontline workers with little formal education are capable of being empowered at work. The goal of the campaign should be to raise employees' expectations for meaningful participation. In addition to showing employees the possibility of true empowerment, the announcements can also warn them away from sham programs with little long-term prospect of success. (Awareness campaigns have a mixed record of success. For example, they worked well in increasing the proportion of drivers who wear seat belts but have had much less effect on getting Americans to quit smoking.)

Employee training should also raise the cost to employers offering low-skill jobs and low wages who are trying to take advantage of employees. The Internet should include easily accessible information on workers' rights and on safety and health issues. For example, workers should be able to type in a simple series of commands followed by a chemical name and receive clearly written information on the hazards associated with that chemical.

The Internet should also contain sufficient information to let frontline employees judge the quality of the workplace innovations they are being asked to adopt. Specifically, if workers are asked to put enormous energy into a consultant's quality program that has a long history of leading to job loss, or short-run results followed by decline of the program, they should have this information up front. Government-maintained directories of training providers and consultants should include space for user reviews from all those who have experience with that service provider.

Continuing Education of Managers

> *"Shut up!" he explained.*
>
> —RING LARDNER

A host of state, local, and federal government programs teach managers how to improve their workplace, but they do not form a coherent whole. For example, NIST sponsors a number of Manufacturing Extension Partnerships to assist companies in upgrading their technology. Numerous states run similar programs. Most of these programs focus on new technology as the solution to manufacturing problems, with little emphasis on work organization. However, although 40 percent of respondents to a survey of two thousand firms with new office technology found the systems were below expectations, only 10 percent attributed failure to technical problems. The majority of reasons given involved human and organizational factors.[12]

The many government programs must be tied together to provide a coherent system that supports high-involvement workplaces. The goal should be taking companies from the initial stages of awareness and interest in new work organizations and providing them with the motivation and the low-cost tools needed to introduce new work practices. Furthermore, the companies should be informed about the various resources that can help them through each step of the way.

The first step is raising managers' awareness of new work practices. The Malcolm Baldrige National Quality Award is an example of a successful tool for raising awareness. More than 1 million copies of the award criteria have been distributed, suggesting that many managers have seen at least one outline of new work practices.

In addition, the government should continue to publicize the successes of high-quality employee involvement programs. Managers, union leaders, and employees of award-winning workplaces should be showcased. For example, the government can subsidize documentaries and case studies of successful cases of workplace reorganization. A high-profile executive should join the government as a spokesperson for the high-involvement workplace.

Once managers are aware of the new work practices, their interest must be engaged. A detailed write-up of the experience of a workplace with high-involvement work practices can be effective in showing the possibilities of the best in employee involvement. Plant tours of similar enterprises can be of help. The government should subsidize groups that organize these tours. The Department of Labor is creating a database of innovative firms, which should facilitate interested companies in contacting those who have gone before them. The database will point users to companies in their industry and region. Substantial evidence exists that managers learn best from those who are most similar to them. The government also has a role in disseminating research relating high-involvement workplaces to organizational performance.[13]

Once managers are interested, providing them with assessment tools that evaluate the readiness of their company for various forms of change is often useful. The first stages of assessment and feedback can be automated via the Internet and performed at no cost by managers in the privacy of their offices or local libraries. The automated assessment should then provide information on appropriate resources for the next step, whether these resources are elsewhere in the computerized database or elsewhere in the public or private sectors.

After the assessment, managers will want to introduce the appropriate form of employee involvement. The current industrial extension services can help firms learn how to implement high-involvement management. The key is to make sure that the various extension officers are familiar with the interactions of technology and workplace issues.

Access to an up-to-date directory of consultants and training providers will lower the costs of introducing high-involvement workplaces. The Department of Labor is building a database of innovative workplace practices and of providers of consulting and training services.

In addition, the Clinton administration has proposed integrating numerous programs operated at the state and federal levels with One-Stop Career Centers that offer job counseling and allow workers to apply for jobless benefits and sign up for training programs all in one place. These career centers will build a database of training providers, including the completion and placement rates and the average starting wages of their participants. In addition, the database will be on the Internet, permitting users easy access to information. Finally, the costs of implementing employee participation could be lowered further if the government published training materials on the skills needed for high-involvement workplaces.

Education for Unions

Education programs also should be established for unions. The Department of Labor's Labor Quality Institute trains union leaders so that they can return to their union and teach the skills needed for high-involvement union-management relations. This program is a good start and should be expanded by encouraging unions to introduce and expand their own training programs. The government should sponsor research and dissemination of best practices for the internal operations of unions. The goal is for union-management relations to be based on high levels of joint problem solving and for unions to increase their reliance on high-involvement practices.

Company Networks

In addition to the direct education of managers, workers, and union leaders, government agencies can help organizations create self-help networks. Such networks have been successful in Europe in increasing the quality and productivity of small firms, and they can provide important support for the high-involvement workplace.[14] In Japan, for example, an average of two conferences are held by problem-solving teams every day.[15] Teams are motivated partly by the opportunity to make a presentation on their successful problem solving. The conferences also promote cross-company learning on techniques of effective employee involvement.

The Department of Labor is working with several business organizations and industry associations to identify and publicize high-performance workplace practices relevant to their member firms. Plans include providing articles in partners' newsletters, furnishing speakers for their events, creating industry-specific case studies and how-to guides, and helping partners' members to benchmark and network for high performance.

As with other forms of teaching, the Internet can play a role. In many highly computer-networked companies, managers use the company's network to exchange information and answer each other's questions about high-performance management. In addition, several networks of companies have introduced intercompany computer networks. The Department of Labor should also provide resources for computerized bulletin boards and mailing lists on topics relating to high-involvement workplaces. For example, one list might cover reinventing government— government managers, employees, and union officials would pass on hints on how their offices are reinventing themselves. They would submit queries for information and discuss the merits of possible ideas before implementation. Another list might be focused on the different industries or technologies within the private sector (hospitals, manufacturing), and managers, employees, and union officials would communicate what they have learned about high-involvement workplaces.

Certification

> *The secret of life is honesty and fair dealing. If you can fake that, you've got it made.*
>
> —GROUCHO MARX

In addition to its role in educating employees, the government issues certifications—from high school diplomas to licenses to practice medicine. The government also certifies companies—from sanctioning of the International Standards Organization (ISO) 9000 quality standard to suppliers for military and other government purchases to cosponsorship with the American Society for Quality Control of the Baldrige award. The government should consistently certify individuals and organizations that have the skills and motivation to continuously improve products and processes and that proactively solve problems. These are the qualities that purchasers (whether employers hiring labor or companies choosing suppliers) need for long-run success.

Certifying Employees' Skills

Employers in the United States train less than their foreign competitors and less than is socially optimal.[16] A national strategy to improve workplaces should greatly increase worker training throughout the economy. A key step in increasing training is establishing national standards in worker training for employee involvement.

The United States is unique among its major competitors for its lack of certifications for worker skills, which diminishes the portability of training and reduces the incentives for employees to invest in increasing their skills.[17] Employees prefer jobs that provide certification, and costs are lowered for employers that train. Training could also be provided by unions, small businesses, consultants, junior colleges, high schools, and business schools. (The federal government could provide a fixed amount per certification if it wanted to subsidize training. Subsidies may be called for because of the numerous imperfections in the market for training.)

Currently, employers' selection rules for employees must pass stringent tests to ensure they are valid predictors of job performance. As part of the effort to promote high-involvement workplaces, the government should presume that the high-involvement skills are helpful and not require each employer to validate the usefulness of the certification in predicting performance at each workplace. To the extent that any groups that have historically faced discrimination receive disproportionately few certifications, the government can provide subsidies to training providers who provide skills to these groups.

As with recent approaches to standards in science education, certification in involvement skills would not rely on passing a single test. Instead, each set of skills would have an appropriate set of training exercises, experience in implementation, and written or oral tests. The goal is closer to the Boy Scouts' merit badge approach to measuring achievement.[18] For example, a high school student could achieve a certification in basic involvement skills such as identifying the root cause of problems and teamwork skills. In her first year on the job, her employer could provide classroom training in the skills for the intermediate-level certification (for example, running a meeting, plus more problem-solving tools). She would also have to participate at work in a problem-solving group and make a presentation about a successful process of problem identification and solution. Later in her career, she would return to a junior college for a certification in training, qualifying her to teach basic employee involvement skills. A colleague with a similar career path might instead attend a local university extension to acquire advanced problem-solving skills in experimental design and data analysis. In either case, the certifications would be recognized across industries because the skills are useful in many jobs.

This proposal builds on, but is distinct from, the existing set of industry-based skill standards because it focuses on the general skills of the high-involvement workplace.[19] Currently, for example, the electronics industry and the retail industry have separate certifications that include similar skills in problem solving, working in groups, and decisionmaking. Unfortunately, the component of the certification that reflects these general skills will not be transferable across industries; that is, no standardization has been established. The proposed certification in involvement skills can be integrated with the current industry standards by encouraging industries to use merit badges in general skills as building blocks for their own certifications (as well as industry-specific components). Although some loss of flexibility for the industries will result, costs should be reduced because the industries do not each need to redefine and revalidate their measures of the general high-involvement skills.

Several benefits would accrue from national employee certifications. For example, they will greatly lower the costs of training employees, because a standard set of skills will be widely taught. The costs of selecting employees will also drop because employers can easily compare skills.

Employers are often unwilling to provide high levels of training for fear that employees will receive the valuable training and then quit. Certifications will reduce this market imperfection, because employees would be willing to pay to receive the training if it led to a certificate that other companies would recognize. (The payments may be made through lower wages during the training period, as is done with apprentices or medical residents. Employers thus are not taking a risk when providing training.) While some economic theories predict that making general training more visible to the market will increase turnover, turnover is lower at companies that pay for publicly certified training.[20] As an additional incentive for employers, the proportion of workers certified could eventually be integrated into the supplier certification.

In addition, achieving a quality certification will require basic reading and math skills. As quality certification becomes more valuable, it indirectly rewards students for achieving basic skills. Many students who perform poorly in traditional classrooms may learn more readily when academic training is combined with the process of solving real-world problems.

Certifying High-Quality Suppliers

For most businesses, more than half the value of their final products is purchased from suppliers.[21] In successful high-involvement companies, "the organization establishes a partnership with suppliers and customers to assure continuous improvement in the quality of the end products and services."[22] Long-term, information-rich relationships between suppliers and customers lead to faster product development, increased flexibility, and higher quality.

High levels of involvement between suppliers and customers are the rule in many successful businesses. Toyota has been a pioneer in creating supplier relations that add value. Toyota also requires all of its suppliers (and their suppliers) to apply for the Deming Award, Japan's highest quality prize. Ford and the other U.S. auto companies have followed Toyota's example of certifying suppliers. Many companies use Ford's Q1 certification, for example, as an indicator of which companies are high-quality suppliers. Motorola, a winner of the United States' Baldrige award, is one of several companies that has required their suppliers to apply for the award to evaluate their own TQM efforts.[23]

Despite the evidence concerning the benefits of close supplier relations, the public sector has done relatively little to involve suppliers in quality programs. About half of the government agencies in a 1992 General Accounting Office survey reported that they had worked with suppliers to improve quality to any degree, and few had close relations.[24]

Given the pattern of successful companies promoting total quality in suppliers, the federal government should initiate a voluntary supplier certification. This certification should increase the quality of both processes and outputs of government contractors and suppliers. Incorporating high Baldrige scores could be one element in the federal procurement process.

The Baldrige award measures companies' progress on a number of quality goals. The company or division must provide evidence that it incorporates quality into management practices, works closely with suppliers, trains workers in quality techniques, and meets customers' desires. The completed application must be less than eighty-five pages, and even shorter for small companies. The process begins with a Board of Examiners (a cross section of recognized quality experts) scoring the written application. High scorers then have site visits led by a senior examiner, and finalists are judged by a panel of judges. (An alternative model would be for the government to certify private sector companies that performed the judging.) Historically, up to six winners were designated among several categories (for example, large versus small businesses); in the future, as many winners in a given category will be permitted as there are outstanding applicants.

Perhaps a 2 percent preference on price would be given for companies scoring more than 450 out of 1,000 (an above-average score), and a 5 percent preference on price would be given for companies scoring more than 600 (an excellent score—winners typically score between 700 and 800). (The government uses similar price differentials to encourage purchases from businesses that are small or that have minority and female owners.)

In the short run, in addition to the Baldrige award, the government can give preferences to existing private sector quality certifications, such as the automobile industry's QS 9000 quality standard and the QSSR quality standard promulgated by Sematech and a consortium of computer chip makers. The multi-industry National Process Certification Standard (ANSI/EIA 599) is also becoming widely accepted in the private sector and should be utilized in government procurement.[25]

The government would benefit from quality certification of suppliers in several ways. When a product's expected life-cycle costs (including repairs, late deliveries, and cost overruns) are taken into account, the increase in quality of supplies used will more than repay the small price difference. Because of fear of favoritism and corruption, government procurement offices are often constrained to rely almost entirely on price in choosing suppliers. The procedures do not permit decisionmakers to consider suppliers' ability to deliver high quality, on time, and within budget.[26] The Baldrige ratings will permit purchasing departments to incorporate nonprice factors that predict total cost, which should increase the quality and decrease the long-run expense of government service.

For example, the Madison, Wisconsin, city government found that one reason broken-down city vehicles required an average of nine days to be repaired was that the parts department found it impossible to keep in stock components for each of the 440 different types of vehicles the city owned. The city owned so many different models because it had a policy of buying the one with the lowest sticker price on the date of purchase.[27]

The price premium corrects for a difficulty that Congress and the president face in ensuring that an agency only accepts a high bid if the supplier is of high quality, not a friend of the purchasing agency. The Baldrige score permits quality factors to be incorporated into the bidding process without corruption and favoritism. This process does not mandate any particular management practices but does reward high quality. Fortunately, high-involvement workplaces that continuously improve lead to lower costs as well as higher quality. Thus as more companies achieve the top rankings, the lowest bids on most contracts will be those with high quality rankings.

Suppliers also would benefit from quality certification. Establishing a common supplier certification will reduce the burden on the supplying companies. Today, many agencies within the federal government have their own supplier certification programs, with differing requirements. A standardized certification will lower these suppliers' costs.

Encouraging suppliers to apply for the Baldrige award will help diffuse best practices throughout the economy. For example, when Cummins Engine was having quality problems, the company applied for the Baldrige award as a way of "turning a harsh spotlight on itself." Although it did not come close to winning, the feedback led to valuable new practices concerning worker training and sources of truckers' complaints. Defect rates declined from 10 percent to below 1 percent in only two years. Baldrige examiners are respected practitioners, which makes their feedback both useful to and respected by recipients.

In addition, the nation as a whole would benefit from quality certification of suppliers. The Baldrige program could be made more useful if companies' scores were publicly available—at least for those that are highly ranked. Certification serves as a credible indicator of companies' quality and flexibility.

A national rating of quality efforts will reduce the costs of all businesses buying from companies in the United States. In Japan and Taiwan, for example, government policies discourage low-quality exports via certification procedures. These policies are intended to enhance national quality reputations.

Publicizing companies' investments in human resources will also help alleviate serious informational problems for potential employees and owners. When the Federal Aviation Administration began publishing on-time statistics for airlines, airlines immediately began improving the proportion of their flights that arrived on time. Similarly, publication of a score that depends partly on training and employee satisfaction will give managers incentives to improve these measures.

Making Baldrige scores public will also improve workers' ability to choose a company that is a good fit with their needs, raising labor market efficiency. In addition, this information will better permit owners and boards of directors to measure how well managers are investing for long-term success by building up their organization's capabilities.

A nationally accepted quality certification will also greatly facilitate the job of industrial extension services, performed, for example, by the Department of Commerce and a number of states. They will be able to focus their energies on helping companies meet the Baldrige criteria's standards of excellence.[28]

The Baldrige award is useful for spreading quality techniques but can be improved. The International Standards Organization has proposed quality standards—ISO 9000 series—that are being widely adopted, particularly by nations of the European Community. Any U.S. supplier certification should be made compatible with ISO 9000 certification, to reduce the costs of complying with both.

The ISO 9000 series primarily requires that an organization have and follow standard procedures for what it does. The ISO standard requires neither that the standard procedures be sensible nor that they be constantly improved. In short, ISO 9000 is an incomplete basis for judging the quality of an organization's process or output. Nevertheless, ISO 9000 is widely accepted and is becoming a management fad for many medium-sized companies that feel they must have ISO 9000 certification to compete. Basing the government's requirements on an extension of the ISO 9000 criteria may make more sense than building ISO 9000 into the Baldrige (see box on proposed additions to ISO 9000 series).

Both the Baldrige criteria and ISO 9000 give insufficient emphasis to the human resource practices that are important for almost all successful quality programs. Specifically, the Baldrige award gives only 15 percent of its points for human resource practices, including training and em-

Proposed Additions to ISO 9000 Series

The International Standards Organization (ISO) 9000 series requires that the companies establish, maintain, and follow documented procedures for almost everything they do. Unfortunately, the ISO standard has no requirement that the procedures be continuously improved. The following proposed additions are intended to increase the usefulness of the ISO standard in identifying which companies are excellent suppliers.

Improving Quality Plans

The supplier shall establish and maintain documented procedures for continuously improving all documented procedures. The supplier shall ensure that this procedure is understood, implemented, and maintained at all levels of the organization. (Guidance on procedures for continuous improvement is given in ISO 9004-4, *Guidelines for Quality Improvement.*)

The supplier shall establish and maintain documented procedures to track suggestions (whether from individuals or teams) and to give replies that either approve suggestions or give feedback on reasons that suggestions have not been approved. (Feedback on rejected suggestions is important to facilitate resubmission of an improved suggestion.)

The supplier shall establish and maintain documented procedures for motivating employees (individually, in groups, or both) to continuously improve all documented procedures. The supplier shall establish and maintain documented procedures for evaluating employee efforts for continuous improvement. (Motivational techniques vary widely and include financial rewards [for example, gainsharing and profit sharing] and nonfinancial rewards [for example, prizes and recognition.] Evaluation of employee efforts can be with, for example, confidential employee surveys or records of number of suggestions submitted and implemented per employee.)

Training

The supplier shall establish and maintain documented procedures for identifying training needs and provide for the training of all personnel performing activities affecting quality, including training in the procedures for continuous improvement. The supplier shall establish and maintain documented procedures for evaluating the effectiveness of training. (This section builds on an existing section in the ISO 9000 series.)

The supplier shall establish and maintain documented procedures for identifying information needs and communicating appropriate information to all levels of the organization and to all personnel performing activities affecting quality. Appropriate records of information shared shall be maintained. (Methods of communication include, but are not limited to, newsletters, meetings, and E-mail. Relevant information may include, but is not limited to, the quality policy, quality results and standards, customer needs, and the organization's goals, mission, and values.)

Subcontractor and Customer Relations

The supplier shall establish and maintain documented procedures for cooperating with customers and subcontractors to share information on needs and costs as well as to create methods for cooperative product improvement.

ployee involvement; human resources are even less important in ISO 9000.

In practice, Baldrige award winners have typically moved to a high-skill work force operating with high levels of employee involvement and trust.[29] The Baldrige award should be modified to increase its emphasis on these practices. Unfortunately, any single measure of employee involvement could be implemented by a company that had low levels of employee involvement but wanted to gain points in the award process.

One solution is to encourage a number of additional policies that are particularly valuable to a company that is serious about employee involvement but are costly to companies only going through the motions. For example, Baldrige award points should be given to companies that allot employees one or more seats on the board of directors, elect an employee relations committee at each establishment, institute a health and safety committee at each establishment, have an employee stock ownership or profit-sharing plan, have no labor law violations, and implement a formal procedure for dispute resolution. The policies can be adopted by companies with low levels of employee involvement, but they are particularly valuable to employers who are moving to high levels of employee involvement.

The U.S. Department of Labor is also considering a certification of excellent workplaces (as are Great Britain and Australia).[30] The Baldrige award and the proposed Labor Department certification should maximize the overlap of their criteria. Regardless of the particular changes made in ISO 9000 or in Baldrige, the standards should be continuously improved as experience continues to accumulate.

Quality certification can also improve intergovernmental relations. The federal government is moving away from micromanaging state-level programs and increasing the fraction of funds for fighting poverty or training workers that states may allocate. Allocations often are made as part of a planning process, in which states, cities, or other organizations must show a strategic plan and lay out evaluation criteria (for example, changes in literacy rates). The federal government should give preference to funding projects that have active employee involvement and quality programs. Although success is not guaranteed by the active involvement of frontline employees, it is difficult without their help. In selecting programs that will receive block grants and waivers from detailed regulations, the federal government should consider the presence and success of involvement programs.

As with procurement, Baldrige scores can be a measure of success on institutionalizing a customer-focused high-involvement organization. Although the Baldrige award recently added health care and education categories, it does not cover state or local governments. However, state and local governments can contract with Baldrige examiners to perform an evaluation In addition, the Baldrige award should expand to cover state and local governments.

Regulation

The world will always be governed by self-interest. We should not try to stop this, we should try to make the self-interest of cads a little more coincident with that of decent people.

—SAMUEL BUTLER

Even if the world is not governed purely by self-interest, enough of it exists to require government regulations when markets reward socially undesirable behavior. Workplace safety is largely regulated by the Occupational Safety and Health Administration (OSHA) and by workers' compensation laws. The Environmental Protection Agency regulates environmental issues. Product safety is regulated by the Consumer Product Safety Commission and a variety of product-specific regulators, such as the Food and Drug Administration for food and pharmaceuticals and the Federal Aviation Administration for air traffic safety. In addition, product liability laws, which stipulate the standard of guilt and determine penalty levels, are shaped both by the courts and by state and federal laws.

A regulator has a problem similar to that of a company buying from a supplier. The company would like the supplier to produce high-quality products, just as the regulator would like the supplier to produce safe ones. Traditionally, American companies have relied on fines or dismissal of underperforming suppliers. This is precisely the penalty-oriented approach of modern regulators. However, modern supplier relations are moving away from reliance on arm's-length relations based on outcomes alone (for example, price). Instead, companies are becoming more knowledgeable about the internal processes of their suppliers, requiring them to continuously improve the product and process and to perform root cause analysis of any quality problems. The promise of the new approach is fewer quality problems and higher profits for both companies and suppliers.

A similar logic applies to regulation. OSHA should concern itself less with the required width of a ladder's step and more with the process by which the width is chosen. Regulators must recognize that internal quality procedures are useful predictors of future quality problems. That is, a workplace with continuous improvement will have fewer internal problems, such as workplace safety, and few external problems of unsafe products or services. Moreover, companies with proactive problem-solving processes are trying to avoid safety problems, which should serve as a mitigating factor in case of trouble.

Regulators should require a report of the root cause for all accidents and product safety problems. Evidence exists that a more problem-solving approach to regulation is partially responsible for the lower accident rates in Japan and that both U.S. and Japanese managers and regulators prefer the problem-solving approach.[31]

A focus on process does not imply that outcomes can be ignored. If companies claim they have effective safety committees, they should demonstrate measurable progress toward creating a safe workplace.

Regulators also face the problem of cost. Many regulations (including civil rights and illegal dismissal) are enforced via the courts—a time-consuming and costly endeavor. Many disputes could be fruitfully addressed with alternative procedures for resolution, including mediation (when an outside party helps the disputants find a mutually agreeable resolution) and arbitration (when an outside party can impose a resolution on the disputants). The promise of these procedures includes lower costs, quicker resolution, dispute resolution procedures tailored to the needs of the workplace, better outcomes with lower acrimony, and an unclogging of the court system (especially if the alternative dispute resolution procedures carry a presumption to the court that their decision is correct).

Currently, these procedures are rarely used for employment cases, and when they are used, employers may impose unreasonable procedures that deprive employees of their right to a fair trial.[32] A company with a certified employee representation council could mitigate these problems. The employee representation council (which would need to meet certain standards concerning the fairness of its election to be qualified) could, in turn, certify the dispute resolution procedures. And only certified procedures would have the presumption in the court system of being fair.

Structuring Capital Markets

The fundamental problems with capital markets are that they focus on short-run returns and do not sufficiently reward managers who make hard-to-monitor investments in workers' skills, motivation, and trust. Underlying these problems are weak boards of directors, accounting information that is incomplete and backward-looking, and few investors focused on the long run. The capital market barriers to participatory firms could be reduced by measures that lengthen the perspectives of both managers and investors and that increase the information flows between these groups.

The Securities and Exchange Commission makes the rules that govern what information publicly traded corporations must disclose on their quarterly and annual reports. The SEC rules also influence voluntary disclosure, and they sometimes act as barriers to reporting on internal business conditions. Currently, managers report that they are afraid to mention any forward-looking data for fear of shareholder lawsuits. Lawsuits are filed when shareholders claim that the annual reports contain misleading statements. Certain sections of the annual report are required by the SEC, and they are given protection from shareholder lawsuits (other than for fraud). The SEC should clarify that reporting of current business conditions (for example, trends in quality or in customer or employee satisfaction) or current business programs (for example, training, employee involvement, or new product development procedures) are similarly protected.

The SEC could ask for more detailed information about the board members and the structure of boards. It could begin by returning to requiring that companies list each director's mailing address, so they can be contacted directly by major shareholders. When directors run for election, a 150–word statement of their goals and strategy might be helpful, as would a description of their credentials. Additional disclosure of the board's structure would also be useful, including, for example, whether outside board members meet independently and whether the board conducts a self-evaluation.

Disclosure could also be expanded for some leading indicators, such as employee and customer satisfaction. *Capital Choices,* the report of the Council of Competitiveness, recommends treating training costs as investments on corporate balance sheets to make human resource investments more visible.[33] Any move to improve the measurement of human resources will discourage managers from reaping short-run gains by depreciating these now-invisible assets.

Training (like other investments such as plant and equipment or R&D) is difficult to measure. A Bush administration Department of Labor report, in recommending a subsidy on training, suggested defining training as expenditures in the following categories: compensation of employees whose sole duties are the design, implementation, or presentation of training programs; the purchase or development of instructional materials and equipment; and payments to third parties (for example, schools) that provide education or training services.[34] The number of hours of training the company provides also should be disclosed. Because new lines of accounting add to costs, the new requirements should pertain only to companies above a certain size.

At a minimum, the government should work with private sector standards-setting organizations to produce voluntary disclosure standards. Financial market analysts only value information if they can compare it with other companies within the industry using a common definition. In those rare instances when data on training are shared in corporate reports, for example, they are sometimes reported as number of employees trained or as number of hours spent or as dollars expended. Thus analysts cannot meaningfully compare the data.[35] A common language is lacking for reviewing nontraditional measures of performance and investments. Ideally, such a language should be compatible with any government-collected statistics, so that the broad government surveys can provide an industry-specific benchmark for the voluntary disclosures.

The government's promotion of workplace certification also has a role in facilitating disclosure. The certifications will measure investment in hard-to-observe aspects of a company and will be comparable over time and across companies. They will serve as a useful summary for boards of directors and owners.

A crucial role for government is to remove barriers to good corporate governance. Currently, pension funds can spend resources trading shares of stock, but some are unsure that spending funds on corporate governance issues falls within their duties as defined by law regulating pension funds (Employee Retirement Income Security Act—ERISA).

Thus as a first step, the Department of Labor must clarify that ERISA fiduciaries can spend fund resources on corporate governance, as well as on trading costs.

ERISA requires pension trustees to maximize the returns to beneficiaries. Until recently, this law had the practical effect of focusing trustees on short-run returns, so they would not be sued for poor investment strategy. The Clinton administration has interpreted their fiduciary duty more broadly to stress pension funds' role as owners, in terms of voting proxies and encouraging pension funds to become well informed about the long-run investments of the companies in which they have large ownership stakes. This interpretation can be extended to include a responsibility for pension funds that have major investments in a company to be well informed about what directors know and do before electing them.

In addition to encouraging long-term owners to act more as owners, additional changes can discourage short-run traders. Proposals include adjusting stock voting rights so that they increase with length of ownership, removing the tax subsidy on financing with junk bonds, changing the tax laws to encourage remuneration of executives based on long-run performance, and introducing a graduated capital gains tax that declines the longer an asset is held.

Perhaps the simplest idea is introducing a small transactions tax on stock sales to reduce speculation. This tax could be low, perhaps returning total brokerage fees back to the levels of the 1960s, before they were deregulated. Even at the 0.5 percent rate charged by Great Britain and Japan, the tax would raise as much as $10 billion per year.[36]

A weaker variant of this idea is removing the tax preferences that pension funds enjoy on their short-run trading profits. The result would be a reduction in massive trading by pension fund managers—a set of investors whose liabilities are of long duration.

A stronger form of discouragement may be appropriate for plans covered by ERISA. Plans with trading volumes consistently above average and that consistently achieve returns below the market level operate counter to the evidence that most trading plans will lose compared with a buy-and-hold strategy. Enforcement actions may be called for because ERISA requires a prudent approach to trading.

The Council on Competitiveness report *Capital Choices* recommended that corporate ownership

be expanded to include directors, managers, employees, and even customers and suppliers. Expanded ownership will foster commonality of interest and help make investors more aware of the value of investment spillovers (such as highly skilled workers), which strengthen firms and benefit related industries and the economy as a whole.[37]

Workers' willingness to invest in their employer is greater with a good social insurance system, because stock ownership is risky. Workers' willingness is also higher with a more equal wealth distribution; 39 percent of Americans have no financial assets.[38] Income distribution, in turn, is affected by many policies, including the tax and education systems. Any policy to create a social safety net and increase the equality of income will have a collateral benefit of increasing workers' willingness to invest in their employer. Because the typical employee expects to be working at the company far longer than the typical CEO intends to hold his or her job, employee ownership can increase companies' emphasis on long-run success.

Currently ESOP trustees are chosen solely by management. They can be company officers or outsiders such as banks. However, these outsiders often receive large fees and can be replaced at will by management. The potential conflicts of interests are clear, and ESOP trustees often act more for the benefit of managers than for either shareholders or employee-owners. Thus the rules of fiduciary duty for ESOP trustees must also be clarified (and some enforcement actions may be necessary).

Some conflicts would be reduced if employees voted all the shares of stock in the ESOP. The initial stock purchase that establishes an ESOP is usually largely funded by bank loans; as the loan is paid off, the shares that are purchased are allocated to accounts of individual employees. The shares that are collateral for the loan (called unallocated shares) are voted by the trustees. Employees vote only the allocated shares—those that come from the paid-off portion of the loan. A simple solution to the conflict between management-appointed trustees and employees is to permit employees to vote the unallocated shares as well.[39] Alternatively, employees could be given a role in nominating and electing the trustees who vote their shares.

Structuring Labor Markets

> *Not often has the power of one man over another been used more callously than in the American labor market after the rise of the large corporation.*
>
> —JOHN KENNETH GALBRAITH

Government policies toward the labor market range from regulating plant closures to subsidizing employee stock ownership to regulating the formation and actions of unions. All of these policies must encourage long-run horizons, cooperation, and continuous improvement. If the education and certification policies are successful, many employees will have the skills for high involvement. What is needed are policies that encourage managers to make full use of these skills.

Some of the demand for employee involvement will arise from the supplier certification. Additional demand can be generated by focusing the current subsidies for ESOPs on those companies that are also implementing employee involvement. This will directly encourage employee involvement. Furthermore, high-involvement companies are the ones where ESOPs appear to raise productivity.

Additional restructuring of labor market policies includes modifying the National Labor Relations Act to remove barriers to labor-management cooperation, modifying policies that affect employee turnover to encourage long-run horizons, and discouraging employers from following a low-skill, low-involvement strategy that raises the costs of high-involvement workplaces.

Subsidizing Employee Involvement

Virtually everything is under federal control . . . except the federal budget.

—HERMAN TALMADGE

The United States has a long, if inconsistent, tradition of encouraging employee involvement, at least in times of war. During both world wars, for example, national policy promoted labor-management cooperation.[40] In the First World War, the National War Labor Board required the establishment of shop committees where unions did not exist.[41] In the Second World War, the War Production Board urged plants to voluntarily introduce labor-management committees, and most complied.[42] In addition, the War Production Board provided training materials for the committees.[43] These committees were somewhat successful in improving workplaces for both workers and managers (although few were successful enough to be sustained after the war ended).[44]

A national policy has never existed to promote high-involvement workplaces in the nonunion sector or in times of peace. A straightforward approach to increasing participation would be to subsidize it through the tax system. Unfortunately, any simple subsidy would only encourage companies to go through the motions of participation. Most participation plans give little power to workers, and plans that are promoted externally would be especially likely to be ineffective. In spite of the problems, a tax subsidy could be effective. The key is to make the subsidy contingent upon implementing a variety of other institutions that are only valuable to a company that is serious about participation.

One possibility is an ESOP tax subsidy for companies that also allot employees one seat on the board of directors, permit employees to elect an employee relations committee in each establishment, institute a health and safety committee at each establishment, have a profit-sharing plan, and implement a formal procedure for dispute resolution.[45] The subsidy could be either in addition to the current tax system's subsidies or a replacement.

The measurable characteristics of a participatory labor-relations system discussed below are representative and could be modified. Any one of them could easily be adopted by a company with no intention of implementing participation. Nevertheless, a company is unlikely to implement all of them just to receive a tax credit on ESOPs. These characteristics are valuable for participatory firms, and most firms implement the policies voluntarily.

THE ESOP REQUIREMENT. To receive a tax subsidy, a company must establish an ESOP with more than 5 percent of its stock. Furthermore, employees will vote all shares of stock held by any ERISA-covered plan. (ERISA is the law granting tax benefits to retirement plans, including ESOPs, 401-K defined contribution pension plans, stock bonus plans, savings plans, defined-benefit pension plans that own company shares, and any deferred profit-sharing plans). Workers will vote all the shares of the ESOP, including those allocated to the ESOP but used as collateral for a loan and not yet purchased by company contributions to the ESOP. (In technical terms, the workers can vote both allocated and unallocated shares of the ESOP.)

For each 10 percent of company stock voted by the workers, workers will elect an additional 10 percent of the corporation's board of directors.

PROFIT SHARING PLAN. To receive the subsidy, a company must set up a profit-sharing or gainsharing plan with average payout (averaging over good and bad years) equal to 5 percent of wages. Profit sharing can act to build identification with the company and may have favorable macroeconomic consequences.[46] More directly, it is a prerequisite to effective long-lasting participation.

EMPLOYEES ON THE BOARD OF DIRECTORS. Regardless of stock ownership, each company receiving the tax subsidy will preserve 10 percent of the corporation's board of directors for representatives of the employees. Employees on boards of directors are typically not very powerful. Nevertheless, such representation can further participation, promote information interchange, and indicate a firm's seriousness about participation. Perhaps most important, requiring an employee on the board will discourage nonparticipatory companies from attempting to gain the tax subsidy.

EMPLOYEE RELATIONS COMMITTEE. Each establishment with more than fifty employees or company with more than one hundred employees will be required to establish an employee relations committee. The committee will be elected on a one-person one-vote basis, and professional and managerial employees will vote for their representatives separately from other employees. The committee will meet at least one hour per quarter.

Particular duties are not assigned to the committee (although members would be protected against reprisals for any actions they take on the committee). The committee will be valuable for high-commitment firms; they can use it for management information sharing, for upward communication, for appeals from shop-floor participatory bodies (for example, when a work team and its supervisor disagree), and for higher-level participation in decisionmaking. Conversely, the committee will be a burden for companies merely trying to gain the subsidy.[47]

HEALTH AND SAFETY COMMITTEE. Each establishment with more than fifty employees or company with more than one hundred employees will be required to set up a health and safety committee. (This requirement might only apply in industries with above-average injury rates or in companies or establishments with above-average injury rates for their industry.) The committee will encourage labor and management to resolve their health and safety problems privately, outside the purview of the federal regulatory apparatus.

Health and safety committees are already common. In one recent survey, 75 percent of establishments with more than fifty employees and 31 percent of smaller establishments had safety committees. In addition, ten states require such committees. Evidence also exists that in several states as well as the province of Ontario such committees can reduce workplace hazards, OSHA fines, and workers' compensation costs.[48]

Information about workplace hazards is underprovided by the free market, because no single worker has a strong incentive to collect the information that is valuable to everyone. The health and safety committee will provide knowledge about safety and health concerns. It will also voice employees' concerns to management.

FORMAL DISPUTE RESOLUTION PROCEDURE. A company would be required to establish a formal procedure for dispute resolution. The procedure would qualify if the decisionmaker is impartial and the process provides due process, the decision is based on a full record, the employee implicitly or expressly agrees to be bound by the results of the dispute settlement mechanism, and the decision is consistent with public policy in the state in which the complaint arose.[49]

As with safety committees, formal procedures for resolving complaints are already common in large U.S. companies—45 percent of large nonunion employers and virtually all union employers have these procedures.[50]

Procedures for dispute resolution should reduce the explosion of litigation and labor-management disputes in the nonunion sector, reducing the time and legal fees spent by employees, the economic costs for firms, and the overcrowding in the judicial system. Furthermore, the presence of a written record will speed trials when they occur.[51]

TRAINING AS SUBSIDY TARGET. An alternative formulation based on a contingent training subsidy has several desirable features. The proposed credit would be a 10 percent tax credit for training programs. The 1990 report of the Department of Labor's Commission on Labor Force Quality and Labor Market Efficiency also recommended a subsidy on training to address imperfections in the market for human capital. The report noted that because

many categories of expenditures could be distantly related to training, the credit must be based on fairly narrow and specific expenditure categories. In the absence of such limitations, firms would have incentives to adopt extremely broad definitions of training expenses.[52]

The report recommended limiting the tax credit to compensation of employees whose sole duties are the design, implementation, or presentation of training programs; the purchase or development of instructional materials and equipment; and payments to third parties (for example, schools) that provide education or training services.[53]

Any training subsidies must require an explanation of how the training will be tied to the job. For example, training in decisionmaking must be linked to introducing procedures that permit employees to make decisions. The training subsidy program might also require managers to take a free course in how to use training as part of an integrated process of workplace transformation. In addition, because designing training and transforming a workplace is a lengthy process, any training subsidies must be for longer than a one-year period.

Because training costs are highest when participation is introduced, subsidizing training will focus the money on new plans and reduce the subsidy to existing plans. Thus the subsidy will maximize the amount of new participation introduced per dollar spent.

If Congress decides to focus training subsidies on participatory firms, the problem of measuring participation will arise. The strategy requiring several imperfect indicators of participation that are beneficial for participatory firms yet costly for firms merely trying to win a tax advantage would be appropriate for training as well. Training subsidies could be limited to firms that implement the five policies suggested for the ESOP subsidy. In addition, to receive the subsidy employers would be required to create an ESOP.

Furthermore, the employee relations councils can be given a role in approving subsidized training programs. This monitoring will restrict employers' ability to receive the subsidy while not providing training.

ALTERNATIVE REQUIRED POLICIES. Many alternative policies could be linked to an ESOP or training subsidy. Each shares the crucial characteristics of being valuable to participatory companies but costly for employers merely going through the motions to gain a subsidy. Any of three alternative policies—supplemental unemployment benefits, employee representatives sitting on the company board of directors' executive compensation committee, and tying the subsidy to lack of labor law violations—could be added to the list of required policies or could act as substitutes for any policies that were either difficult to monitor or overly costly to implement.

The first policy is to require subsidized companies to provide a specified level of supplemental unemployment benefits (that is, benefits to laid-off employees above the government-provided minimum). A participatory company's stable employment lowers the cost for other companies to provide employment security; thus layoffs have a greater social cost than private cost. Supplemental unemployment benefits will stabilize aggregate demand both by lowering the rate of layoffs and by maintaining the purchasing power of those employees who are laid off. Because high-involvement employers provide high levels of employment security, supplemental benefits are relatively low-cost for them to provide.

A second alternative policy is to require that at least one employee representative sit on the board of directors' executive compensation committee. The differential between blue-collar and CEO pay in the United States has almost doubled since the early 1980s, with predictable effects on employee morale.[54] No clear economic rationale exists for the rapid increase in top executive compensation, leading many commentators to suspect a worsening of company owners' ability to restrain managers.[55] Employees share with company owners an interest in restraining excessive executive compensation. Furthermore, owners of high-commitment companies (where large wage differentials have the added impact of reducing valuable cohesiveness) are particularly interested in ending excess payments to executives.

The third proposed alternative policy is to eliminate the ESOP or training subsidy for a period of time if the employer was found guilty of labor law violations. (A maximum penalty would be set per violation.) In the United States, for example, a common labor law violation is dismissing an employee who was engaged in legally protected prounion activities. No effective penalty for this crime exists under current labor law.

There are several related reasons for eliminating or reducing the subsidy for companies that violate labor laws. Employees will be reassured that their employer is not only superficially listening to workers, while trying to deny them the representative of their choice. Union leaders and activists also will be assured that employee involvement activities such as employee relations councils are not intended to create company unions that replace effective independent unions. The administrative costs will be negligible, because the relevant records of violations are readily available.

The initial effect of any participation-linked tax subsidy would be modest. Few companies will rush to change their labor relations system merely for a subsidy on ESOPs or on training expenses. However, to the extent that participatory firms stabilize aggregate demand, provide economic above-market wages to low-wage workers, and provide other positive spillovers, these contingent subsidies can increase productivity, worker fulfillment, and labor market efficiency.

Labor Law

Existing labor law provides a number of obstacles to employee involvement. The United States' tradition of worker representation revolves around collective bargaining between an employer and a single worker representative, the union. Furthermore, the relevant laws implicitly assume that this relationship is hostile, leading to a variety of limitations on who can be in a union and what forms of representation are legal in nonunion settings. The U.S. legal system must be redirected to promote cooperation at work and to provide employees with organizations that can represent their interests.

The law concerning union organizing—the National Labor Relations Act—should be modified to make clear that labor-management cooperation is legal unless it is implemented specifically to avoid unions.

Because so many worker involvement programs result in little true empowerment or management commitment, exempting companies from the restrictions of the current labor law only if they signify their seriousness about transforming the workplace might make more sense. One possibility is to permit direct employee involvement in nonunion workplaces only if it is also accompanied by several of the proposed policies to limit the ESOP tax subsidy: an employee on the board of directors, an employee relations committee in each establishment, a health and safety committee at each establishment, a profit-sharing plan, and a formal procedure for dispute resolution. Not all of these need be required; perhaps the employer could choose any two it preferred.

The law must also permit employee representatives to sit on boards of directors without fear of conflict-of-interest penalties. Finally, the law must clarify that highly skilled workers who collectively undertake tasks traditionally performed by management (such as hiring and disciplining employees) can still maintain their union membership.

Currently, only 11 percent of the private sector work force is in a union. The vast majority of the work force is not represented. Substantive employee involvement requires that employees have an independent voice, so that management faces a penalty if it breaks its promises, and a means for participation in higher-level decisions.

One form of nonunion employee representation is the club or interest group that forms spontaneously or with company sponsorship around different issues or for different groups. These groups range from softball teams and motorcyclists to female engineers and libertarians. The government should promote the growth of employee groups of all forms, because they help workers feel comfortable when expressing their views.

Computer networks greatly facilitate the formation of interest groups.[56] The government should ensure that space on the Internet is available that is both confidential and reasonably priced so that interested employees can discuss their workplace.

Employment and Turnover

Current macroeconomic and labor market policies discourage workers from looking at the long term. Fluctuating aggregate demand raises fears of layoffs, fears of attracting a disproportionate share of poorly qualified workers discourage employers from implementing just-cause employment policies, and lax international standards lead employers to close plants and relocate overseas.

The effects of product market conditions on a firm's level of employee involvement implies that policies to maintain high and steady aggregate demand and to ease the transition of resources out of declining industries would enhance the relative efficiency of participatory workplaces as opposed to workplaces that rely on fear of dismissal to motivate. Employers that avoid layoffs pay an implicit subsidy to employers that lay off workers. This subsidy would be reduced if the unemployment insurance system granted partial unemployment insurance for partial layoffs (that is, job sharing) and increased the portion of unemployment insurance that is paid by the company that lays off workers. In addition, all state and federal funds for retraining workers should be released for workers who have not yet been laid off. Such policies would stabilize aggregate demand and encourage long-term employment relations, to the relative advantage of participatory workplaces. They have been used by labor-hoarding employers such as Motorola and Hewlett-Packard in several of the few states that permit partial unemployment insurance. More states should do so.

Just-cause employment policies lead to a concentration of poorly qualified applicants. In addition, just cause is more important for participatory firms than for traditional firms. Participatory firms would be indirectly encouraged if just cause were required by law for all employers. A similar argument applies to a host of policies that are important at IMMUN-style companies providing long-term employment, including anti-AIDS discrimination and a national family leave policy.

Finally, international competition is blamed for a much larger share of the United States' problems than is its due. Nevertheless, some companies relocate plants to nations that do not respect basic human rights in the workplace, and a much larger number of plants operate with the threat of relocation. When countries can compete for foreign investment on the basis of encouraging slave labor, child labor, and violence against union organizers, a vicious spiral is set into motion. The United States should encourage the creation of a forum to enact multilateral sanctions against nations that routinely and egregiously violate International Labor Organization standards for human rights in the workplace. For example, the International Labor Organization's reports on human rights violations could be tied to penalties under the General Agreement on Tariffs and Trade and its successor World Trade Organization.

One of the distinctive roles of the federal government is determining the macroeconomic policy of the nation: using monetary, taxing, and spending policies to influence the rates of unemployment and inflation in the economy. Building a high-involvement workplace requires a long perspective and large investments in workers. These investments depreciate if the company is situated in an environment with wide fluctuations, so layoffs are costly to avoid. The macroeconomic authorities must understand that the cost of recessions does not stop at the lost output but includes the lower incentives in the future to build high-skill, high-involvement workplaces.

The news is not all bad. The changes in the workplace created by the policies suggested here will make macroeconomic problems less severe. As more enterprises avoid layoffs, recessions will be less severe. As companies invest more in their work force and turnover declines, the average rate of unemployment should decline as well, because fewer people will be between jobs. Finally, as fewer enterprises rely on the threat of dismissal to motivate workers, the economy will be tolerant of operating at lower average rates of unemployment.

High Involvement in the U.S. Government

I'm from the government, and I'm here to help you.
—ONE OF "THE GREATEST LIES"

The public sector should also encourage employee involvement.[57] The federal government is trying to reinvent itself, and 68 percent of respondents to a 1992 GAO survey of federal installations report some involvement in quality programs. Unfortunately, only 4 percent report that they have "incorporated all of the principles and operating practices of TQM throughout much of the organization." These few high-involvement workplaces report improved customer service and reduced costs; they have also implemented substantial changes in human resource policies.[58] For example, after the Internal Revenue Service began TQM in 1986, it reduced mailing costs by $11 million. Naval Air Systems claimed to have saved $1.8 billion from better supplier relations.[59]

Conversely, the majority of government agencies, which have not implemented substantial changes in customer focus and in human resource policies, report much lower success with their quality efforts.[60] Government policies must support the full range of changes, not accept superficial efforts.

A CUSTOMER FOCUS. Successful innovations in government usually begin with a focus on the customers: the taxpayers, automobile drivers, check recipients, or students that an agency serves.[61] A key issue in designing a quality program is "Who is the customer?" An important insight of the quality movement is that most employees and departments have many customers; that is, many other people both inside and outside the organization would notice if a person or group ceased showing up at work. Successful reinvention will focus on identifying the needs of all customers and meeting as many as possible.

In the private sector, although many customers are internal to the organization, the ultimate customer is the one paying for the product. The government's customers include the citizenry in general—an extremely diffuse group. (Even in the private sector, regulators, communities, suppliers, and employees are additional stakeholders in a corporation.) Because of the diffuse nature of the citizen-customer, an agency can emphasize the wrong customer.[62] In such a case, increased efficiency resulting from employee involvement could lead to a worse outcome—perhaps more trade protection of inefficient companies or more environmentally harmful logging on sensitive public lands.

When customers are defined as those concentrated groups with a strong interest in the decisions of an agency, an increased focus on satisfying customers can lead to worse goals than the old system. These new customers are precisely the old lobbyists and special interest groups that have long plagued government's search for the general good.

However, one benefit of a quality program is that it forces an agency to define explicitly who its customers are. This process gives employees the tools to recognize the needs of customers (such as the citizenry in general) whose interests are more diffuse than those directly regulated or served by an agency. Any quality program in the federal government must require agencies to explicitly state how they are choosing the trade-offs between the general interest of employees, citizens, and consumers against the specific interests of a particular industry or sector.[63]

The quality movement's tools for investigating customers' needs are well suited for trading off conflicting interests and searching for integrative (win-win) solutions to conflicts.[64] Even when interests conflict, increased efficiency in meeting one group's goals can simultaneously lead to improvements in meeting the goals of other groups.

An important purpose of a democratic government is to provide a forum for resolving conflicting interests among different groups of citizens. Having a high-involvement workplace can neither resolve political disputes nor choose the appropriate priorities and customers of government. What employee involvement does offer is a more efficient way to achieve those goals chosen by the political process.

Another important advantage of stressing quality is that it provides a single goal on which workers, managers, voters, and customers agree. Having a focus has shown tangible results in the private sector: Managers whose companies stressed quality as the motivation for promoting employee involvement reported greater success than those companies that were motivated by the desire to increase productivity or to reduce cost.[65]

Workers are in favor of high quality for several reasons.[66] First, most workers like to do a good job and to satisfy customers. In addition, quality programs lead to substantially higher skill and autonomy for workers: Workers perform their own quality control, understand the role of their task in the production of a good or service, influence their immediate work environment, and decide how to increase quality.

Workers are rewarded for their quality efforts by the satisfaction inherent in designing their own workplaces and in knowing their products perform well. In a successful program, these intrinsic rewards are combined with extrinsic rewards such as increased job security and higher pay. When the whole package works, the outcome is higher quality and productivity coupled with higher worker satisfaction, lower turnover, and increased take-home pay. These motivators should succeed as well in the public as in the private sector.

CHANGES IN HUMAN RESOURCE POLICIES. Unfortunately, many commonly used human resource policies can undercut workers' intrinsic motivation to do a good job.[67] The changes in human resource policies are required for government's reinvention to achieve its potential and to create true high-involvement workplaces.

Most important, the reinvention must provide true empowerment for employees, not just an opportunity to spout off. This empowerment has not been the rule so far. For example, in a large survey of the federal government, agencies reported that the single most common barrier to TQM's success is that employees do not believe they are empowered.[68]

Even when employees generate new ideas at the start of a program, if the ideas lead to layoffs, employees quickly stop participating. Thus employment security has been important in maintaining the flow of ideas at companies such as Hewlett-Packard and NUMMI. Unfortunately, short-run political and budget pressures led the Clinton administration's reinvention plans to emphasize employment reduction, sometimes overpowering the emphasis on a custumer focus and employee-driven continuous improvement.

Pay should be tied to performance as well. Groups need to know that their efforts are valued by the organization, and they need to be rewarded for their extra efforts and tasks. Group- and team-based gainsharing fit well with TQM. Today, fewer than half of federal installations with TQM efforts even grant recognition to successful work teams—far fewer actually provide financial rewards.[69]

In addition to changes in motivation, TQM requires changes in employees' ability to participate. Successful TQM requires high levels of training, so workers can engage in the new problem-solving tasks. Starting TQM is an investment that takes several years to pay off.[70]

TQM also requires changes in the role of public sector unions. Unions are often distrustful of new work practices that may reduce worker loyalty to unions and undercut union contracts. The starting point is, as the Federal Quality Institute recommended, to "include organized labor at all stages in the process so that union leaders understand what is planned and can support the effort."[71]

However, as the Federal Quality Institute's case studies make clear, new roles must be created for unions. At successful TQM sites in the private sector such as NUMMI or GM's Saturn plant, as well as successful TQM sites in the public sector such as the IRS, unions are full partners in designing the quality program.[72] If TQM programs are to gain union support, they must enhance the role of the union and create new sources of power for the unions' leaders. For example, union officials can work with management when ideas span multiple work groups and when employees disagree with their supervisor. These enhancements in the union's role are important because TQM often involves relaxing the work rules that had been protecting employees from arbitrary management actions.

In addition, union enthusiasm can protect an organization from loss of commitment by management. For example, a TQM program at the Air Force Logistics Command center at McClellan Air Force Base in California was threatened by an Air Force reorganization that fragmented the center. The program has been very successful: it saved more than $7 million in four years, raised aircraft mission readiness from 40 to 76 percent, and won a national award from the U.S. Federal Quality Institute. Nevertheless, no support existed for continuing the project at the management level. In the end, "the voice of the local union to keep the project going may turn out to be the greatest asset in terms of extending the project's life."[73]

Quality programs also need to change the role of middle managers. Quality programs push decisionmaking power down to the employees who deal with clients or produce the product. This shift reduces the power of middle-level managers and can threaten their jobs. Adding teaching, coaching, cross-departmental coordination, and problem-solving tasks to middle managers' jobs is crucial. In addition, top managers must push their own decisions downward, so middle managers can address more strategic problems. In short, the key is for managers at each level of the organization to build the skills and motivation of the levels below and then to trust their subordinates. The federal government's attempts at reinvention have not succeeded in rewarding managers for their efforts in decentralization.

Pushing decisions downward is not the only change that TQM requires of top management. Top management should effectively communicate their endorsement of TQM as a serious change in the organization. Communicating this top-management support is a problem in both the private and public sectors.[74] Top management can communicate their enthusiasm for TQM with such actions as sitting on the TQM steering committee, publicly endorsing TQM principles, and implementing TQM principles in their own work.

Most important, top management must communicate through their actions, not just their words. All levels of the organization resent management that does not "walk like it talks." A little training, a few tools, and a set of slogans do not suffice. Long-term success with TQM requires a complete overhaul of how decisions are made.

Integrated Policies

Prediction is difficult, particularly of the future.

—NIELS BOHR

Employee involvement is no panacea. Nevertheless, high-involvement workplaces can help improve the standard of living of all Americans.

The federal government often attempts to adopt best-practice management techniques from the private sector. A national employee involvement program is in one sense a continuation of this sensible approach.

An additional advantage of a national quality program is that it does not require lengthy legislative enactment. A few executive orders can create the framework for a substantial restructuring of how both America's government and businesses operate. Progress can be accelerated by drawing on existing organizations such as the Federal Quality Institute and the Department of Labor's Office of the American Workforce.

Citizens demand and deserve government that uses all of the capabilities of its employees. Fortunately, as the quality of government services increases, citizens' willingness to pay for government services will rise. "The goal of the quality movement is increasing confidence in government," said F. Joseph Sensenbrenner, former mayor of Madison, Wisconsin.[75] No longer will the post office or other government offices serve as synonyms for poor motivation and management.

The positive feedback from a government quality program may improve the entire economy. In the automobile industry, for example, Ford requires an extensive certification procedure to win its Q1 (now QSSR) supplier certification. Successful Q1 suppliers advertise this certification. Certifications can alleviate the market failure caused by the cost of observing supplier quality. As the Baldrige award certification becomes a national standard, even companies that do not sell to the government will want to go through the procedure. (For example, Advanced Micro Devices used to advertise that its chips met the military's strict specifications even when it sold almost no chips to the military.)

Part of the problem of fragmented government policies—many of which work against the interests of citizens and against the interests of high-involvement workplaces—stems from the power of special interest groups, typically those with disproportionate access to wealth, to prevail over portions of the government. The proposed policies cannot solve all the problems of unresponsive bureaucracy or of special interest groups. Nevertheless, taken as whole, they can greatly improve the effectiveness of government. Frontline employees will be more empowered. Compared with high-level bureaucrats and political appointees, frontline employees have more contact and more in common with typical citizens.

Furthermore, the benefits of high-involvement workplaces will make high-level bureaucrats and political appointees more sensitive to how their policies affect workplaces. The high-involvement workplace coupled with total quality management gives government employees the necessary decisionmaking tools to integrate the needs of different constituencies and make sensible trade-offs. Moreover, these tools imply that the trade-offs are made explicitly, which increases government accountability. Finally, the proposed policies will increase all employees' empowerment on the job and will enhance independent employee voices. These new sources of power can help offset the disproportionate power of wealthy entrenched special interests in political battles. In short, the problems of American democracy will not be solved by workplace reform. Nevertheless, workplace reform can help mitigate some of the problems of the U.S. political system.

A national policy to promote employee involvement promises more than just good management. Since the mid-1980s debate has raged about how to increase the quantity of good jobs in the American economy. Employee involvement and total quality management programs depend on the energy and skills of American workers. Correctly implemented employee involvement has the potential of greatly increasing both wages and worker satisfaction.

An involvement focus in the training program avoids a common problem with government-subsidized training. These funds are often used to teach skills that are routine and useful only at the current employer—not the advanced skills needed for continuous improvement of workers' learning and earning capacity throughout life.[76] Unlike training programs in which the topics are chosen solely by management, the quality certification program teaches general problem-solving skills. While some managers will try to use workers with these skills in jobs that do not permit problem solving, they will be at a competitive disadvantage to companies whose employees are continuously improving the production process.

The proposed focus on problem-solving skills will also avoid the difficulty encountered by other programs operating under the rubric of TQM and employee involvement. Specifically, many TQM-type programs give employees tools to solve the quality and productivity problems of concern to management, but they lead to a speed-up that can decrease workers' wages, safety, and quality of worklife.[77] Fortunately for the employees, social science theory and evidence agree with common sense: Workers will not consistently contribute their ideas and energy if the company does not reward them. Companies giving employees more autonomy and opportunity for problem solving will soon find it in their best interest to increase the pay and status of these employees.[78]

Traditional American management has focused on dividing workers and keeping their skill levels low. This management style implicitly teaches the workers that they have no valuable ideas and are incapable of doing more complicated tasks.[79] Management will find treating workers with such a low level of respect costly, once the workers are trained and experienced with high-involvement tools such as problem solving and running meetings. Employees who succeed in high-involvement workplaces have different skills and a different self-image than the traditional U.S. worker. They are accustomed to working together in groups to solve problems, and they know their ideas can be effective.

For example, when workers at Mazda's U.S. plant became dissatisfied with the plant's safety record and pace of work, the shop-floor workers applied the skills they had learned in their training for employee involvement. They held meetings that used the TQM procedures, analyzed root causes, brainstormed possible solutions, and followed the steps they had learned for solving problems. As Mazda management learned, training in problem solving can be applied to problems chosen by the workers, not just those chosen by management.[80]

Most TQM programs (like a host of employee involvement programs before them) are poorly implemented and do not survive more than a few years. In general, these programs ask workers for their good ideas but give employees neither power nor rewards. A national quality program that supports substantive participation by employees can increase productivity while raising the quality of worklife for American workers.

9

Conclusion

If hard work were such a wonderful thing, surely the rich would have kept it all to themselves.

—LANE KIRKLAND

The new workplace at the NUMMI auto plant combined high-involvement management and former GM workers and UAW union leaders. The system succeeded beyond anyone's expectations. However, tensions have made maintaining continuous involvement difficult.

Successful Employee Involvement

Success at NUMMI allows for an examination of whether theories of employee involvement accurately foretell a raise in productivity. Unfortunately, organizational theories do not provide an unambiguous prediction. Whether participation has a positive effect on performance is an empirical question, not a theoretical one. Moreover, it is difficult to answer. Nonetheless, the literature yields a fairly consistent set of conclusions.

In most American companies, participation plans are introduced without substantially changing the organization of the workplace. The effect on productivity is usually positive and often small, sometimes zero or statistically insignificant, and almost never negative. The size and statistical significance of the effect are contingent on the type of participation involved and on other aspects of the company's management system.

In a minority of cases, employee involvement is implemented as part of a fundamental shift in management strategy. In the high-involvement workplace, workers or work groups have substantive decisionmaking

164

rights instead of purely consultative arrangements such as suggestion systems or quality circles. Changes in how workers learn and how they are rewarded accompany the increased involvement. Typically, these changes are integrated into the strategy of the enterprise and are reflected in changed roles for other stakeholders in the organization—managers, union leaders, and business partners.

Few companies have achieved results comparable to NUMMI, with its 40 percent reduction in the time needed to build a car as well as quality improvement from GM's worst to its best. Nevertheless, in a number of industries, the companies, divisions, and government installations that have made the shift to employee involvement have experienced impressive gains in productivity, quality, and worker satisfaction.

On the basis of the evidence from all industrialized nations, a number of management policies are required to maintain support for participation from employees, managers, unions, and business partners. The policies to maintain employee support require giving employees the ability, incentive, and power to improve their workplace. Forms of empowerment vary widely but include establishing work teams and creating forms of representative participation. Incentive schemes vary even more widely but typically reward individuals for learning new skills, reward groups of workers for their collective success, and build cohesiveness and solidarity more than competition and individualism. Workers are motivated by assurances that they will not lose their jobs as a result of the suggestions they make. Workers' ability to provide valuable suggestions is usually enhanced by high levels of training and information sharing. A number of data sets provide evidence on the relationship between employee involvement, business policies, and corporate performance.

While most participation plans reward neither individual workers nor work groups for their ideas, successful participation plans share the gains from new ideas with workers. While most participation plans leave the us-versus-them division between workers and managers intact, successful participation reduces pay and status divisions between levels of the company. While workers in most participation plans fear that productivity improvements may lead to fewer workers being employed, successful participatory firms typically increase job security and avoid laying off workers. While workers often fear they will be punished for their ideas that are critical of existing procedures, successful participation plans typically guarantee individual rights and ensure that workers will not be dismissed or transferred arbitrarily.

While many participation plans are implemented to avoid unions or to circumvent the union contract, at unionized establishments successful substantive participation is usually designed with the help of union officials. While all employee involvement plans remove old roles, sources of power, and sources of security from managers and union leaders, successful plans create new roles for these stakeholders. For unions, these roles involve higher levels of information sharing, problem solving, and trust, usually accompanied by new structures such as safety and technology committees through which unions help formulate employment and business policies.

Similarly, high-involvement workplaces involve suppliers and customers as business partners. In the new workplaces, business partners as well as workers enjoy higher levels of communication, trust, commitment, and involvement.

Most successful cases of employee involvement rely on integration of human resource policies with the rest of what a company does: Managers often receive rewards based on their success with involving employees; the product market strategy often stresses the quality and flexibility that involved employees create; and all stakeholders in the business, from unions to investors to customers, are brought into the high-involvement framework.

Implications for Business Leaders

Sustaining a successful, high-involvement, high-performance work organization is difficult. It requires changes in human resource policies such as pay and training, changes in management style, and changes in supplier relations. At the same time, research has produced evidence that the results can be worth it: Organizations that have invested in their people have, on average, enjoyed impressive rewards. The road to high performance is a long one, and U.S. employers should embark on it now.

Implications for Union Leaders

In years past, union leaders fought to protect the status quo—the jobs, work rules, and wages that limited arbitrary management discretion and kept workers' living standards high. A generation of union decline and a decade of concession bargaining weakened the tenability of the old strategies. At the same time, many managers implement employee involvement as a strategy to avoid or weaken unions.

However, substantive employee involvement can revitalize the union movement. In most unionized settings with successful employee involvement, unions acquire new roles that are based on much higher levels of information sharing and consultation before decisions are made. More important, unions have the right to negotiate not only about traditional bargaining topics, but also about production methods and strategic issues such as new technology and marketing. When managers suggest employee involvement programs, unions must act quickly to ensure that the program enhances the role of the union and promotes work force solidarity.

Especially for smaller companies, unions can play a role in training and certifying workers in employee involvement skills. Unions must take a proactive stance in training their members in the skills needed for the twenty-first century, and improve the management of companies at the same time.

As workplaces become more democratic and workers acquire new skills in decisionmaking and teamwork, unions must change as well. Employee involvement opens new areas for the union to play a role and provides a new resource of more highly trained members. The union must open itself up to more access by interested members and must find new methods of staying in touch with the concerns of its members.

Change Is Slow

Although substantive employee participation can have positive effects on productivity, it has not become commonplace.

One reason is the limited incentives provided to American managers. Managers have been trained and selected for success in a hierarchical setting. A number of other technological and organizational innovations have taken a generation or longer to spread throughout industry, and employee involvement is no exception.

In addition, employee involvement requires investing in employees' skills and in a company's reputation as a trustworthy employer. These are investments that only pay off in the long term. American managers, however, are often punished for the immediate decline in profits, because investors usually cannot observe long-term investments in human resources. Therefore, any manager can increase current earnings by curtailing training or by breaking commitments to workers or suppliers. The result is little employee involvement, because investors have trouble monitoring and rewarding managers for investing for the long run.

Implications for Investors

For the new work organization to succeed, a variety of business stakeholders must change their behavior. Financial market stakeholders such as large investors (particularly pension funds), boards of directors, commercial and investment banks, and stock analysts must learn to evaluate human resource investments. Most very large U.S. employers have a TQM program somewhere in their company. Stakeholders must request information to evaluate if the managers are investing in the long run or merely following a management fad. This information should include both management practices, such as training budgets and gainsharing programs, and management outcomes, such as product quality and worker satisfaction. Financial stakeholders will enjoy higher returns if they reward companies that invest in the long term and punish those managers that pump up current earnings while failing to invest in human resources.

Managers and investors have an interest in boards of directors that are independent and well informed enough to certify credibly that managers are making long-run nonfinancial investments. Boards and managers must craft measurement and reward systems that create incentives to build up product quality, customer satisfaction, and human resources, even at the occasional expense of short-run accounting measures. These incentive systems usually should be benchmarked to the company's past and to its competitors, and they also must be extended down into the corporation—to reward all managers and frontline employees for actions that lead to long-term success.

Public Policies

Employee involvement is slow to spread partly because of problems within a company. A second set of reasons for the slow dissemination of high-involvement workplaces concerns a company's environment—the labor, capital, and product market conditions in which it functions, as well as the legal and political environment. Because these characteristics vary widely across economies, workplaces, not surprisingly, also differ significantly. As a result, public policies may be called for to increase the number of high-involvement workplaces that provide desirable, high-productivity jobs. The free market can be biased against high-involvement workplaces, and such workplaces provide benefits that are not rewarded by the free market.

BARGAINING PROBLEMS. Highly profitable enterprises flourish in free markets. In most high-involvement enterprises, workers can bargain (often implicitly) for some of the gains from employee involvement, often received via higher wages, satisfaction, and safety. The market ignores these benefits when evaluating which companies are sufficiently profitable to survive. Thus some efficient high-involvement enterprises will not be profitable enough to survive.

PRODUCT MARKET CONDITIONS. The environment of a company also affects its viability. Closer supplier relations raise productivity through better communication and problem solving. They also usually involve a reduction in the number of suppliers, because a high-involvement employer will get its parts from a single source. This change increases the bargaining power of suppliers. Companies with high profits from other sources, perhaps from a monopoly in the final product market, will forgo efficient supplier relations to maximize its bargaining power and its profits.

The variability of product demand matters, too. Because they avoid laying off workers, high-involvement companies flourish when recessions are shallow and rare. Macroeconomic policies that encourage stable employment and demand can increase the use of participation. At the same time, high-involvement employers usually try to minimize their layoffs. Each company that switches to a no-layoff policy stabilizes demand for other companies and makes recessions less of a problem.

Product market conditions affect the viability of high-involvement employers because businesses must often choose a strategy of relying on high or low flexibility from all of their suppliers or customers. For example, in making high-fashion clothing, high-skill workers can quickly switch models to adapt to consumers' demands. This quick response system works best with expensive information interchange between customers and suppliers. Few suppliers want to build this capacity for a single customer, and few customers want to build this capacity for a single supplier. Only the creation of flexible high-skill networks of suppliers and customers can bring about an industry with high skills, high flexibility, and rapid response to consumers' demands.

LABOR MARKET CONDITIONS. High-involvement enterprises tend to motivate with the intrinsic interest of the work, long-term commitments, and rewards paid to successful work groups. High unemployment works to the relative advantage of more traditional employers that rely on the threat of unemployment to motivate workers. When unemployment is low, participatory firms gain in relative productivity. At the same time, encouraging participation may be a requirement for maintaining low unemployment. As long as many companies rely upon fear of unemployment to motivate workers, high employment will lead to falling productivity and rising inflation, and it will not be sustainable.

High-involvement companies tend to emphasize equality of status. This work system is more likely to succeed when other organizations are also emphasizing equality; otherwise, high-involvement companies tend to lose their best employees.

High-involvement companies are likely to emphasize due process in dismissals, which attracts a disproportionate number of poorly motivated workers who fear being dismissed. High-involvement companies will incur lower costs in selecting their work force when many companies have similar policies of due process.

High-involvement companies often provide training that is useful to many employers. When the trained workers quit, the training dollars are a loss to high-involvement employers and a gain to others. Some training dollars from high-involvement employers end up benefiting other employers.

In addition, because so many other employers have reneged on their promises to train or to avoid layoffs, workers discount high-involvement companies' promises of training or job security and, by extension, their reputations.

CAPITAL MARKET CONDITIONS. High-involvement businesses often have difficulty raising capital, because control rights are shared with workers. Even if the efficiency gains from employee involvement outweigh any efficiency losses from the shortage of capital, less efficient traditional companies with fewer difficulties raising capital will be able to grow faster. This faster growth may lead the economy to be dominated by inefficient traditional firms, not more efficient high-involvement enterprises.

POLITICAL ENVIRONMENT. Employees who are involved at work are better trained in the political process and make better decisions. Employees' involvement also makes their workplaces a little less likely to pollute or cause other negative spillovers to their communities. In addition, workers in rigid jobs are often alienated and are more likely to engage in destructive behaviors at home. The benefits of employee involvement to the political environment are not incorporated into the balance sheets that determine which companies will survive.

LEGAL ENVIRONMENT. Finally, many high-involvement workplaces run afoul of U.S. labor law, which is based on a confrontational system of worker-management relations. Specifically, most forms of substantive employee involvement are illegal, because they are too close to being company-dominated unions or they blur the line between workers and managers.

Lessons for Government

The development of successful participatory systems in the United States has public policy implications. Hundreds of laws and programs affect workplaces, from accounting rules that fail to measure training as an investment, to tax laws that subsidize employee ownership without participation, to schools that train future workers to show up on time but do not emphasize problem solving or working together in groups. Understanding the hundreds of programs is made simpler by focusing on the primary functions of government: research, teaching, certification, regulation of workplaces and products, structuring the markets for labor and capital, and acting as an employer for approximately 20 percent of the work force.

What is lacking within each of these functions is a consistent interest in encouraging high-involvement workplaces. A coordinated approach can be devised to promote workplaces where all employees have the skills, incentives, and authority to constantly improve the work process and product. The approach could create a win-win policy that fosters the goals of government, business, and employees.

RESEARCH. While government-supported research has traditionally focused on increasing profitability and managerial control, research must be retargeted so that new technologies enhance workers' ability to continuously improve the work process. Research that creates skill-enhancing technologies will lead to higher productivity, new technology that is more likely to be implemented, and better jobs. In addition, research must help provide an understanding of what management practices and new technology support the high-involvement workplace and how government policies are affecting workplaces.

TEACHING. The government engages in teaching at a host of levels: kindergarten through high school, subsidizing both public and private universities, retraining workers, subsidizing on-the-job training, and training union leaders and managers. These various forms of training have to focus consistently on the skills needed for the high-involvement workplace, such as problem solving, working in groups, and continuous learning. For engineers and managers, the skills must include learning how to listen and appreciating the importance of structuring technology and the business to take advantage of all employees' contributions.

American schools have come under enormous criticism in recent decades. Fortunately, the set of high-involvement skills is not an additional burden for schools, but an overarching focus that will alleviate the difficulties schools have in everything from retention rates to school-to-work transitions.

After schooling is completed, learning must continue in high-involvement workplaces. Ongoing training for managers and union leaders must create an integrated framework to move decisionmakers from being aware of new work practices to becoming competent to introduce and sustain the new work practices within their company. This training must be matched with continuous resources for education for all workers in the appropriate skills of the high-involvement workplace.

CERTIFICATION. The government also certifies employees' qualifications. Certification occurs when schools give diplomas and when groups sanctioned by the states certify occupations such as barbers, medical doctors, and carpenters. The government also certifies businesses when it grants the Baldrige award and when it approves certifiers who, in turn, attest that plants are in compliance with the international ISO 9000 standard for quality. The government should consistently certify individuals and organizations that have the skills and motivation to continuously improve products and processes and that proactively solve problems. These are the qualities that purchasers (whether employers hiring labor or companies choosing suppliers) need for long-term success.

REGULATION OF WORKPLACES AND PRODUCTS. The government regulates the safety of workplaces and products in a variety of fashions, including through the Occupational Safety and Health Administration, the Consumer Product Safety Commission, and product liability laws. Regulators must reward businesses with proactive problem-solving methods, which search out issues before they cause problems and resolve the root cause of problems that are identified. The rewards (for example, fewer inspections or lower fines) should be based in part on the lower probability of future violations in workplaces where all employees continuously identify and resolve problems.

STRUCTURING CAPITAL AND LABOR MARKETS. Perhaps most important, the government regulates and structures capital and labor markets. In both settings, regulations must be reformed to encourage long-term perspectives, trust, and abundant flow of information.

For too long, managers have operated in an environment that discouraged investment in employees, because these investments are difficult to monitor. While the public sector is not primarily at fault, a number of government policies should be modified to encourage these investments. For example, accounting rules can place training investments on an equal footing with investments in R&D and plant and equipment. The government can also encourage pension funds and other investors to measure investments in human resources, while pension funds and other shareholders should be discouraged from frequent trading that lowers average returns. ESOP laws should remove restrictions that impede workers from voting their shares and acting like owners.

Within labor markets, regulations must be modified to remove barriers to labor-management cooperation and to discourage employers from raising the costs of high-involvement workplaces. In addition, the government can design the information superhighway to promote the creation of employee groups, enhancing their power to participate effectively.

Current subsidies for employee stock ownership plans can be focused on companies that are implementing employee involvement—the subset of companies in which ESOPs appear to raise productivity. One possibility is a tax credit on ESOPs that is available for companies that also allot employees one seat on the board of directors, elect an employee relations committee in each establishment, institute a health and safety committee at each establishment, have a profit-sharing plan, and implement a formal procedure for dispute resolution. Alternatively, a training subsidy could require a similar list of policies.

Macroeconomic policies must be refocused on maintaining high employment, because the costs of recession are particularly high for high-involvement companies that invest heavily in their work force and that avoid layoffs.

REINVENTING GOVERNMENT. Reinvention of government is a major theme of the Clinton administration. Nevertheless, current efforts fall short of the full-scale transformation that is required. Higher levels of employee involvement can enhance efforts to promote a productive and responsive government.

Participation can increase organizational performance, but the relationship is affected by the form and scope of participation, the supporting employment practices of the employer, and the external environment in which the employer operates. This volume emphasizes a particular aspect of the economics of companies, the interaction of companies and their environments. Several theories reviewed here address the classic question, Why is work so rarely organized in a participative fashion? To the extent that these theories receive empirical support, the policies proposed here can both improve macroeconomic performance and raise worker productivity and satisfaction.

Appendix

Research Method for the NUMMI Case Study

The management practices that have been developed since the mid-1980s at New United Motor Manufacturing Inc. (NUMMI) are the focus of the case study presented in chapter 2. Paul S. Adler, Barbara Gold-oftas, and I conducted extensive interviews and gathered data from NUMMI, the United Auto Workers (UAW), the California state Occupational Safety and Health Administration (Cal-OSHA), and historical documents.

Approximately sixty individuals representing NUMMI, UAW Local 2244, and Cal-OSHA were interviewed in 1993. We spoke with people from all ranks of the company (team member, team leader, skilled trades worker, group leader, assistant manager, manager, and vice president) and who served a variety of functions (assembly, pilot team, quality and assembly engineering, labor relations, safety, and training). Interviews with union members included the leadership of both the Administrative Caucus and People's Caucus as well as rank-and-file members. We also interviewed a number of injured workers. Each interview typically lasted thirty to sixty minutes, although key respondents were interviewed at greater length or multiple times.[1]

For supplementary and historical material, company and union documents were reviewed, including union newspapers; company reports on ergonomic and workability problems; and training materials for workers, managers, and ergonomics evaluators. We also relied on previous case studies describing NUMMI's early years.[2] To supplement documentation of the September 1992 OSHA citation, we used the extensive materials

175

the union and management submitted to the state agency to support the complaint.

Bargaining Problems and Up-Front Bonds

Several economists have argued that bargaining problems, among other market failures, could be alleviated if workers or their union could directly pay management to choose efficient technology (see table 6-1, high employee involvement). This payment, called an up-front bond, would be made before the change to the new work organization or before a new worker was hired. In this example, workers and managers would both be better off if workers could pay management an up-front bond of $30 million to implement the efficient high-involvement technology. (Any payment between $20 million and $60 million would leave both parties better off.) Efficient bonding is unlikely, for reasons closely paralleling those that workers are unable to purchase their training.

First, after receiving the bond, management has an incentive to renege and implement low-involvement technology anyway—pocketing the bond and retaining high bargaining power.[3]

If management knows more about the surplus available from each technology than the workers, then workers often cannot pay a mutually beneficial bond to buy the efficient technology. Because of the asymmetric information, workers will be afraid to pay a high bond; they fear that management will only accept the bond if the total surplus to be created by technology is unusually low.[4]

In any case, employees are unable to pay large bonds, because they have few liquid assets. The typical family has less than $4,000 liquid assets.[5]

That managers or owners will choose work organization to maximize profits, but that this work organization may not maximize total surplus, is relevant to other settings even without bargaining. Employers with employee involvement may have to pay above-market wages to their low-wage workers to reduce inequality and promote cohesiveness. Managers disregard the benefits to workers of above-market wages when choosing their production technology.

Michael A. Conte noted that labor-owned cooperatives appear to be more productive than their capitalist-owned counterparts. Correspondingly, high productivity translates into higher pay for the worker-owners of the cooperatives. Nevertheless, little incentive exists for anyone to found new cooperatives. The problems that prohibit large bonds imply

that founders are unable to charge prospective worker-owners the entire value of the future high compensation they will receive. The asymmetric information problem in particular appears to be severe—
founders know more about the value of the new enterprise than do
prospective worker-owners. In the Pacific Northwest, several plywood
cooperatives were founded by entrepreneurs who then sold shares to
worker-owners; most of these new cooperatives were poorly designed
and soon went bankrupt. Potential future worker-owners are now leery
of all prospective cooperatives, and the rate of founding has dropped.

Checklist for the High-Involvement Workplace

While not a definitive assessment tool, the following checklist can be
used by anyone in a company to evaluate how closely the work practices are to the model of high involvement presented in this book.[6]
Score 1 for "Strongly agree," 2 for "Agree," 3 for "Neither agree nor
disagree," 4 for "Disagree," and 5 for "Strongly disagree." Evaluate the
reasons for those items that earn a 4 or 5. Can changes be made to move
the company in the direction of the high-involvement model?

Explanations are required for how some work practices are implemented. The checklist will be most useful if all employees give
similar answers about the extent and methods of implementing high
involvement.

Empowering Employees

DIRECT PARTICIPATION.   Frontline employees are actively involved in continuously improving their work process.
[How?]   _____

Frontline employees can rapidly modify their work processes to correct quality, safety, or other problems. [How?]   _____

Frontline employees are actively involved in selecting
new technology, modifying the product or service, and
meeting with customers. [How?]   _____

When individuals or teams make suggestions, managers always either approve the suggestions or give feedback on
reasons that suggestions have not been approved.   _____

Most frontline employees are organized into work teams
with substantial autonomy.   _____

Frontline employees are involved in determining their work and quality performance goals and operating standards. [How?] _____

REPRESENTATIVE PARTICIPATION. Workers have effective mechanisms of representative participation that voice their concerns directly to upper management, that address issues that span multiple work groups, and that can act as an appeals process when lower levels disagree. _____

Motivating Employees

REWARDS. Employees or work groups receive financial and nonfinancial rewards when they improve the work process or make other improvements. [How?] _____

PAY FOR SKILL. Workers are rewarded when their work-related skills increase, even if those skills cannot be used at the job they are currently performing. [How?] _____

REDUCING DIFFERENCES. The company reduces differences in pay and status to enhance cohesiveness. [How?] _____

EMPLOYMENT SECURITY. The company has a stated policy that employees will not be laid off as a result of productivity improvements that follow from their suggestions. _____

The company has policies that minimize or avoid laying off employees. [How?] _____

The company actively helps laid-off workers find new employment. (Answer if applicable.) _____

GUARANTEED RIGHTS. The company has a stated policy that employees will not be punished for their suggestions. _____

The Ability to Participate

TRAINING. The company spends a higher proportion of payroll on training its frontline work force than does the rest of the industry. (Most large companies allocate 1.5 percent of payroll for training; 3–5 percent is typical for high-performance companies.) _____

The company measures the effectiveness of training and finds the programs effective. _____

The company has programs to support continuous learning (for example, job rotation and cross-training). _____

SHARING INFORMATION. All employees in the company are given information on operating results and goals as well as on organizational performance compared with the competition. [How?] _____

All employees are trained to use this information. [How?] _____

Multiple formal and informal mechanisms exist by which information flows up, down, and across the company. _____

Management Support

Managers are rewarded for their success in promoting high involvement and are given training in the new roles demanded of them. [How?] _____

Departments or divisions are evaluated on a variety of nonfinancial performance measures to supplement financial measures (for example, customer satisfaction, employee satisfaction, innovation, and training investments). [What are the measures and how are they related to managerial evaluations?] _____

The company communicates a variety of nonfinancial performance measures to its stakeholders (such as the board of directors or corporate central headquarters). [How?] _____

Union Support

The union-management relationship has moved away from traditional collective bargaining toward interest-based bargaining and cooperative problem solving, with the union involved in nontraditional topics such as choice of new technology. _____

The union is a partner in the high-involvement workplace. [How?] _____

Business Partner Support

The company exchanges detailed information with major suppliers and customers on the process of making and using its products. This information is analyzed to maximize the joint benefits of the relationship. [How?] _____

The company regularly measures defect rates and customer satisfaction, and these rates are high and improving. _____

Strategic Integration

The company integrates human resource concerns and practices into its long-term strategy. [How?] _____

Notes

Chapter 1

1. Department of Labor and Department of Commerce, Commission on the Future of Worker-Management Relations, *Fact Finding Report* (May 1994), p. 52.

2. This section draws on David I. Levine and George Strauss, "Employee Participation and Involvement," in Commission on Workforce Quality and Labor Market Efficiency, *Investing in People: A Strategy to Address America's Workforce Crisis,* background papers, vol. 2, paper 35b (Department of Labor, September 1989), pp. 1893–948.

3. Some authors distinguish participation from employee involvement; I use the terms interchangeably.

4. S. Wyatt and J. N. Langdon, *Fatigue and Boredom in Repetitive Work,* Reprint 77, prepared for the Industrial Health Research Council (London: Her Majesty's Stationery Office, 1933).

5. F. J. Roethlisberger and W. J. Dickson, *Management and the Worker* (Harvard, 1939).

6. Motohiro Morishima, "Information Sharing and Firm Performance in Japan," *Industrial Relations,* vol. 30 (Winter 1991), pp. 37–61.

7. Keith Bradley and Alan Gelb, *Worker + Capitalism = The New Industrial Relations* (MIT Press, 1983).

8. Kurt Lewin, "Studies in Group Decision," in Dorwin Cartwright and Alvin Zander, eds., *Group Dynamics* (Evanston, Ill.: Harper, 1953), pp. 287–301; and Renis Likert, *New Patterns of Management* (McGraw-Hill, 1961).

9. Special Task Force to the Secretary of Health, Education, and Welfare, *Work in America* (MIT Press, 1973), p. 186.

10. J. Richard Hackman and Edward E. Lawler III, "Employee Reactions to Job Characteristics," *Journal of Applied Psychology,* monograph 55 (1971), pp. 259–86.

11. This theory was developed in England by Eric Trist and others, *Organizational Choice* (New York: Garland, 1987), and in Norway by Fred Emery and

Einar Thorsrud, *New Designs for Work Organizations* (Oslo, Norway: Tannum Press, 1969).

12. Lester Coch and John R. P. French, "Overcoming Resistance to Change," *Human Relations,* vol. 1, no. 4 (1948), pp. 512-32; Nancy Morse and Everett Reimer, "The Experimental Change of a Major Organizational Variable," *Journal of Abnormal and Social Psychology,* vol. 52 (January 1956), pp. 120-29; and Alfred Marrow, David Barrows, and Stanley Seashore, *Management by Participation* (Harpers, 1967).

13. R. N. Ford, *Motivation through Work Itself* (New York: American Management Association, 1969); Scott Myers, *Every Employee a Manager: More Meaningful Work through Job Enrichment* (McGraw-Hill, 1970); and Richard Walton, "Establishing and Maintaining High Commitment Work Conditions," in John R. Kimberly, Robert H. Miles, and associates, eds., *The Organizational Life Cycle: Issues in the Creation, Transformation, and Decline of Organizations* (San Francisco: Jossey-Bass, 1980), pp. 208-90.

14. Michael Hammer and James Champy, *Reengineering the Corporation: A Manifesto for Business Revolution* (Harper Business, 1993).

15. Paul Osterman, "How Common Is Workplace Transformation and Who Adopts It?" *Industrial and Labor Relations Review,* vol. 47 (January 1994), pp. 173-88. Osterman defines *core employees* as "the largest group of non-supervisory, non-managerial workers at this location who are directly involved in making the product or in providing the service at your location" (p. 175).

16. Edward E. Lawler III, Gerald Ledford, and Susan A. Mohrman, *Employee Involvement in America* (Houston: American Productivity and Quality Center, 1989).

17. Sum of percentages does not represent total number of employees covered by employee involvement because those covered by multiple programs were counted more than once. A conservative measure of incidence is to examine the maximum value among the programs for workers covered by employee involvement. Excluding surveys, the average across all respondents is 28 percent, which represents a lower bound for the percentage involved in employee involvement. David I. Levine and Douglas Kruse, "Employee Involvement Efforts: Incidence and Effects," Working Paper OBIR-49 (University of California at Berkeley, Haas School of Business, 1991).

18. William Cooke, *Joint Labor-Management Relations and Company Performance: New Paths or Going in Circles?* (Kalamazoo, Mich.: Upjohn Institute, 1987); Paula B. Voos, "Managerial Perceptions of the Economic Impact of Labor Relations Programs," *Industrial and Labor Relations Review,* vol 40 (January 1987), pp. 195-208; and Edward E. Lawler III, Susan A. Mohrman, and Gerald Ledford, *Employee Involvement and Total Quality Management* (San Francisco: Jossey-Bass, 1992).

19. Richard B. Freeman and Joel Rogers, "Who Speaks for Us? Employee Representation in a Nonunion Labor Market," in Bruce E. Kaufman and Morris M. Kleiner, eds., *Employee Representation: Alternatives and Future Directions* (Madison, Wis.: Industrial Relations Research Association, 1993), p. 28.

20. Marshall Sashkin, "Participative Management Is an Ethical Imperative," *Organizational Dynamics,* vol. 12 (Spring 1984), pp. 5-22. Even if empower-

ment at work is not a fundamental right and does not raise efficiency, it still may be socially desirable if it raises wages. Assume that a high-involvement alternative to a sweatshop raised the wages of one hundred minimum-wage workers by $1,000 a year each, and profits declined by $101,000. In total, gross national product (GNP) has fallen by $1,000 (workers gained $100,000 and the owner lost $101,000). Nevertheless, most of the $101,000 decline in profits came from the pockets of the wealthy, while most wage income is received by the nonwealthy. Encouraging employee involvement may be desirable on equity grounds to the extent that it raises workers' skills and wages.

21. The argument in this section is drawn from Robert Dahl, *Preface to Economic Democracy* (University of California Press, 1985).

22. Armen A. Alchian and Harold Demsetz, "Production, Information Costs, and Economic Organization," *American Economic Review,* vol. 62 (December 1972), pp. 777-95.

23. Juliet Schor, "Social Wages and the Business Cycle: Measuring the Cost of Job Loss," in Marc Jarsulec, ed., *Money and Macro Policy* (Boston: Kluwer-Nijhoff, 1983), pp. 135-54; and Jack Steiber, "Employment-at-Will: An Issue for the 1980s," *Proceedings of the 1983 Annual Spring Meeting of the Industrial Relations Research Association* (Madison, Wis., 1984), pp. 1-5.

24. Dahl, *Preface to Economic Democracy.*

Chapter 2

1. J. Patrick Wright, *On a Clear Day You Can See General Motors: John Z. de Lorean's Look inside the Automotive Giant* (Avon Books, 1979).

2. Ben Hamper, *Rivethead* (Warner Books, 1991), p. 46.

3. Charles R. Walker and Robert H. Guest, *The Man on the Assembly Line* (Oxford University Press, 1952), pp. 51 and 60.

4. Paul Adler, "The 'Learning Bureaucracy': New United Motor Manufacturing Inc.," in Larry L. Cummings and Barry M. Shaw, eds., *Research in Organizational Behavior,* vol. 15 (Greenwich, Conn.: JAI Press, 1992), p. 185.

5. John F. Krafcik, "A New Diet for U.S. Manufacturing: The Auto Industry Enters the 1990s," *Technology Review,* vol. 92 (January 1989), pp. 28-36.

6. John Holusha, "No Utopia, But to Workers It's a Job," *New York Times,* January 29, 1989, p. C1; and Adler, "The 'Learning Bureaucracy.' "

7. Lindsay Chappell, "Labor Rules Are Model for Partners, Transplants," *Automotive News* (October 19, 1992), p. 39.

8. Krafcik, "A New Diet for U.S. Manufacturing," p. 36.

9. Taichi Ohno, *Toyota Production System: Beyond Large-Scale Production* (Cambridge, Mass.: Productivity Press, 1988); Taichi Ohno, *Just-in-Time for Today and Tomorrow* (Cambridge, Mass.: Productivity Press, 1988); Y. Monden, *Toyota Production System* (Atlanta, Ga.: Institute of Industrial Engineers, 1983); and Adler, "The 'Learning Bureaucracy.' "

10. "Collective Bargaining Agreement between New United Motor Manufacturing Inc. and International Union, United Automobile, Aerospace and Agricultural

Implement Workers of America, UAW, and Its Affiliated Local Union, 2244," July 1, 1991.

11. "Collective Bargaining Agreement between New United Motor Manufacturing Inc. and International Union, United Automobile, Aerospace and Agricultural Implement Workers of America, UAW, and Its Affiliated Local Union, 2244," p. 1.

12. Krafcik, "A New Diet for U.S. Manufacturing," p. 33.

13. The typical GM plant is a composite of the experience at many U.S. auto plants and does not represent any particular plant. Clair Brown and Michael Reich, "When Does Union-Management Cooperation Work? A Look at NUMMI and GM-Van Nuys," *California Management Review*, vol. 31 (Summer 1989), pp. 26–44.

14. Kim B. Clark, Takahiro Fujimoto, and Bruce W. Chew, "Product Development in the World Auto Industry," *Brookings Papers on Economic Activity*, vol. 3 (1987), pp. 729–71.

15. California Occupational Safety and Health Administration, "Citation against NUMMI," no. 2 (Oakland, Calif., January 6, 1993).

16. Richard E. Wokutch, *Worker Protection, Japanese Style: Occupational Health and Safety in the Auto Industry* (Ithaca, N.Y.: ILR Press, 1992).

17. Mike Parker and Jane Slaughter, *Choosing Sides: Unions and the Team Concept* (Detroit, Mich.: Labor Notes, 1988); and Knuth Dohse, U. Jurgens, and Thomas Malsch, "From 'Fordism' to 'Toyotism'? The Social Organization of the Labor Process in the Japanese Automobile Industry," *Politics and Society*, vol. 14, no. 2 (1985), pp. 115–46.

18. Louis Uchitelle, "Union Leaders Fight for Their Place in Clinton's Workplace of the Future," *New York Times*, August 8, 1993, p. A32.

19. This example is drawn from Department of Labor, Office of the American Workplace, *Integrating Workers and Technology in the New American Workplace* (1994).

20. "When GM's Robots Ran Amok," *Economist*, August 10, 1991, p. 64.

Chapter 3

1. Adam Smith, *An Inquiry into the Nature and Causes of the Wealth of Nations*, ed. Edwin Cannan (Random House, Modern Library, 1937), p. 734.

2. Aaron Lowin, "Participative Decisionmaking: A Model, Literature Critique, and Prescription for Research," *Organizational Behavior and Human Performance*, vol. 3 (1968), pp. 68–106; and Edwin Locke and David M. Schweiger, "Participation in Decisionmaking: One More Look," in Barry Staw and L. L. Cummings, eds., *Research in Organizational Behavior*, vol. 1 (1978).

3. The review of evidence in this and the following chapter is not exhaustive, but it does indicate the broad range of methods used and the general tenor of the results found.

4. A number of other studies have outlined preconditions for the success of employee involvement that are similar to those presented here, including Edward E. Lawler III, Susan A. Mohrman, and Gerald Ledford, *Employee Involvement and Total Quality Management* (San Francisco: Jossey-Bass, 1992); David I. Levine and George Strauss, "Employee Participation and Involvement," in Commission on

Workforce Quality and Labor Market Efficiency, *Investing in People: A Strategy to Address America's Workforce Crisis,* background papers, vol. 2, paper 35b (Department of Labor, September 1989), pp. 1893-948; Department of Labor, Office of the American Workplace, *Road to High-Performance Workplaces* (1994); and Jeffrey Pfeffer, *Competitive Advantage through People: Unleashing the Power of the Work Force* (Harvard Business School Press, 1994). The Department of Labor report was undergoing revisions while I was a visitor in the department's Office of the American Workplace and revising this book, which led to some convergence.

5. Statistical research on consultative participation generated generally positive results in Michael Schuster, "The Impact of Union-Management Cooperation on Productivity and Employment," *Industrial and Labor Relations Review,* vol. 36 (April 1983), pp. 413-30; only short-lived positive results in John Accordino, "Quality of Working Life Systems in Large Cities: An Assessment," *Public Productivity Review,* vol. 12 (Summer 1989), pp. 345-60, and Cortlandt Cammann and others, *Management-Labor Cooperation in Quality of Worklife Experiments: Comparative Analysis of Eight Cases* (University of Michigan, Institute for Social Research, 1984); and small negative effects in Harry C. Katz, Thomas A. Kochan, and Jeffrey Keefe, "Industrial Relations and Productivity in the U.S. Automobile Industry," *Brookings Papers on Economic Activity,* vol. 3 (1988), pp. 685-727. M. L. Marks and others, "Employee Participation in a Quality Circle Program: Impact on Quality of Worklife, Productivity, and Absenteeism," *Journal of Applied Psychology,* vol. 71 (1986), pp. 61-69. Studies of voluntary participation are subject to the problem of highly motivated volunteers, those who are likely to increase their productivity regardless of quality circle membership.

6. Maryellen Kelley, "Unions, Technology, and Labor-Management Cooperation," in Lawrence Mishel and Paula B. Voos, eds., *Unions and Economic Competitiveness* (Washington: Economic Policy Institute, 1992); and William N. Cooke, "Employee Participation Programs, Group-Based Incentives, and Company Performance: A Union-Nonunion Comparison," *Industrial and Labor Relations Review,* vol. 47 (July 1994), pp. 594-609.

7. Accordino, "Quality of Working Life Systems in Large Cities"; Cammann and others, *Management-Labor Cooperation in Quality of Worklife Experiments;* Schuster, "The Impact of Union-Management Cooperation on Productivity and Employment"; and Ricky Griffin, "Consequences of Quality Circles in an Industrial Setting: A Longitudinal Assessment," *American Management Journal,* vol. 31, no. 2 (1988), pp. 338-58.

8. Keith Bradley and Stephen Hill, "Quality Circles and Managerial Interest," *Industrial Relations,* vol. 26 (Winter 1987), pp. 68-82.

9. Edward E. Lawler III and Susan A. Mohrman, "Quality Circles after the Fad," *Harvard Business Review,* vol. 63 (January 1985), pp. 65-71; Thomas A. Kochan, Harry C. Katz, and Robert B. McKersie, *The Transformation of American Industrial Relations* (Basic Books, 1986); Thomas A. Kochan, Joel Cutcher-Gershenfeld, and John Paul MacDuffie, *Employee Participation, Work Redesign, and New Technology: Implications for Public Policy in the 1990s* (Commission on Workforce Quality and Labor Market Efficiency, 1989); and Joel Cutcher-Gershenfeld, *Tracing a Transformation in Industrial Relations: The Case of Xerox Corpora-*

tion and the Amalgamated Clothing and Textile Workers Union (Department of Labor, Bureau of Labor-Management Relations and Cooperative Programs, 1988). All the reviews of the effects of participation alone (that is, without additional changes in the workplace that give workers motivation or ability) reveal a fairly consistent pattern: Participation raised productivity on average, but the relationship was too weak to be important in actual organizations. John A. Wagner III, "Participation's Effects on Performance and Satisfaction: A Reconsideration of the Research Evidence," *Academy of Management Journal*, vol. 19, no. 2 (1994), pp. 312-30.

10. Lester Coch and John R. P. French, "Overcoming Resistance to Change," *Human Relations*, vol. 1, no. 4 (1948), pp. 512-32; E. A. Fleishman, "Attitude versus Skill Factors in Work Group Productivity," *Personnel Psychology*, vol. 18 (1965), pp. 253-66; Nancy Morse and Everett Reimer, "The Experimental Change of a Major Organizational Variable," *Journal of Abnormal and Social Psychology*, vol. 52 (January 1956), pp. 120-29; L. L. Neider, "An Experimental Field Investigation Utilizing an Expectancy Theory View of Participation," *Organizational Behavior and Human Performance*, vol. 26 (1980), pp. 425-42; and A. K. Rice, "Productivity and Social Organization in an Indian Weaving Shed," *Human Relations*, vol. 6 (1953), pp. 297-329.

11. Daniel Mitchell, David Lewin, and Edward E. Lawler III, "Alternative Pay Systems, Firm Performance, and Productivity," in Alan Blinder, ed., *Paying for Productivity* (Brookings, 1990), pp. 15-87.

12. John R. Cable and Felix R. FitzRoy, "Cooperation and Productivity: Some Evidence from West German Experience," *Economic Analysis and Workers' Management*, vol. 14, no. 2 (1980), pp. 163-80; and John R. Cable and Felix R. FitzRoy, "Productive Efficiency, Incentives, and Employee Participation: Some Preliminary Results for West Germany," *Kyklos*, vol. 33, no. 1 (1980), pp. 100-21. In a more recent article, Cable presented some criticisms of the methods used to define and measure the participation index in the 1980 Cable and FitzRoy studies. John R. Cable, "Some Tests of Employee Participation Indices," in Derek C. Jones and Jan Svejnar, eds., *Advances in the Economic Analysis of Participatory and Labor-Managed Firms*, vol. 2 (Greenwich, Conn.: JAI Press, 1985), pp. 79-80.

13. John F. Krafcik, "A New Diet for U.S. Manufacturing: The Auto Industry Enters the 1990s," *Technology Review*, vol. 92 (January 1989), pp. 28-36.

14. Katz, Kochan, and Keefe, "Industrial Relations and Productivity in the U.S. Automobile Industry," pp. 685-727.

15. Kochan, Katz, and McKersie, *The Transformation of American Industrial Relations.*

16. Kelley, "Unions, Technology, and Labor-Management Cooperation."

17. Kelley, "Unions, Technology, and Labor-Management Cooperation."

18. Anthony Carnevale and others, *What Works in High-Performance Workplaces* (Department of Labor, Employment and Training Administration, 1994).

19. Daniel Denison, *Corporate Culture and Organizational Effectiveness* (John Wiley and Sons, 1990); and Gary S. Hansen and Birger Wenerfelt, "Determinants of Firm Performance: Relative Importance of Economic and Organizational Factors," *Strategic Management Journal*, vol. 10 (1989), pp. 399-411.

20. George Strauss, "Workers Participation in Management: An International Perspective," in Barry Staw and L. L. Cummings, eds., *Research in Organizational Behavior*, vol. 4 (1982), pp. 173-265; and Robert N. Stern, "Participation by Representation," *Work and Occupations*, vol. 15 (November 1988), pp. 396-422.

21. Derek C. Jones, "The Productivity Effects of Worker Directors and Financial Participation by Employees in the Firm: The Case of British Retail Cooperatives," *Industrial and Labor Relations Review*, vol. 41 (October 1987), pp. 79-92.

22. Jan Svejnar, "Codetermination and Productivity: Empirical Evidence from the Federal Republic of Germany," in Derek C. Jones and Jan Svejnar, eds., *Participatory and Self-Managed Firms: Evaluating Economic Performance* (Lexington, Mass.: Lexington Books, 1982), pp. 199-212; and Felix R. FitzRoy and Kornelius Kraft, "Economic Effects of Codetermination," *Scandinavian Journal of Economics*, vol. 95, no. 3 (1993), pp. 365-75.

23. The case study evidence is surveyed in Strauss, "Workers Participation in Management." No positive relationship was found between works councils and productivity in Cable and FitzRoy, "Productive Efficiency, Incentives, and Employee Participation," and John T. Addison, Kornelius Kraft, and Joachim Wagner, "German Works Councils and Firm Performance," in Bruce E. Kaufman and Morris M. Kleiner, eds., *Employee Representation: Alternatives and Future Directions* (Madison, Wis.: Industrial Relations Research Association, 1993), pp. 305-38. A modest effect was found in Stephen Smith, "Employee Participation Rights, Training, and Efficiency: Hypotheses and Preliminary Evidence from Germany," George Washington University, Department of Economics, 1994.

24. Motohiro Morishima, "Information Sharing and Firm Performance in Japan," *Industrial Relations*, vol. 30 (Winter 1991), pp. 37-61.

25. This is an instance of the more general result from property rights economics: It is efficient when residual claimants have some control rights over the company. See Eric Furubotn and Svetovar Petrovich, *The Economics of Property Rights* (Ballinger Press, 1974). See also Alfred Steinherr, "On the Efficiency of Profit Sharing and Labor Participation in Managment," *Bell Journal of Economics*, vol. 82 (August 1977), pp. 545-55.

26. Evidence in Martin Weitzman and Douglas Kruse, "Profit Sharing and Productivity," in Alan Blinder, ed., *Paying for Productivity* (Brookings, 1990), pp. 95-140. See also, for example, General Accounting Office, *Employee Stock Ownership Plans: Little Evidence of Effects on Corporate Performance*, GAO-PEMD-88-1 (October 1987); Michael Quarrey and Corey Rosen, *Employment Ownership and Corporate Performance* (Oakland, Calif.: National Center for Employee Ownership, 1986); and Richard J. Long, "Worker Ownership and Job Attitudes: A Field Survey," *Industrial Relations*, vol. 21, no. 2 (1982), pp. 196-215.

27. Derek C. Jones and Jeffrey Pliskin, "The Effects of Worker Participation, Employee Ownership, and Profit Sharing on Economic Performance: A Partial Review," in Raymond Russell and Veljko Rus, eds., *International Handbook of Participation in Organizations for the Study of Organizational Democracy, Cooperation, and Self-Management*, vol. 2 (Oxford University Press, 1991), pp. 43-63.

28. Joseph M. Juran, *Juran on Planning for Quality* (Free Press, 1988).

29. Edward E. Lawler III, Gerald E. Ledford, and Susan A. Mohrman, *Employee Involvement in America* (Houston, Texas: American Productivity and Quality Center, 1989), pp. 21-25.

30. Casey Ichniowski, Kathryn Shaw, and Giovanni Prennushi, "The Effects of Human Resource Management Practices on Productivity," Columbia University, Graduate School of Business, 1994.

31. Lawler, Ledford, and Mohrman, *Employee Involvement in America,* pp. 21-25.

32. Author's calculations based on Robert P. Quinn and Graham Staines, *Quality of Employment Survey 1973-77: Panel,* survey conducted by University of Michigan, Survey Research Center (Ann Arbor, Mich.: Inter-University Consortium for Political and Social Research, 1979). The survey was made on a representative sample of the U.S. population.

33. Ichniowski, Shaw, and Prennushi, "The Effects of Human Resource Management Practices on Productivity."

34. Mark Huselid, "The Impact of Human Resource Management Practices on Turnover, Productivity, and Corporate Financial Performance," *Academy of Management Journal* (forthcoming); and Paul Osterman, "How Common Is Workplace Transformation and Who Adopts It?" *Industrial and Labor Relations Review,* vol. 47 (January 1994), p. 185.

35. Richard J. Long, "Patterns of Workplace Innovation in Canada," *Relations Industrielles,* vol. 44, no. 4 (1989), pp. 805-25.

36. Lawler, Mohrman, and Ledford, *Employee Involvement and Total Quality Management.*

37. Pfeffer, *Competitive Advantage through People,* p. 39.

38. Even majority ownership of companies by employee stock ownership plans (ESOPs) rarely brings about any substantial increase in the participation of rank-and-file employees. For example, only 4 percent of companies with ESOPs had union or other representatives of nonmanagerial employees elected to serve on company boards. See General Accounting Office, *Employee Stock Ownership Plans.* For details, see Michael A. Conte and Jan Svejnar, "The Performance Effects of Employee Ownership Plans," in Alan Blinder, ed., *Paying for Productivity* (Brookings, 1990), pp. 143-82. "[Michael] Quarrey found that neither the size of the company's contribution to the ESOP[,] . . . the percentage of employee ownership or board participation . . . nor a change in key management personnel was a factor in predicting the superior performance of a firm. Instead, the amount of concrete worker participation in management, along with a management team that believed employees should be owners and actively sought to integrate them into the corporate culture, powerfully explained better performance. Participation was measured by the presence of company working groups involving both managers and workers in seven substantive areas of company operations as well as by management's perception of workers' influence." Quoted in Joseph Blasi, *Employee Ownership: Revolution or Ripoff?* (Harper Collins, 1990), p. 230.

39. Derek C. Jones and Takao Kato, "Employee Stock Ownership Plans and Productivity in Japanese Manufacturing Firms," *British Journal of Industrial Relations,* vol. 31 (September 1993), p. 331.

40. For excellent reviews of the empirical findings on the performance of worker-owned companies, see John Bonin, *Economics of Cooperation and the Labor-Managed Firm* (Harwood Press, 1987); Derek C. Jones and Jeffrey Pliskin, "The Effects of Worker Participation, Employee Ownership, and Profit Sharing on Employee Performance: A Partial Review," Working Paper 88/13 (Hamilton College, Department of Economics, 1988); and Conte and Svejnar, "The Performance Effects of Employee Ownership Plans."

41. Saul Estrin and Derek C. Jones, "The Viability of Employee-Owned Firms: Evidence from France," *Industrial and Labor Relations Review,* vol. 45 (January 1992), pp. 323-38; Richard J. Long, "Job Attitudes and Organizational Performance under Employee Ownership," *Academy of Management Journal,* vol. 23 (December 1980), pp. 726-37; and Bodil Thordarson, "A Comparison of Worker-Owned Firms and Conventionally Owned Firms in Sweden," in Derek C. Jones and others, eds., *Advances in the Economic Analysis of Participatory and Labor-Managed Firms,* vol. 2 (Greenwich, Conn.: JAI Press, 1987), pp. 225-42.

42. The European producer co-ops have several distinguishing features: Employees can become members by buying into the enterprises; worker-members participate in the control and management of the enterprises; control is usually on the basis of one-member, one-vote and may be exercised indirectly on most matters through an elected board of directors; and worker-members and often workers who are not members share in the firms' profits. Workers receive only limited returns on their capital contribution (returns that are below returns on alternative assets) and they cannot sell their shares back to the enterprise or on the secondary market as long as they remain employees.

43. C. J. Bellas, *Industrial Democracy and the Worker-Owned Firms: A Study of Twenty-One Plywood Companies in the Pacific Northwest* (Praeger, 1972); Avner Ben-Ner and Saul Estrin, "Unions and Productivity: Unionized Firms versus Union-Managed Firms," Working Paper 88-01 (University of Minnesota, Industrial Relations Center, 1988); Michael A. Conte and Jan Svejnar, "Productivity Effects of Worker Participation in Management, Profit Sharing, Worker Ownership of Assets, and Unionization in U.S. Firms," *International Journal of Industrial Organization,* vol. 6 (1988), pp. 139-51; Janez Jerovsek and Stane Mozina, "Efficiency and Democracy in Self-Managing Enterprises," in Josip Obrdovic and William Dunn, eds., *Workers' Self-Management and Organizational Power in Yugoslavia* (University of Pittsburgh, University Center for International Studies, 1978); Derek C. Jones, "British Producer Cooperatives, 1948-68: Productivity and Organization Structure," in Derek C. Jones and Jan Svejnar, eds., *Participatory and Self-Managed Firms: Evaluating Economic Performance* (Lexington, Mass.: Lexington Books, 1982); Derek C. Jones, "The Productivity Effects of Worker Directors and Financial Participation by Employees in the Firm: The Case of British Retail Cooperatives," *Industrial and Labor Relations Review,* vol. 14 (October 1987), pp. 79-92; and Juan G. Espinosa and Andrew S. Zimbalist, *Economic Democracy: Workers' Participation in Chilean Industry 1970-73* (Academic Press, 1978). A similar conclusion is supported by empirical research on the Mondragon producer cooperatives in Spain. Studies of the Mondragon co-ops suggested that they have higher productivity than comparable conventional companies operating in the same economic environment. See, for example, Henk Thomas and Chris Logan,

Mondragon: An Economic Analysis (Boston: G. Allen and Urwin, 1982); and Keith Bradley and Alan Gelb, "Motivation and Control in the Mondragon Experiment," *British Journal of Industrial Relations*, vol. 19 (July 1981), pp. 211-31.

44. Department of Labor, Bureau of Labor-Management Relations and Cooperative Programs, *Exploratory Investigations of Pay-for-Knowledge Systems* (1986).

45. Lawler, Mohrman, and Ledford, *Employee Involvement and Total Quality Management.*

46. Osterman, "How Common Is Workplace Transformation and Who Adopts It?" p. 185.

47. Long, "Patterns of Workplace Innovation in Canada," pp. 805-25.

48. Irving Bluestone, "Comments on Job Enrichment," *Organizational Dynamics*, vol. 2 (Winter 1974), pp. 46-47.

49. Joanne Martin, "When Expectations and Justice Do Not Coincide," in H. W. Bierhoff, R. L. Cohen, and J. Greenberg, eds., *Justice in Social Relations* (Plenum Press, 1986), pp. 317-35; Joanne Martin and others, "Now That I Can Have It, I'm Not So Sure I Want It: The Effects of Opportunity on Aspirations and Discontent," in Barbara A. Gutek and Laurie Larwood, eds., *Women's Career Development* (Newbury Park, Calif.: Sage, 1987), pp. 42-65; Wayne M. Alves and Peter H. Rossi, "Who Should Get What? Fairness Judgments of the Distribution of Earnings," *American Journal of Sociology*, vol. 84 (November 1978), pp. 541-64; Thomas A. Mahoney, "Organizational Hierarchy and Position Worth," *Academy of Management Journal*, vol. 22 (1979), pp. 726-37; Edward J. Lawler and Martha E. Thompson, "Impact of Leader Responsibility for Inequity on Subordinate Revolts," *Social Psychology*, vol. 41 (September 1978), pp. 264-68; and Elaine Hatfield and Susan Sprecher, "Equity Theory and Behavior in Organizations," in Samuel B. Bacharach and Edward J. Lawler, eds., *Research in the Sociology of Organizations*, vol. 3 (Greenwich, Conn.: JAI Press, 1984), pp. 95-124.

50. Donald A. Dye, "The Trouble with Tournaments," *Economic Inquiry*, vol. 22 (January 1984), pp. 147-49; and Edward Lazear, "Pay Equity and Industrial Politics," *Journal of Political Economy*, vol. 97 (June 1989), pp. 561-80.

51. Quoted in Morton Deutsch, "Is There a Trade-off between Economic Efficiency and Equity?" paper prepared for the 1988 Asilomar Conference on Organizations, Asilomar, Calif. See Morton Deutsch, *Distributive Justice: A Social Psychological Perspective* (Yale University Press, 1985); and Karen Cook and Karen Hegtvedt, "Distributive Justice, Equity, and Equality," *American Review of Sociology*, vol. 9 (1983), pp. 217-41. For a review of the early literature on this subject, see Albert Lott and Bernice Lott, "Group Cohesiveness as Interpersonal Attraction," *Psychological Bulletin*, vol. 64, no. 4 (1965), pp. 259-309. See also William J. Goode, "The Protection of the Inept," *American Sociological Review*, vol. 32 (February 1967), pp. 5-19; and Ivan D. Steiner, ed., *Group Process and Productivity* (Academic Press, 1972).

52. John F. Witte, *Democracy, Authority, and Alienation in Work: Workers' Participation in an American Corporation* (University of Chicago Press, 1980), p. 162; Katrina Berman, "The Worker-Owned Plywood Cooperatives," in Frank Lindenfeld and Joyce Rothschild-Whitt, eds., *Workplace Democracy and Social Change* (Boston: Porter Sargent Publishers, 1982), p. 171; and Keith Bradley and Alan Gelb, *Cooperation at Work: The Mondragon Experience* (London: Heinemann Edu-

cational Books, 1983). On Japan, see William Ouchi, *Theory Z* (Avon, 1981); Ezra F. Vogel, *Japan as Number 1* (Harvard University Press, 1979), pp. 120, 140-41; and Thomas Rohlen, "The Company Work Group," in Ezra F. Vogel, ed., *Japanese Organization and Decisionmaking* (University of California Press, 1975). See also Edward E. Lawler III, *Pay and Organization Development* (Reading, Mass.: Addison-Wesley, 1981), p. 225; and Michael Beer and others, *Managing Human Assets* (Free Press, 1984), p. 145. For a more detailed review of the evidence, see David I. Levine, "Cohesiveness, Productivity, and Wage Dispersion," *Journal of Economic Behavior and Organizations*, vol. 15 (March 1991), pp. 237-55.

53. Lawler, Ledford, and Mohrman, *Employee Involvement in America*.

54. Carnevale and others, *What Works in High-Performance Workplaces*, table V-20.

55. Author's calculations based on data described in James Lincoln and Arne Kalleberg, *Culture, Control, and Commitment* (Cambridge University Press, 1990).

56. Author's calculations based on data described in Lawler, Mohrman, and Ledford, *Employee Involvement and Total Quality Management*.

57. Douglas Cowherd and David I. Levine, "Product Quality and Pay Equity between Low-Level Employees and Top Management: An Investigation of Distributive Justice Theory," *Administrative Science Quarterly*, vol. 37 (June 1992), pp. 302-20.

58. Stanley Mathewson, *Restriction of Output among Unorganized Workers* (Viking Press, 1931), chapter 5; F. J. Roethlisberger and W. J. Dickson, *Management and the Worker* (Harvard University Press, 1939); Michael Schuster, "The Impact of Union-Management Cooperation on Productivity and Employment," *Industrial and Labor Relations Review*, vol. 36 (April 1983), pp. 415-30; and Thomas Kochan, Harry Katz, and Nancy Mower, "Worker Participation and American Unions," in Thomas Kochan, ed., *Challenges and Choices Facing American Labor* (MIT Press, 1985), p. 290.

59. For a description of the many policies companies use to avoid layoffs when product demand declines, see Gary B. Hansen, *Preventing Layoffs: Developing an Effective Job Security and Economic Adjustment Program*, reprint US DOL BLMR 102 (Department of Labor, Bureau of Labor-Management Relations in Cooperative Programs, 1988).

60. Ouchi, *Theory Z*, p. 118.

61. George Nano, presentation before the *Labor Center Reporter* editorial board, University of California at Berkeley, September 12, 1988.

62. James Bolt, "Job Security: Its Time Has Come," *Harvard Business Review*, vol. 61 (November-December 1983), p. 120.

63. Bolt, "Job Security," p. 116.

64. Keith Bradley and Alan Gelb, "Cooperative Labour Relations: Mondragon's Response to Recession," *British Journal of Industrial Relations*, vol. 25 (January 1985), pp. 77-97.

65. Author's calculations based on data described in Lawler, Ledford, and Mohrman, *Employee Involvement in America*.

66. Lincoln and Kalleberg, *Culture, Control, and Commitment*; and author's calculations.

67. Huselid, "Estimates of the Impact of Human Resource Management Practices on Turnover, Productivity, and Corporate Financial Performance."

68. Lawler, Mohrman, and Ledford, *Employee Involvement and Total Quality Management;* and author's calculations.

69. Osterman, "How Common Is Workplace Transformation and Who Adopts It?"

70. Michael Hammer and James Champy, *Reengineering the Corporation: A Manifesto for Business Revolution* (Harper Business, 1993).

71. Paul Bernstein, *Workplace Democratization: Its Internal Dynamics* (New Brunswick, N.J.: Transaction Books, 1980), p. 75.

72. James Baron, "The Employment Relation as a Social Relation," *Journal of Japanese and International Economics,* vol. 2 (December 1988), pp. 492-525.

73. Frank Lindenfeld and Joyce Rothschild-Whitt, "Reshaping Work: Prospects and Problems of Workplace Democracy," in Frank Lindenfeld and Joyce Rothschild-Whitt, eds., *Workplace Democracy and Social Change* (Boston: Porter Sargent Publishers, 1982), pp. 1-20; Shoshana Zuboff, *In the Age of the Smart Machine* (Basic Books, 1984); and Fred Foulkes, *Personnel Policies in Large Nonunion Companies* (Englewood Cliffs, N.J.: Prentice Hall, 1980). See also Bernstein, *Workplace Democratization,* p. 75. Individual rights as prerequisites for participation also listed in Cammann and others, *Management-Labor Cooperation in Quality of Worklife Experiments.*

74. For a discussion on how guaranteed individual rights increased commitment, see Richard T. Mowday, Lyman Porter, and Richard M. Steers, *Employee-Organization Linkage* (Academic Press, 1982), pp. 33, 34.

75. Richard Freeman and James Medoff, *What Do Unions Do?* (Basic Books, 1984).

76. Jack Steiber, "Employment-at-Will: An Issue for the 1980s," *Proceedings of the 1983 Annual Spring Meeting of the Industrial Relations Research Association* (Madison, Wis., 1984), p. 2.

77. Huselid, "Estimates of the Impact of Human Resource Management Practices on Turnover, Productivity, and Corporate Financial Performance."

78. Saul Rubinstein, Michael Bennett, and Thomas Kochan, "The Saturn Partnership: Co-Management and the Reinvention of the Local Union," in Bruce E. Kaufman and Morris M. Kleiner, eds., *Employee Representation: Alternatives and Future Directions* (Madison, Wis.: Industrial Relations Research Association, 1993), p. 350.

79. Ouchi, *Theory Z.*

80. John Bishop, "A Program of Research on the Role of Employer Training in Ameliorating Skill Shortages and Enhancing Productivity and Competitiveness," Education and the Quality of the Workforce Working Paper 7 (University of Pennsylvania, 1993); and Laurie Bassi, "Reorganization of Work and Workplace Education: Scope and Impact," Georgetown University, Department of Economics, 1993.

81. John F. Krafcik, *Training and the Automobile Industry: International Comparisons,* Contractor Report (Office of Technology Assessment, February 1990); John Paul MacDuffie and Thomas Kochan, "Human Resources, Technology, and Manufacturing Performance: Evidence for the Automobile Industry,"

Proceedings of the 1987 Annual Spring Meeting of the Industrial Relations Research Association (Madison, Wis., 1988); Ramchandran Jaikumar, "Postindustrial Manufacturing," *Harvard Business Review*, vol. 64 (November-December 1986), pp. 69-76; and Bishop, "A Program of Research on the Role of Employer Training in Ameliorating Skill Shortages and Enhancing Productivity and Competitiveness," p. 11.

82. Author's calculations based on data described in Lawler, Mohrman, and Ledford, *Employee Involvement and Total Quality Management.*

83. Author's calculations based on data described in Lincoln and Kalleberg, *Culture, Control, and Commitment.*

84. Carnevale and others, *What Works in High-Performance Workplaces*, table V-20; and Ichniowski, Shaw, and Prennushi, "The Effects of Human Resource Management Practices on Productivity."

85. Huselid, "Estimates of the Impact of Human Resource Management Practices on Turnover, Productivity, and Corporate Financial Performance"; and Osterman, "How Common Is Workplace Transformation and Who Adopts It?".

86. Author's calculations based on data described in Lawler, Mohrman, and Ledford, *Employee Involvement and Total Quality Management.*

87. Author's calculations based on data described in Lawler, Mohrman, and Ledford, *Employee Involvement and Total Quality Management.*

88. Huselid, "Estimates of the Impact of Human Resource Management Practices on Turnover, Productivity, and Corporate Financial Performance"; Ichniowski, Shaw, and Prennushi, "The Effects of Human Resource Management Practices on Productivity" (correlation = .24).

Chapter 4

1. Janice Klein, "Why Supervisors Resist Employee Involvement," *Harvard Business Review*, vol. 62 (September 1984), pp. 87-95; Keith Bradley and Stephen Hill, "'After Japan': The Quality Circle Transplant and Productive Efficiency," *British Journal of Industrial Relations*, vol. 21, no. 3 (1983); Thomas Kochan, Harry Katz, and Nancy R. Mower, *Worker Participation and American Unions: Threat or Opportunity?* (Kalamazoo, Mich.: Upjohn Institute, 1984); and Richard Walton, "Establishing and Maintaining High Commitment Work Conditions," in John R. Kimberly, Robert H. Miles, and associates, eds., *The Organizational Life Cycles: Issues in the Creation, Transformation, and Decline of Organizations* (San Francisco: Jossey-Bass, 1980).

2. David Kusnet, "Worker Ideas Shape a Better Workplace," *AFL-CIO News,* vol. 34 (January 21, 1989), p. 6.

3. Keith Bradley and Stephen Hill, "Quality Circles and Managerial Interest," *Industrial Relations*, vol. 26 (Winter 1987), pp. 68-82.

4. Robert Ruh, Roger Wallace, and Carl Frost, "Management Attitudes and the Scanlon Plan," *Industrial Relations,* vol. 12 (1973), pp. 282-88.

5. Frank Heller, *Managerial Decision Making* (London: Tavistock, 1971).

6. Renis Likert, *New Patterns of Management* (McGraw-Hill, 1961).

7. Joseph Hoerr, *And the Wolf Finally Came: The Decline of the American Steel Industry* (University of Pittsburgh Press, 1988), p. 465.

8. Author's analysis of data described in Edward E. Lawler III, Gerald Ledford, and Susan A. Mohrman, *Employee Involvement in America* (Houston, Texas: American Productivity and Quality Center, 1989).

9. Empirical data on the role of international union support in sustaining labor-management cooperation can be found in Adrienne Eaton, "The Extent and Determinants of Local Union Control of Participative Programs," *Industrial and Labor Relations Review*, vol. 43 (July 1990), pp. 604-20. See also AFL-CIO, Committee on the Evolution of Work, "The New American Workplace: A Labor Perspective," Working Paper (Washington, February 1994); Harry Katz, "The Debate over the Reorganization of Work and Industrial Relations within the North American Labor Movement," paper prepared for the 1986 Conference on Trade Unions, New Technology, and Industrial Democracy, University of Warwick; and Walter Gershenfeld, "Employee Participation in Firm Decisions," in Morris Kleiner and others, eds., *Human Resources and Performance of the Firm* (Madison, Wis.: Industrial Relations Research Association, 1987), pp. 123-58.

10. The position of the critics mentioned in this section is summed up in Mike Parker, *Inside the Circle: A Union Guide to Worker Participation in Management* (Boston: South End Press, 1985); and Mike Parker and Jane Slaughter, *Choosing Sides: Unions and the Team Concept* (Detroit, Mich.: Labor Notes, 1988).

11. Robert Drago, "Quality Circle Survival: An Exploratory Analysis," *Industrial Relations*, vol. 27 (Fall 1988), pp. 336-51.

12. Commission on the Future of Worker-Management Relations, *Fact Finding Report* (Department of Labor and Department of Commerce, May 1994), p. 60.

13. Author's analysis of data described in Lawler, Ledford, and Mohrman, *Employee Involvement in America.*

14. Maryellen Kelley, "Unions, Technology, and Labor-Management Cooperation," in Lawrence Mishel and Paula B. Voos, eds., *Unions and Economic Competitiveness* (Washington: Economic Policy Institute, 1992); and William N. Cooke, "Employee Participation Programs, Group-Based Incentives, and Company Performance: A Union-Nonunion Comparison," *Industrial and Labor Relations Review*, vol. 47 (July 1994), pp. 594-609.

15. Federal Quality Institute, *Introduction to Total Quality Management in the Federal Government*, US GPO 299-9960 (1991), p. 13.

16. Susan Helper and David I. Levine, "Long-Term Supplier Relations and Product Market Structure," *Journal of Law, Economics, and Organization*, vol. 8 (October 1992), pp. 561-81.

17. "Cookie Mix, Dry," *Harper's*, vol. 271 (October 1985), pp. 25-26.

18. John F. Krafcik, "A New Diet for U.S. Manufacturing: The Auto Industry Enters the 1990s," *Technology Review*, vol. 92 (January 1989), pp. 28-36.

19. Susan Helper, "Comparative Supplier Relations in the U.S. and Japanese Auto Industries," *Business and Economic History*, 2d series, vol. 19 (1990), pp. 153-62.

20. Susan Helper and Mari Sako, "Supplier Relations in the Auto Industry: A Limited Japanese-U.S. Convergence?" *Sloan Management Review* (forthcoming), figure 1.

21. Kim Clark, "Project Scope and Project Performance: The Effects of Parts Strategy and Supplier Involvement on Product Development," *Management Science,* vol. 35 (December 1989), pp. 1247-63.

22. Mitsubishi Research Institute, *The Relationship between Japanese Auto and Auto Parts Makers* (Tokyo, 1987); and Michael Cusumano and Akira Takeishi, "Supplier Management and Performance at Japanese, Japanese-Transplant, and U.S. Auto Plants," Working Paper (Massachusetts Institute of Technology, Sloan School of Management, 1990).

23. Susan Helper, "How Much Has Really Changed between U.S. Automakers and Their Suppliers?" *Sloan Management Review,* vol. 32 (Summer 1991), pp. 15-28; and Susan Helper, "Comparative Performance of U.S. and Japanese Transplant Suppliers in the Auto Industry," Working Paper (Case Western Reserve University, 1992).

24. Michael Smitka, "Competitive Ties: Subcontracting in the Japanese Automobile Industry," Ph.D. dissertation, Yale University, Department of Economics, 1991.

25. Michael Smitka, *Competitive Ties: Subcontracting in the Japanese Automobile Industry* (Columbia University Press, 1991); Toshihiro Nishiguchi, "Strategic Dualism: An Alternative in Industrial Society," Ph.D. dissertation, Oxford University, Department of Economics, 1990; and Michael Cusumano, *The Japanese Automobile Industry* (Harvard University Press, 1985).

26. Helper, "How Much Has Really Changed between U.S. Automakers and Their Suppliers?"

27. This section draws on Susan Helper and David I. Levine, "Supplier/Customer Participation and Worker Participation: Is There a Linkage?" *Proceedings of the Annual Meeting of the Industrial Relations Research Association* (Madison, Wis., forthcoming).

28. Mitsubishi Research Institute, *The Relationship between Japanese Auto and Auto Parts Makers.*

29. Masahiko Aoki, "The Japanese Firm in Transition," in Kozo Yamamura and Yasukichi Yasuba, eds., *The Political Economy of Japan,* vol. 1: *The Domestic Transformation* (Stanford University Press, 1987), p. 265.

30. Helper and Levine, "Supplier/Customer Participation and Worker Participation."

31. Maryellen Kelley, Bennett Harrison, and Cathleen McGrath, "Collaborative Practices within and between U.S. Manufacturing in 1991," *Proceedings of the Annual Meeting of the Industrial Relations Research Association* (Madison, Wis., 1994).

32. Anthony Carnevale and others, *What Works in High-Performance Workplaces* (Department of Labor, Employment and Training Administration, 1994), table V-19.

33. Carnevale and others, *What Works in High-Performance Workplaces,* table V-19.

34. A longer review is provided in Department of Labor, *High Performance Work Practices and Firm Performance* (July 1993).

35. Casey Ichniowski, Kathryn Shaw, and Giovani Prennushi, "The Effects of Human Resource Management Practices on Productivity," Columbia University, Graduate School of Business, 1994.

36. Jeffrey B. Arthur, "Effects of Human Resource Systems on Manufacturing Performance and Turnover," *Academy of Management Journal*, vol. 37, no. 3 (1994), pp. 670-87.

37. John Paul MacDuffie, "Human Resource Bundles and Manufacturing Performance," University of Pennsylvania, Wharton School of Management, June 1993.

38. Joel Cutcher-Gershenfeld, "The Impact on Economic Performance of a Transformation in Workplace Relations," *Industrial and Labor Relations Review*, vol. 44 (January 1991), pp. 241-60; and Ramchandran Jaikumar, "Postindustrial Manufacturing," *Harvard Business Review*, vol. 64 (November-December 1986), pp. 69-76.

39. Jeffrey Pfeffer, *Competitive Advantage through People: Unleashing the Power of the Work Force* (Harvard Business School Press, 1994).

40. Mark Huselid, "The Impact of Human Resource Management Practices on Turnover, Productivity, and Corporate Financial Performance," *Academy of Management Journal* (forthcoming).

41. Casey Ichniowski, "Human Resource Management Systems and the Performance of U.S. Manufacturing Businesses," Working Paper 3449 (National Bureau of Economic Research, 1990).

42. Department of Labor, *High Performance Work Practices and Firm Performance*.

43. Daniel Denison, *Corporate Culture and Organizational Effectiveness* (John Wiley and Sons, 1990).

44. Dennis Kravetz, *The Human Resource Revolution* (San Francisco: Jossey-Bass, 1988).

45. Barry Macy and Hiroaki Izumi, "Organization Change, Design, and Work Innovation: A Meta-Analysis of 131 North American Field Studies—1961-91," in Richard N. Woodman and William A. Pasmore, eds., *Research in Organizational Change and Development* (Greenwich, Conn.: JAI Press, 1993), pp. 235-313.

46. Eileen Appelbaum and Rosemary Batt, *The New American Workplace: Transforming Work Systems in the United States* (Ithaca, N.Y.: ILR Press, 1994).

47. General Accounting Office, *Management Practices: U.S. Companies Improve Performance through Quality Efforts*, GAO/NSIAD-91-190 (1991), p. 2.

48. For additional information on Japan, see Robert E. Cole, *Strategies for Learning: Small-Group Activities in American, Japanese, and Swedish Industry* (University of California Press, 1989); on large U.S. employers, Edward E. Lawler III, Susan A. Mohrman, and Gerald Ledford, *Employee Involvement and Total Quality Management* (San Francisco: Jossey-Bass, 1992); on reports of quality programs from around the world, "The Quality Imperative," *Business Week*, October 25, 1991 (special issue); and on case studies within the federal government, Federal Quality Institute, *Federal TQM Documents Catalog and Database User Guide*, US GPO 313-893 (1992).

49. David Osborne and Ted Gaebler, *Reinventing Government* (Addison-Wesley, 1992).

50. Personal communication from Ken Stockbridge, total quality management expert, General Accounting Office, 1992.

51. Parker, *Inside the Circle.*

52. General Accounting Office, *Quality Management: Survey of Federal Organizations,* GAO/GGD-93-9BR (1992).

53. Barbara Flynn, Roger Schroeder, and Sadao Sakakibara, "The Impact of Quality Management Practices on Performance and Competitive Advantage," Working Paper (University of Minnesota, Carlson School of Management, 1994).

54. Sherry Jarrell and George Easton, "An Exploratory Empirical Investigation of the Effects of Total Quality Management on Corporate Performance," in Phil Lederer, ed., *The Practice of Quality Management* (Harvard Business School Press, forthcoming).

55. Kevin Hendricks and Vinod Singhal, "Quality Awards and the Market Value of the Firm," Working Paper (College of William and Mary, Graduate School of Business, 1994).

56. "TQM Companies' Stock Outperforms S&P 500, Dow Jones, and NASDAQ," *AQP Report* (February-March 1994), p.1.

57. David I. Levine and Laura D'Andrea Tyson, "Participation, Productivity, and the Firm's Environment," in Alan Blinder, ed., *Paying for Productivity* (Brookings, 1990), pp. 203-04.

58. For example, Ichniowski, Shaw, and Prennushi, "The Effects of Human Resource Management Practices on Productivity"; and Hendricks and Singhal, "Quality Awards and the Market Value of the Firm."

59. Arthur, "Effects of Human Resource Systems on Manufacturing Performance and Turnover"; Huselid, "The Impact of Human Resource Management Practices on Turnover, Productivity, and Corporate Financial Performance"; James Lincoln and Arne Kalleberg, *Culture, Control, and Commitment* (Cambridge University Press, 1990); and J. L. Cotton and others, "Employee Participation: Diverse Forms and Different Outcomes," *Academy of Management Review,* vol. 13, no. 1 (1988), pp. 8-22.

60. For example, Cooke, "Employee Participation, Group-Based Pay Incentives, and Company Performance."

61. Aoki, "The Japanese Firm in Transition," pp. 283-84.

Chapter 5

1. Armen A. Alchian and Harold Demsetz, "Production, Information Costs, and Economic Organization," *American Economic Review,* vol. 62 (December 1972), pp. 777-95; and Michael C. Jensen and William H. Meckling, "Rights and Production Functions: An Application to Labor-Managed Firms and Codetermination," *Journal of Business,* vol. 52 (October 1979), pp. 469-506.

2. Walter Powell and Paul DiMaggio, *The New Institutionalism in Organizational Analysis* (University of Chicago Press, 1991).

3. Zvi Grilliches, "Hybrid Corn: An Exploration in the Economics of Technological Change," *Econometrics* (October 1957), pp. 501-22.

4. Henry Ogden Armour and David J. Teece, "Organizational Structure and Economic Performance: A Test of the Multidivisional Hypothesis," *Bell Journal of Economics,* vol. 9 (Spring 1978), pp. 106-22.

5. I thank Jim Rebitzer for pointing out this argument.

6. A formal model of managers choosing to diminish employees' input to maximize their power at the expense of efficiency and profits is presented in Richard Freeman and Edward Lazear, "An Economic Analysis of Works Councils," in Joel Rogers and Wolfgang Streeck, eds., *Works Councils* (University of Chicago Press, 1994).

7. Edward E. Lawler III, *The Ultimate Advantage: Creating the High-Involvement Organization* (San Francisco: Jossey-Bass, 1992).

8. The arguments in this paragraph are drawn from Stephen Smith, "Employee Participation Rights, Training, and Efficiency: Hypotheses and Preliminary Evidence from Germany," George Washington University, Department of Economics, 1994.

9. Kenneth A. Froot, Andre F. Perold, and Jeremy C. Stein, "Shareholder Trading Practices and Corporate Investment Horizons," *Journal of Applied Corporate Finance*, vol. 5 (Summer 1992), pp. 42-58.

10. Jeremy Stein, "Takeover Threats and Managerial Myopia," *Journal of Political Economy*, vol. 96 (February 1988), pp. 61-80; and Jeremy Stein, "Efficient Capital Markets, Inefficient Firms: A Model of Myopic Corporate Behavior," *Quarterly Journal of Economics*, vol. 104 (November 1989), pp. 655-69.

11. Baruch Lev, "On the Usefulness of Earnings and Earnings Research," *Journal of Accounting Research*, supplement (1989), pp. 153-92.

12. Froot, Perold, and Stein, "Shareholder Trading Practices and Corporate Investment Horizons," p. 55.

13. James V. McGee and Robert G. Eccles, *Business Models and Performance: Improving Dialog about Measurement*, report prepared for the Financial Executives Research Foundation (1993).

14. Stein, "Efficient Capital Markets, Inefficient Firms."

15. Eric G. Flamholz, *Human Resource Accounting* (San Francisco: Jossey-Bass, 1985), p. 27.

16. Su H. Chan, John Kensigner, and John D. Martin, "The Market Rewards Promising R&D—And Punishes the Rest," *Journal of Applied Corporate Finance*, vol. 5 (Summer 1992), pp. 56-66.

17. Michael T. Jacobs, *Short-Term America: The Causes and Cures of Our Business Myopia* (Harvard Business School Press, 1991).

18. John M. Conley and William M. O'Barr, "The Culture of Capital," *Harvard Business Review*, vol. 69 (March-April 1991), p. 111.

19. Association for Investment Management and Research, *The CFA Candidate Study and Examination Program Review* (Charlottesville, Va., 1994), p. 113.

20. Robert Eccles and Sarah Mavrinac, "Improving the Corporate Disclosure Process," Working Paper (Harvard Business School, 1994), table 6.

21. Thomas Kochan and Paul Osterman, *The Mutual Gains Enterprise: Forging a Winning Partnership among Labor, Management, and Government* (Harvard Business School Press, 1994), p. 114.

22. Eccles and Mavrinac, "Improving the Corporate Disclosure Process," p. 13.

23. Jacobs, *Short-Term America.*

24. Chee W. Chow, "The Use of Organizational Controls and Their Effects on Data Manipulation and Management Myopia: A U.S. versus Japan Comparison," CEO Discussion Paper 93-7, University of Southern California, 1993.

25. Department of the Treasury, Financial Management Services, *Performance Measurement: Report on a Survey of Private Sector Performance Measures* (January 1993).

26. Alfred Rappaport, "Better Incentives at the Divisional Level," *New York Times,* April 5, 1992, p. C15.

27. Gunnar Eliasson, *Business Economic Planning: Theory, Practice, and Compensation* (London: Wiley and Sons, 1976).

28. Harold Salzman and Robert Lund, "Skill-Based Technology Design," paper prepared for the 1994 Integrating People and Technology in High Performance Work Systems conference held by Department of Commerce, National Institute for Standards and Technology, p. 10.

29. Carliss Y. Baldwin and Kim B. Clark, "Capabilities and Capital Investment: New Perspectives on Capital Budgeting," *Journal of Applied Corporate Finance,* vol. 5 (Summer 1992), pp. 67-82.

30. For investors and board members who are interested in the long-term success of companies, see the appendix for a discussion on evaluating the management practices of companies.

31. John C. Bogle, Sr., "Is a Long-Term Time Frame for Investing Affordable and Even Relevant?" *Investing for the Long Term* (Charlottesville, Va.: Association for Investment Management and Research, 1992), p. 14.

32. Bogle, "Is a Long-Term Time Frame for Investing Affordable and Even Relevent?" p. 14.

33. Josef Lakonishok, Andrei Shleifer, and Robert Vishney, "The Structure and Performance of the Money Management Industry," University of Chicago, Department of Economics, November 1991.

34. Jacobs, *Short-Term America,* pp. 18-19.

35. Michael Porter, *Capital Choices* (Washington: Council on Competitiveness and Harvard Business School Press, 1992), p. 84.

36. Susan Helper, "Comparative Performance of U.S. and Japanese Transplant Suppliers in the Auto Industry" Working Paper (Case Western Reserve University, 1992); and Annalee Saxenian, *Regional Advantage: Culture and Competition in Silicon Valley and Route 128* (Harvard University Press, 1994).

37. Rappaport, "Better Incentives at the Divisional Level."

38. Increasing the power of boards and shareholders only makes sense if they are more interested than managers in long-term performance. Unfortunately, many pension funds focus entirely on short-run returns from their fund managers. Changes in pension fund governance to emphasize long-run value creation also are needed.

39. For example, for management writers, see Peter F. Drucker, "Reckoning with the Pension Fund Revolution," *Harvard Business Review,* vol. 69 (March-April 1991); for pension fund managers, Edward V. Regan, "Nonfinancial Measures of Corporate Performance," speech prepared for the 1993 Forum of Chief Financial Officers held by *Business Week;* for total quality management consultants, Ivor S. Francis, "Measurement and Enhancement of Corporate Performance," paper prepared for the 1994 Conference Board; and for experts on management accounting, H. Thomas Johnson, *Relevance Regained* (Free Press, 1992).

40. Competitiveness Policy Council, *The Will to Act*, final report of the Sub-council on Corporate Governance and Financial Markets (December 1992).

41. Flamholz, *Human Resource Accounting*.

42. Council of Institutional Investors, "Shareholder Bill of Rights," Washington, 1989; and TIAA-CREF, *Policy Statement on Corporate Governance* (New York, 1993).

43. Stephen L. Nesbitt, *Long-Term Rewards from Corporate Governance* (Santa Monica, Calif.: Wilshire Associates, January 1994).

44. Asra Nomani, "CalPERS Says Its Investment Decisions Will Reflect How Firms Treat Workers," *Wall Street Journal*, June 17, 1994, p. A5.

45. Sherry Jarrell and George Easton, "An Exploratory Empirical Investigation of the Effects of Total Quality Management on Corporate Performance," in Phil Lederer, ed., *The Practice of Quality Management* (Harvard Business School Press, forthcoming); Kevin Hendricks and Vinod Singhal, "Quality Awards and the Market Value of the Firm," Working Paper (College of William and Mary, Graduate School of Business, 1994); and Association for Quality and Participation, "TQM Companies' Stock Outperforms S&P 500, Dow Jones, and NASDAQ," *AQP Report* (February-March 1994), p.1.

Chapter 6

1. The description of bargaining problems derives from Stephen Marglin, "What Do Bosses Do?" *Review of Radical Political Economics*, vol. 6, no. 2 (1974), pp. 33-60. It was later formalized in Richard Freeman and Edward Lazear, "An Economic Analysis of Works Councils," Harvard University, May 1992; and Gilbert Skillman, "Constituting the Employment Relation: A Strategic Bargaining Analysis," Brown University, Department of Economics, December 1990. Marglin, Freeman, Lazear, and Skillman generalize the simple example presented in this section.

2. The results discussed in this section are formally presented in Susan Helper and David I. Levine, "Long-Term Supplier Relations and Product Market Structure," *Journal of Law, Economics, and Organization*, vol. 8 (October 1992), pp. 568-81.

3. Kim Clark, "Project Scope and Project Performance: The Effects of Parts Strategy and Supplier Involvement on Product Development," *Management Science*, vol. 35 (December 1989), pp. 1247-63.

4. C. Cline, "Cumberland Metal Industries (A)," Case Number 9-578-170, Harvard Business School, 1978, p. 6.

5. The results discussed in this section are formally presented in David I. Levine and Richard Parkin, "Work Organizations, Employment Security, and Macroeconomic Stability," *Journal of Economic Behavior and Organizations* (forthcoming).

6. This assumes that workers reduce their consumption during layoffs, which is consistent with the evidence. See, for example, John Y. Campbell and N. Gregory Mankiw, "Permanent Income, Current Income, and Consumption," *Journal of Business and Economic Statistics*, vol. 8 (July 1990), pp. 265-79.

7. Daniel Mitchell, "Gainsharing: An Anti-Inflation Reform," *Challenge*, vol. 25 (July-August 1982), pp. 18-25.

8. Thomas Bailey, "Discretionary Effort and the Organization of Work," Columbia University, Department of Philosophy and Social Science, 1993.

9. For elaboration on points made in this section, see David Stern, *Managing Human Resources: The Art of Full Employment* (Boston: Auburn House Publishing, 1982).

10. Samuel Bowles, David Gordon, and Thomas Weisskopf, *Beyond the Waste Land* (Garden City, N.Y.: Anchor Press, 1984), p. 303. Michael Beer and James W. Driscoll noted how "high rates of turnover or absenteeism, high grievance rates, sabotage, complaints and hostility, and labor problems can create *internal* pressures for improving the quality of work life." Michael Beer and James W. Driscoll, "Strategies for Change," in J. Richard Hackman and J. Lloyd Suttle, eds., *Improving Life at Work: Behavioral Science Approaches to Organizational Change* (Santa Monica, Calif.: Goodyear Publishing Co., 1977), pp. 364-453. The situation with high unemployment and use of traditional monitoring techniques will be stable only if participatory companies pay wages that are comparable to market wages. Otherwise, participatory companies will open paying low wages, hiring the unemployed, and putting traditional firms out of business. Because participatory companies require that workers feel they are treated fairly and because they have high costs of employee turnover, they may not be able to provide their workers with below-market utility levels.

11. The basic result of efficiency-wage models is that if firms require unemployment to motivate, the macroeconomy will endogenously create unemployment. The issues discussed in this paragraph are formally presented in, for example, Carl Shapiro and Joseph Stiglitz, "Equilibrium Unemployment as a Worker Discipline Device," *American Economic Review*, vol. 74 (June 1984), pp. 433-44; and Samuel Bowles, "The Production Process in a Competitive Economy: Walrasian, Neo-Hobbesian, and Marxian Models," *American Economic Review*, vol. 75 (March 1985), pp. 16-36.

12. For elaboration, see David I. Levine, "Cohesiveness, Productivity, and Wage Dispersion," *Journal of Economic Behavior and Organizations*, vol. 15 (March 1991), pp. 237-55.

13. In this model, participatory companies pay "efficiency wages" to low-end workers; that is, wages that increase workers' efficiency. As in other efficiency wage models, the market leads to too few workers receiving the relatively high wage. Shapiro and Stiglitz, "Equilibrium Unemployment as a Worker Discipline Devise"; and Bowles, "The Production Process in a Competitive Economy."

14. Elaboration on the results discussed in this section is in David I. Levine, "Just-Cause Employment Policies in the Presence of Worker Adverse Selection," *Journal of Labor Economics*, vol. 9 (July 1991), pp. 294-305.

15. Edward E. Lawler III, *The Ultimate Advantage: Creating the High-Involvement Organization* (San Francisco: Jossey-Bass, 1992), p. 242.

16. Steve Prokesch, "Levi's Broad AIDS Program," *New York Times*, March 12, 1987, pp. D1, 33.

17. Prokesch, "Levi's Broad AIDS Program," p. 33.

18. H. Shimada and J. MacDuffie, "Industrial Relations and Humanware," Working Paper 1855-7 (Massachusetts Institute of Technology, Sloan School of Management, 1986); and Commission on Workforce Quality and Labor Market Efficiency,

Investing in People: A Strategy to Address America's Workforce Crisis (Department of Labor, September 1989).

19. Gary Becker, *Human Capital*, 2d ed. (University of Chicago Press, 1975).

20. Ronald Dore, *Taking Japan Seriously* (Stanford University Press, 1987); and Gary Herrigel, "Industrial Order and the Politics of Industrial Change: Mechanical Engineering in the Federal Republic of Germany," in Peter Katzenstein, ed., *Industry and Politics in West Germany: Toward the Third Republic* (Cornell University Press, 1989), pp. 185-220.

21. *Statistical Abstract of the United States* (Department of Commerce, 1993), table 788. In 1989, 39 percent had no liquid assets other than their checking account.

22. Benjamin Hermalin, "Three Essays on the Theory of Contracts," Ph.D. dissertation, Massachusetts Institute of Technology, 1988.

23. Josef Ritzen, "Market Failure for General Training and Remedies," in David Stern and Josef Ritzen, eds., *Market Failure in Training* (New York: Springer-Verlag, 1991), pp. 185-214.

24. John Bishop, "A Program of Research on the Role of Employer Training in Ameliorating Skill Shortages and Enhancing Productivity and Competitiveness," Education and the Quality of the Workforce Working Paper 7 (University of Pennsylvania, 1993).

25. Eliakim Katz and Adrian Ziderman, *General Training under Asymmetric Information* (Washington: World Bank, Education and Employment Division, 1988).

26. Stephen L. Mangum, "Evidence on Private Sector Training," in Commission on Workforce Quality and Labor Market Efficiency, *Investing in People: A Strategy to Address America's Workforce Crisis*, background papers, vol. 1, paper 7b (Department of Labor, September 1989), p. 358.

27. Bishop, "A Program of Research on the Role of Employer Training in Ameliorating Skill Shortages and Enhancing Productivity and Competitiveness."

28. Andrei Shleifer and Lawrence Summers, "Breach of Trust in Hostile Takeovers," in Alan Auerbach, ed., *Corporate Takeovers: Causes and Consequences* (University of Chicago Press, 1988), pp. 35-56.

29. Shleifer and Summers, "Breach of Trust in Hostile Takeovers."

30. See, for example, proposals that the participatory firm be financed by external debt finance, including so-called risk-participation bonds, which differ from ordinary equity only in that their owners have no voting control over enterprise decisions: Roger McCain, "On the Optimum Financial Environment for Worker Cooperatives," *Zeitschrift für Nationalokonomie*, vol. 37 (1977), pp. 354-84; and Louis Putterman, "On Some Recent Explanations of Why Capital Hires Labor," *Economic Inquiry*, vol. 22 (1984), pp. 171-87.

31. J. E. Stiglitz and A. Weiss, "Credit Rationing in Markets with Imperfect Information," *American Economic Review*, vol. 71 (June 1981), pp. 393-410.

32. Michael C. Jensen and William H. Meckling, "Rights and Production Functions: An Application to Labor-Managed Firms and Codetermination," *Journal of Business*, vol. 52 (October 1979), pp. 469-506; and Armen A. Alchian and Harold Demsetz, "Production, Information Costs, and Economic Organization," *American Economic Review*, vol. 62 (December 1972), pp. 777-95.

33. Gregory Dow, "Can Labor-Managed Firms Flourish in a Capitalist World?" in Samuel Bowles, Herbert Gintis, and Bo Gufstafsson, eds., *Markets and Democracy: Participation, Accountability, and Efficiency* (Cambridge University Press, 1993), pp. 176-96.

34. Michael Porter, *Capital Choices* (Washington: Council on Competitiveness and Harvard Business School, 1992).

35. Roger M. Atherton and Dennis M. Crites, "Hewlett-Packard Company (A)," Case 0208 (Harvard Business School, 1976), p. 4; and Roger M. Atherton and Dennis M. Crites, "Hewlett-Packard: A 1975-78 Review," Case 0209 (Harvard Business School, 1980), p. 5.

36. Carol Pateman, *Participation and Democratic Theory* (Cambridge University Press, 1970).

37. Adam Smith, *An Inquiry into the Nature and Causes of the Wealth of Nations,* ed. Edwin Cannan (Random House, Modern Library, 1937); and Richard B. Freeman and Joel Rogers, "Who Speaks for Us? Employee Representation in a Nonunion Labor Market," in Bruce E. Kaufman and Morris M. Kleiner, eds., *Employee Representation: Alternatives and Future Directions* (Madison, Wis.: Industrial Relations Research Association, 1993), p. 9.

38. Robert Dahl, *Preface to Economic Democracy* (University of California Press, 1985), p. 95.

39. Edward S. Greenberg, *Workplace Democracy: The Political Effects of Participation* (Cornell University Press, 1986).

40. John E. Roemer, "Would Economic Democracy Decrease the Amount of Public Bads?" *Scandinavian Journal of Economics,* vol. 95, no. 2 (1993), pp. 227-38.

41. Marshall Sashkin, "Participative Management Is an Ethical Imperative," *Organizational Dynamics,* vol. 12 (Spring 1984), pp. 5-22.

42. Melvin L. Kohn, *Class and Conformity: A Study in Values* (Homewood, Ill.: Dorsey Press, 1969).

43. Like well-meaning parents, well-meaning teachers may be teaching overly authoritarian skills. As long as most jobs are MG-style, teachers will be doing their students a service if they teach obedience. Having graduates whose education emphasized showing up on time and sitting quietly lowers MG's costs because those are the skills needed from its workers. If most jobs were IMMUN-style, well-meaning teachers would emphasize IMMUN's job requirements of creativity and problem solving. Having creative graduates lowers IMMUN's costs. As with earlier cases, multiple stable outcomes are possible. The United States may be caught in the undesirable position of having relatively little emphasis on problem solving both in schools and at work.

44. Department of Health, Education, and Welfare, *Work in America* (1974).

45. This section on labor law draws on Barbara A. Lee, "Collective Bargaining and Employee Participation: An Anomalous Interpretation of the National Labor Relations Act," *Labor Law Journal,* vol. 38 (April 1987), pp. 206-19; Gregory J. Kamer, Scott M. Abbot, and Lisa G. Salevitz, "The New Legal Challenge to Participation," *Labor Law Journal,* vol. 45 (January 1994), pp. 41-48; and Donna Sockell, "The Legality of Employee-Participation Programs in Unionized Firms," *Industrial and Labor Relations Review,* vol. 37 (July 1984), pp. 541-56.

46. Richard Edwards, *Rights at Work: Employment Relations in the Post-Union Era* (Brookings, 1993), p. 191.

47. Edwards, *Rights at Work*, p. 192.

48. Robert B. Reich, *The Resurgent Liberal* (Times Books, 1989), pp. 34-50.

49. Orley Ashenfelter and David Bloom, "Lawyers as Agents of the Devil in a Prisoner's Dilemma Game," Working Paper 4447 (National Bureau of Economic Research, September 1993).

50. Richard E. Wokutch, *Worker Protection, Japanese Style: Occupational Health and Safety in the Auto Industry* (Ithaca, N.Y.: ILR Press, 1992).

51. The record on repetitive motion injuries is more mixed. See Wokutch, *Worker Protection, Japanese Style;* and Paul S. Adler, Barbara Goldaftas, and David I. Levine, "The Toyota Production System, Ergonomics, and Employee Involvement: NUMMI's 1993 Model Introduction," University of Southern California Graduate School of Business, 1995.

Chapter 7

1. See, for example, Kazuo Koike, "Human Resource Development and Labor-Management Relations," in Kozo Yamamura and Yasukichi Yasuba, eds., *The Political Economy of Japan*, vol. 1: *The Domestic Transformation* (Stanford University Press, 1987), pp. 289-330; Robert Cole, *Work, Mobility, and Participation* (University of California Press, 1979); and Tashiro Shirai, ed., *Contemporary Industrial Relations in Japan* (University of Wisconsin Press, 1983). This overview draws from David I. Levine and Laura D'Andrea Tyson, "Participation, Productivity, and the Firm's Environment," in Alan Blinder, ed., *Paying for Productivity* (Brookings, 1990), pp. 183-244.

2. See, for example, James Baron, "The Employment Relations," *American Sociological Review*, vol. 50 (December 1985); and James R. Lincoln and Arne L. Kalleberg, "Work Organizations and Workforce Commitment: A Study of Plants and Employees in the U.S. and Japan," *American Sociological Review*, vol. 50 (December 1985), pp. 738-60.

3. Taishiro Shirai, "A Theory of Enterprise Unionism," in Taishiro Shirai, ed., *Contemporary Industrial Relations in Japan* (University of Wisconsin Press, 1983), pp. 117-44.

4. Lincoln and Kalleberg, "Work Organizations and Workforce Commitment."

5. Chalmers Johnson, "Japanese-Style Management in America," *California Management Review*, vol. 30 (Summer 1988), pp. 34-45; and James Abegglen and George Stalk, Jr., *Kaisha: The Japanese Corporation* (Basic Books, 1985).

6. Richard Freeman and Martin Weitzman, "Bonuses and Employment in Japan," *Journal of the Japanese and International Economics*, vol. 1 (1987), pp. 168-94.

7. Thomas Rohlen, "The Company Work Group," in Ezra F. Vogel, ed., *Japanese Organization and Decisionmaking* (University of California Press, 1975).

8. Koike, "Human Resource Development and Labor-Management Relations."

9. Lincoln and Kalleberg, "Work Organizations and Workforce Commitment"; and James R. Lincoln, Jon Olson, and Hanado Mitsuyo, "Cultural Effects of Organi-

zational Structure: The Case of Japanese Firms in the United States," *American Sociological Review*, vol. 43 (1978), pp. 839-47.

10. Koike, "Human Resource Development and Labor-Management Relations"; and Kazuo Koike, "Internal Labor Markets: Workers in Large Firms," in Taishiro Shirai, ed., *Contemporary Industrial Relations in Japan* (University of Wisconsin Press, 1983), pp. 29-62.

11. Ezra F. Vogel, *Japan as Number 1: Lessons for America* (Harvard University Press, 1979); Rohlen, "The Company Work Group"; Ronald Dore, *British Factory—Japanese Factory: The Origin of National Diversity in Industrial Relations* (University of California Press, 1973); Baron, "The Employment Relations"; Abegglen and Stalk, *Kaisha*, chapter 8; and Arne L. Kalleberg and James R. Lincoln, "The Structure of Earning Inequality in the U.S. and Japan," *American Sociological Review*, vol. 98 (1988), pp.121-53.

12. Michael Gerlach, "Business Alliances and the Strategy of the Japanese Firm," *California Management Review*, vol. 30 (Fall 1987), pp. 126-42; Abegglen and Stalk, *Kaisha*, chapter 8; and Koike, "Human Resources Development and Labor-Management Relations."

13. For more on declining industry law and the benefits it offers to maintain employment or ease transition, see Jimmy W. Wheeler, Merit E. Janow, and Thomas Pepper, *Japanese Industrial Development Policies in the 1980s* (Croton-on-Hudson, N.Y.: Hudson Institute, 1982), chapter 7.

14. Robert Dore, "Japan in Recession," *Dollars and Sense*, no. 192 (March-April 1994), pp. 20-24.

15. Robert Gordon, "Productivity, Wages, and Prices Inside and Outside of Manufacturing in the U.S., Japan, and Europe," *European Economic Review*, vol. 31 (April 1987), pp. 685-733.

16. Abegglen and Stalk, *Kaisha;* Masahiko Aoki, "The Japanese Firm in Transition," in Kozo Yamamura and Yasukichi Yasuba, eds., *The Political Economy of Japan*, vol. 1: *The Domestic Transformation* (Stanford University Press, 1987), pp. 263-88; and Gerlach, "Business Alliances and the Strategy of the Japanese Firm."

17. Masahiko Aoki, *The Economic Analysis of the Japanese Firm* (Amsterdam: North Holland, 1984).

18. Robert E. Cole, *Strategies for Learning: Small-Group Activities in American, Japanese, and Swedish Industry* (University of California Press, 1989).

Chapter 8

1. George J. Stigler, *The Citizen and the State: Essays on Regulation* (University of Chicago Press, 1975), pp. 114-44.

2. David Noble, *Forces of Production: A Social History of Industrial Automation* (Oxford University Press, 1984).

3. Department of Commerce, *Guide to NIST* (Gaithersburg, Md., October 1993), p. 80.

4. Department of Commerce, *Guide to NIST,* p. 45.

5. Department of Commerce, *Guide to NIST,* p. 44.

6. Prabhakar Arafi, director, NIST, "Setting the Framework," remarks prepared for NIST Conference on Integrating Technology and People in High Performance Work Systems, May 1994.

7. Harold Salzman and Robert Lund, "Skill-Based Technology Design," paper prepared for the 1994 Integrating People and Technology in High Performance Work Systems conference held by Department of Commerce, National Institute for Standards and Technology.

8. Barry Staw, "Organizational Psychology and the Pursuit of the Happy/Productive Worker," *California Management Review*, vol. 28 (Summer 1986), pp. 40-53.

9. Department of Labor, Secretary's Commission on Achieving Necessary Skills (SCANS), *Government as a High Performance Employer*, SCANS report for America 2000 (1988).

10. The quote is from Salzman and Lund, "Skill-Based Technology Design," a review of more than two hundred engineering design texts. They concluded that more than three-fourths of the texts had "the complete absence of any engineering consideration of workers" (p. 6). Overall, "the traditional approach to designing industrial systems is to design people out and, for those who are left in, minimize their role" (p. 1).

11. Evelyn Ganzglass, ed., *Excellence at Work* (Kalamazoo, Mich.: Upjohn Institute, 1992).

12. Tora K. Bikson and Barbara Gutek, *Implementation of Office Automation* (Santa Monica, Calif.: Land Corporation, 1984).

13. See, for example, Department of Labor, Office of the American Workplace, *Road to High-Performance Workplaces* (1994).

14. Charles F. Sabel, "Studied Trust," in Stephen R. Sleigh, ed., *Economic Restructuring and Emerging Patterns of Industrial Relations* (Kalamazoo, Mich.: Upjohn Institute, 1993).

15. Robert E. Cole, *Strategies for Learning: Small-Group Activities in American, Japanese, and Swedish Industry* (University of California Press, 1989).

16. John Paul MacDuffie and Thomas Kochan, "Human Resources, Technology, and Manufacturing Performance: Evidence from the Automobile Industry," *Proceedings of the 1987 Annual Meeting of the Industrial Relations Research Association* (Madison, Wis., 1988); Commission on Workforce Quality and Labor Market Efficiency, *Investing in People: A Strategy to Address America's Workforce Crisis* (Department of Labor, September 1989); and John Bishop, "A Program of Research on the Role of Employer Training in Ameliorating Skill Shortage and Enhancing Productivity and Competitiveness," Education and the Quality of the Workforce Working Paper 7 (University of Pennsylvania, 1993).

17. In other industrialized nations, such as Germany, there are certifications in occupation-specific skills, ranging from welding to bank telling. Because each company wants all other companies to train lots of young workers (to hire them away once they are skilled), certifications are only viable when powerful industry groups push employers to train apprentices. Such groups are lacking in the United States, reducing the viability of the German apprenticeship model.

18. Tim Beardsley, "Teaching Real Science," *Scientific American*, vol. 267 (October 1992), p. 101.

19. The new system of voluntary employee skill certification was enacted in the School-to-Work Act of 1994.

20. Michael Feuer, Henry Glick, and Anand Desai, "Firm-Sponsored Education and Specific Human Capital: A Test of the Insurance Hypothesis," in David Stern and Josef Ritzen, eds., *Market Failure in Training* (New York: Springer-Verlag, 1991), pp. 41-60.

21. This section draws on David I. Levine and Susan Helper, "A Quality Policy for America," *Contemporary Economic Policy* (forthcoming).

22. Federal Quality Institute, *Introduction to Total Quality Management in the Federal Government,* US GPO 299-9960 (1991), p. 13.

23. General Accounting Office, *Management Practices: U.S. Companies Improve Performance through Quality Efforts,* GAO/NSAID-91-190 (1991), p. 35.

24. General Accounting Office, *Quality Management: Survey of Federal Organizations,* GAO/GGD-93-9BR (1992), p. 56.

25. See *National Electronic Process Certification Standard: EIA 599* (Washington: American National Standards Institute, Electronic Industry Association, 1992). ANSI/EIA 599 is based on the military's Qualified Manufacturer's Line standard, MIL-I-28535, a standard for semiconductor manufacturing that draws heavily on the Baldrige award criteria. Thus precedent exists for using quality standards in government procurement.

26. Steven Kelman, *The Fear of Discretion and the Quality of Government* (Washington: American Enterprise Institute for Public Policy Research, 1990); and Robert Leone, *Who Profits?* (Basic Books, 1986), p. 183.

27. Joseph Sensenbrenner, "Quality Comes to City Hall," *Harvard Business Review,* vol. 69 (March-April 1991), pp. 65 and 68.

28. Great Britain also has a program to provide twenty to thirty days of free consulting to assist small and medium-sized companies in setting up their quality programs. Unfortunately, virtually all of the approximately ten thousand consultants focused on ISO 9000 certification and not on more effective quality and involvement programs. See Graham Wilson, *Making Change Happen* (London: Pitman, 1994). As an additional benefit, government assistance for exporters can give preference to companies with quality certifications. This targeting will help improve the reputation of U.S. products, just as similar certifications have assisted Japanese and Taiwanese exports.

29. Eileen Appelbaum and Rosemary Batt, *The New American Workplace: Transforming Work Systems in the United States* (Ithaca, N.Y.: ILR Press, 1994).

30. Department of Industrial Relations, Australian Manufacturing Council Secretariat, *Interim Evaluation of the Australian Best Practice Demonstration Program* (Canberra, Australia, September 1993).

31. Accident rates are notoriously difficult to compare across nations. Nevertheless, Japanese auto factories have fatality rates, which are fairly accurately measured, far below the U.S. level, suggesting that they truly are safer workplaces. See Richard E. Wokutch, *Worker Protection, Japanese Style: Occupational Health and Safety in the Auto Industry* (Ithaca, N.Y.: ILR Press, 1992).

32. Jonathan Leonard, *Use of Enforcement Techniques in Eliminating Glass Ceiling Barriers,* Report to the Department of Labor, Glass Ceiling Commission (1994).

33. Michael Porter, *Capital Choices* (Washington: Council on Competitiveness and Harvard Business School, 1992). See also Eric G. Flamholz, *Human Resource Accounting* (San Francisco: Jossey-Bass, 1985).

34. Commission on Workforce Quality and Labor Market Efficiency, *Investing in People: A Strategy to Address America's Workforce Crisis* (Department of Labor, September 1989), p. 17.

35. Robert Eccles and Sarah Mavrinac, "Improving the Corporate Disclosure Process," Working Paper (Harvard Business School, 1994), p. 13.

36. Dan Goodgame, "Losing Big on Capital Gains: Shortsighted Plan to Slash the Tax Rate May Be Unstoppable," *Time,* August 14, 1989, p. 53.

37. Porter, *Capital Choices,* p. 14.

38. *Statistical Abstract of the United States* (Department of Commerce, 1993), table 788.

39. Joseph Blasi and Douglas Kruse, "Employee Ownership and Participation: Trends, Problems, and Policy Options," *Journal of Employee Ownership Law and Finance,* vol. 5 (Spring 1993), pp. 41-73.

40. Sanford M. Jacoby, *Employing Bureaucracy* (Columbia University Press, 1985); and War Production Board, *1,600 Labor-Management Committees in the War Production Drive* (Washington, 1942).

41. Department of Labor and Department of Commerce, Commission on the Future of Worker-Management Relations, *Fact Finding Report* (May 1994), p. 47.

42. Frank McElroy and Alexander Moros, "Joint Production Committees, January 1948," *Monthly Labor Review,* vol. 67 (August 1948), pp. 123-26.

43. War Production Board, *Basic Guide for Labor-Management Committees* (Washington, 1945).

44. McElroy and Moros, "Joint Production Committees."

45. This section draws on David I. Levine, "Public Policy Implications of Imperfections in the Market for Worker Participation," *Economic and Industrial Democracy,* vol. 13 (May 1992), pp. 183-206; and Blasi and Kruse, "Employee Ownership and Participation."

46. Martin L. Weitzman, *The Share Economy: Conquering Stagflation* (Harvard University Press, 1984). For a discussion on the idea that the macroeconomic arguments in favor of profit sharing may not be as strong as Weitzman claimed, see David I. Levine, "Efficiency Wages in Weitzman's Share Economy," *Industrial Relations,* vol. 28 (Fall 1989), pp. 321-34.

47. In nonunion companies, employment relations committees would not be permitted to deal with compensation matters. In unionized companies, the employment relations committees would not be empowered to deal with any matters covered by the collective bargaining agreement, unless that agreement specifically permitted the topic to be discussed. Similar committees, usually called works councils, are mandated in all continental European Community states. In most of these nations, the councils have rights to information and consultation on a variety of issues. In Germany, Denmark, Luxembourg, and the Netherlands, the councils also have codetermination rights (that is, the management of the company must receive the consent of the works councils) concerning a range of personnel issues such as hiring, firing, and work rules. For a description of these policies, see Lowell Turner, "The Single Market and the Social Europe Debate," paper prepared

for the 1991 Labor Responses to Economic Unification in Western Europe conference held by the University of California at Berkeley, Institute of Industrial Relations. For a discussion on independently advocated works councils that are required at companies enjoying the tax incentives for ESOPs, see Richard B. Freeman, "Employee Councils, Worker Participation, and Other Squishy Stuff," in *Proceedings of the Annual Spring Meeting of the Industrial Relations Research Association* (Madison, Wis., 1991), pp. 328-37.

48. Department of Labor and Department of Commerce, Commission on the Future of Worker-Management Relations, *Fact Finding Report,* pp. 121-22.

49. This language is adapted from Richard N. Block and Benjamin W. Wolkinson, "Impediments to Innovative Employee Relations Arrangements," in Commission on Workforce Quality and Labor Market Efficiency, *Investing in People: A Strategy to Address America's Workforce Crisis,* background papers, vol. 2 (Department of Labor, September 1989), p. 2038. For the first three points, they cite Alan F. Westin and Alfred G. Felin, *Resolving Employment Disputes without Litigation* (Washington: Bureau of National Affairs, 1988).

50. David Lewin, "Grievance Procedures in Nonunion Workplaces: An Empirical Analysis of Usage, Dynamics, and Outcomes," *Chicago-Kent Law Review,* vol. 66 (1990), p. 828.

51. Block and Wolkinson, "Impediments to Innovative Employee Relations Arrangements," p. 2039.

52. Commission on Workforce Quality and Labor Market Efficiency, *Investing in People,* p. 17.

53. Department of Labor and Department of Commerce, Commission on the Future of Worker-Management Relations, *Fact Finding Report,* p. 17.

54. Douglas Cowherd and David I. Levine, "Product Quality and Pay Equity between Low-Level Employees and Top Management: An Investigation of Distributive Justice Theory," *Administrative Science Quarterly,* vol. 37 (June 1992), pp. 302-20.

55. Graef S. Crystal, *In Search of Excess: The Overcompensation of American Executives* (Norton, 1991).

56. Elizabeth Bishop and David I. Levine, "Computer Mediated Communication as Employee Voice: A Case Study," *Proceedings of the Conference on NetWORKing,* Working Group 9.1 (Geneva, Switzerland: International Federation for Information Processing, 1993).

57. This section is derived from Susan Helper and David I. Levine, "A Quality Policy for America." See also Department of Labor, Secretary's Commission on Achieving Necessary Skills (SCANS), *Government as a High Performance Employer,* SCANS report for America 2000 (1991).

58. General Accounting Office, *Quality Management.*

59. Christopher Farrell, "Even Uncle Sam Is Starting to See the Light," *Business Week,* October 25, 1991, pp. 132-37.

60. General Accounting Office, *Quality Management.*

61. David Osborne and Ted Gaebler, *Reinventing Government* (Addison-Wesley, 1992).

62. The classic example is the Interstate Commerce Commission, which was established to prevent monopoly pricing in railroads. Instead, it managed to create a cartel for the railroads to keep prices high.

63. Any workplace changes will need to be complemented by additional changes in the political system. Typical changes that will help reduce the power of special interests include limiting their ability to finance politicians and political campaigns, increasing disclosure of lobbying activities by corporations, and restricting the ability of corporations (as opposed to individuals) to influence government.

64. Roger Fisher and William Ury, *Getting to Yes*, 2d ed. (Penguin, 1991).

65. David I. Levine and Douglas Kruse, "Employee Involvement Efforts: Incidence and Effects," Working Paper OBIR-49 (University of California at Berkeley, Haas School of Business, 1991).

66. Robert E. Cole, Paul Bacdayan, and Joseph White, "Quality, Participation, and Competitiveness," *California Management Review*, vol. 35 (Spring 1993), pp. 68-81.

67. David I. Levine and George Strauss, "Employee Participation and Involvement," in Commission on Workforce Quality and Labor Market Efficiency, *Investing in People: A Strategy to Address America's Workforce Crisis*, background papers, vol. 2, paper 35b (Department of Labor, September 1989), pp. 1893-948.

68. General Accounting Office, *Quality Management*, p. 40.

69. General Accounting Office, *Quality Management*, p. 53.

70. General Accounting Office, *Management Practices*, p. 3.

71. Federal Quality Institute, *Introduction to Total Quality Management in the Federal Government*, US GPO 299-9960 (1991), p. 12.

72. Federal Quality Institute, *Introduction to Total Quality Management in the Federal Government*, p. 13; Debbie Goldman and Laura Ginsberg, *Making Government Work* (Washington: AFL-CIO, Public Employees Department, 1991); and Debbie Goldman and Laura Ginsberg, *Reinvigorating the Public Service* (Washington: AFL-CIO, Public Employees Department, 1992).

73. G. R. Gilbert, "Quality Improvement in a Federal Defense Organization," *Public Productivity and Management Review*, vol. 16 (Fall 1992), p. 71. Unions have been effective advocates for total quality principles in the private sector as well. Unions have pushed management to introduce quality programs into plants without them, pressed management to live up to its commitments to train, and fought to protect quality circles and total quality management training from managers intent on showing a short-term profit. See United Auto Workers, "Workers Eager to Produce Quality Products," *UAW Ammo*, vol. 27 (November 1991), p. 8; Steve Babson, "Lean Production at Mazda," Working Paper (Wayne State University, Labor Studies Program, 1992); and Kenneth Coss, "Labor-Management Collaboration," discussion prepared for the 1993 Northeast Ohio Industrial Relations Research Association meeting.

74. Edward E. Lawler III, Susan A. Mohrman, and Gerald Ledford, *Employee Involvement and Total Quality Management* (San Francisco: Jossey-Bass, 1992); and General Accounting Office, *Quality Management*, p. 57.

75. Cited in Farrell, "Even Uncle Sam Is Starting to See the Light," p. 133.

76. Hannah Finan Roditi, "Youth Apprenticeship: High Schools for Docile Workers," *Nation*, vol. 254, March 16, 1992, pp. 340-43.

77. Mike Parker, *Inside the Circle: A Union Guide to Worker Participation in Management* (Boston: South End Press, 1985).

78. Jeremy Burlow and Lawrence Summers, "A Theory of Dual Labor Markets with Application to Industry Policy, Discrimination, and Keynesian Unemployment," *Journal of Labor Economics*, vol. 4, no. 3, part 1 (1986), pp. 376-414.

79. Special Task Force to the Secretary of Health, Education, and Welfare, *Work in America* (MIT Press, 1973).

80. Joseph Fucini and Suzy Fucini, *Working for the Japanese* (Free Press, 1990), p. 194, and chapter 9.

Appendix

1. For a description of interview respondents, see Paul S. Adler, Barbara Goldoftas, and David I. Levine, "The Toyota Production System, Ergonomics, and Employee Involvement: NUMMI's 1993 Model Introduction," University of Southern California Graduate School of Business, 1995.

2. Paul Adler, "NUMMI, Circa 1988," Stanford University, Department of Industrial Engineering and Engineering Management, 1990; Paul Adler, "The 'Learning Bureaucracy': New United Motor Manufacturing Inc.," in Larry L. Cummings and Barry M. Staw, eds., *Research in Organizational Behavior*, vol. 15 (Greenwich, Conn.: JAI Press, 1992), pp. 111-94; and John F. Krafcik, "Learning from NUMMI," International Motor Vehicle Project Working Paper (Massachusetts Institute of Technology, 1986).

3. If companies can acquire reputations, this problem is alleviated. Evidence is available that reputations enforce implicit contracts only at very large employers. For a report on how nonunion employers adjusted the pensions of their retirees during the high and unanticipated inflation period of the 1970s, see Steven G. Allen, Robert L. Clark, and Daniel A. Sumner, "Postretirement Adjustments of Pension Benefits," *Journal of Human Resources*, vol. 21 (Winter 1986), pp. 118-37. For example, only 5 percent of small enterprises (fewer than one hundred employees) adjusted the nominal value of their pensions upward to partially keep pace with the unanticipated inflation of the late 1970s. In contrast, 20 percent of medium-sized enterprises (one hundred to one thousand), 33 percent of large enterprises (one thousand to five thousand), and 43 percent of very large enterprises (more than five thousand) adjusted their nominal pensions upward.

4. A formal model of this "lemons" problem is presented in Susan Helper and David I. Levine, "Long-Term Supplier Relations and Product Market Structure," *Journal of Law, Economics, and Organization*, vol. 8 (October 1992), pp. 561-81.

5. Additional reasons that bonding is rare are discussed in William T. Dickens and others, "Employee Crime and the Monitoring Puzzle," *Journal of Labor Economics*, vol. 7 (July 1989), pp. 331-47.

6. This checklist draws on Department of Labor, Office of the American Workplace, *Road to High-Performance Workplaces* (1994).

Index